Penguin Special
British Capitalism, Workers
and the Profits Squeeze

Andrew Glyn was born in 1943 and read Politics,
Philosophy and Economics at Oxford. He worked as an
economist in the Treasury and the Department of
Economic Affairs. Later on he was employed part-time by
the Board of Trade and the Ministry of Technology. He
did graduate work in economics at Nuffield College,
Oxford, and is now Fellow and Tutor in Economics at
Corpus Christi College, Oxford. An article he published,
with Bob Sutcliffe, in *New Left Review*, March 1971,
formed the basis from which this book eventually
developed.

Bob Sutcliffe was born in 1939 and read Politics, Philosophy
and Economics at Oxford; he obtained his M.A. at Harvard.
He has worked as Research Officer for the Oxford
University Institute of Economics and Statistics and as
consultant in Forest Economics to the United Nations
Food and Agriculture Organization. He was formerly
Fellow and Tutor in Economics at Jesus College, Oxford.
He has edited *Studies in the Theory of Imperialism* (1972.
With Roger Owen), and written *Industry and
Underdevelopment* (1971).

Andrew Glyn and Bob Sutcliffe

British Capitalism, Workers and the Profits Squeeze

Penguin Books

Penguin Books Ltd, Harmondsworth,
Middlesex, England
Penguin Books Inc., 7110 Ambassador Road,
Baltimore, Maryland 21207, U.S.A.
Penguin Books Australia Ltd, Ringwood,
Victoria, Australia

First published 1972

Made and printed in Great Britain by
Cox & Wyman Ltd, London, Reading and Fakenham
Set in Monotype Times

Contents

Part III The Responses

Acknowledgements

We thank the following people for helping us while we were writing this book. We are alone responsible for the contents.

Philip Armstrong, Richard Barratt, Roy Bhaskar, Geoff Brown, Carlyle David, Celia Glyn, James Hamilton-Paterson, Jeremy Hardie, John Harrison, Daniel Jessel, Simon Mahon, Judy Mabro, Steve McDonnell, Bill MacKeith, Luca Meldolesi, Katharine Munby, Ed Nell, Roger Owen, Bernard Reaney, Jonathan Rée, Peter Short, Barry Slater, Paolo Sylos-Labini, John Wolfers.

The diagram on page 179 is used with the permission of the Controller of H.M.S.O.

Chapter 1
Introduction

As British capitalism entered the 1970s the economy appeared to take on a new character. In 1966 unemployment began an upward climb which took it in five years to its highest level since 1940, when the recovery from the long inter-war depression was still incomplete. The previous period of five successive years' rising unemployment had been between 1927 and 1932. By January 1972 more than a million people were without work and the situation showed no sign of improvement. During 1970 and 1971 an average of one thousand people were thrown out of work every day. The rate of bankruptcies reached record heights and included not only tiny firms but supposedly immortal giant industrial companies, some of them, like Rolls-Royce and Upper Clyde Shipbuilders, receiving state support. Not since the slump of 1929–32 had national production grown so slowly as it did in a two-year period between 1969 and 1971. In the same period prices and wages rose faster than at any time since 1920. In short, the British economy was experiencing its biggest crisis since the war.

But this book is not just about the British *economy*; it is about the political economy of British *capitalism*. Books which focus their attention on the economy – on the rate of economic growth, the level of investment, wages and productivity, and on the balance of payments – fail to relate these things to the social system which underlies all economic activity in Britain. Our approach means that we see the economic sphere as a place where different classes – capitalists and workers – pursue their distinct interests and continually come into conflict with each other. Many questions which are often presented as 'purely economic' can only be properly understood as manifestations of this class conflict. Such an understanding is absent from most orthodox economic analysis as taught in schools and colleges and repeated in the press and on TV.

Capitalism is a system of production dependent on private profit. It cannot operate without sufficient profits; they are the incentive which drives capitalists to invest, and they provide much of the finance for investment. A decline in profits, therefore, forces some firms out of existence and, by reducing investment in others, prevents living standards from rising. In these ways it sets up forces which threaten the survival of the capitalist system.

Our argument in this book is that British capitalism has suffered such a dramatic decline in profitability that it is now literally fighting for survival. This crisis has developed because mounting demands from the working class for a faster growth in living standards has coincided with growing competition between capitalist countries. This competition, apparent in conflicts over trade and exchange rates, has prevented British capitalism from simply accommodating successful wage demands by pushing up prices correspondingly. And it has intensified because the other rich countries have been subject to the same pressures from the working class as British capitalism. These pressures have in some instances – France in 1968 and Italy since the autumn of 1969 – already been a cause of major political crises.

We believe that by combining the apparently disconnected pieces of economic information, familiar from the radio, press and TV, with some less known, but central, facts about profitability, we can present a coherent picture of the critical condition of British capitalism and of the possibilities open to it. One of these is that profitability will be restored, but this can only be at the expense of the living standards and political strength of the working class. As in the past, capital will attempt to secure the cooperation of the workers' leaders. Thus the crisis for capitalism is also a crisis for the working class.

Attempts will be made to persuade workers to show moderation, on the grounds that everybody will prosper in a healthy economy. We hope that by analysing the measures now necessary to restore the British economy to health under capitalism, we will help to spread the realization that the best interests of workers lie not in the continuation of capitalism at all, but rather in the control by the working class of its own fate in a democratic socialist system.

Conventional economists rule out this possibility since they assume that capitalism is permanent, and their claim that their analysis is politically neutral is thus incorrect. We claim no bogus political neutrality; indeed we believe that the facts we have assembled and analysed in this book amply confirm the correctness of a socialist viewpoint.

The main text, which should be intelligible to people without formal training in economics, is divided into three parts. Part I documents the historical parallels and beginnings of the present crisis in Britain (chapter 2), gives a detailed account of the collapse of profitability since 1950 and its apparent causes (chapter 3), and surveys the same facts in the other major capitalist countries (chapter 4). Part II describes the effects of the crisis in Britain – on the living standards of workers and capitalists (chapter 5) and on the prospects for investment and the failure of firms (chapter 6). Part III is about the recent and potential reactions to the crisis from capitalist corporations (chapter 7), from the government (chapter 8) and from the working class (chapter 9). It shows how the strategy being followed by the participants is leading to the inevitability of intensified class conflict, and forcing a change in the political situation internationally and in Britain (chapter 10).

The tables and diagrams which punctuate the text can be omitted: they only elaborate or summarize information already in the text. When we have used technical economic terms or mentioned obscure events we have given an explanation or definition in a footnote at the bottom of the page when they first appear. These footnotes are marked with superior numbers: [1], [2], etc. We also use these footnotes to elaborate or qualify a point in the text, in which case we use the asterisk series: *, †, ‡. References to sources of information or quotations are shown by a number in the text [1] and appear at the end of the book. In addition, a number of chapters have appendices which appear together at the end of the book. Except for the first two, these are more difficult than the text and are written for those with some economic training. In the main they are detailed explanations of the methods by which we did our calculations and elaborations of points in the text.

Part One
The Crisis

Chapter 2
The Historical Decline of British Capitalism

1. The start of the decline: 1870–1914

The present crisis, while not a repeat of any previous one, does have many important historical parallels, both in economic conditions and in the responses of capitalists and workers to them. And it has grown out of deep historical roots. The long-term problem of profitability[1] for British capitalism has continuously threatened since sometime late in the nineteenth century to reach crisis proportions. Whenever it has done so, then the commonest results, as we shall see, have been a heightening of the class struggle, the development of slump conditions and some transformation in the involvement of the government in the economy.

By the time the First World War broke out British industrial capital was experiencing immense problems. Britain in 1870 had produced as much as one third of the world's industrial goods; by 1913 it produced only 14 per cent. It had been overtaken in terms of total production by the U.S. and Germany, and more than matched in productivity[2] by the U.S., Germany and Sweden. The profitability of British industrial capitalism, if not its very survival, was threatened by the joint pressures of an increasingly militant working class and growing international competition.

The growth of industrial capital had depended on a high ratio of

[1] The *profitability* of production can be measured by the share of profits in the value of output, or more usually by the rate of profit. The two measures tell very much the same story. The *rate of profit* is the annual amount of profits divided by the total amount of money invested. The *share of profits* is the total amount of profits expressed as a proportion of the national income.

[2] *Productivity* normally refers to productivity of labour and means output produced per person employed. If productivity rises faster than wages per man then total output will be rising faster than total wages paid. Thus wages paid per unit of output produced (i.e. wage costs) will fall. Occasionally productivity of capital is measured and means output produced per unit of capital employed. It is the inverse of the capital/output ratio.

profits to wages, or a high rate of exploitation. In 1870 income from property (profits and rents as opposed to wages and salaries) had still accounted for about half of the total national income.[1] But the maintenance of this position had become more difficult. The economist Alfred Marshall had seen the cause of the Great Depression of 1873 to 1896 in the fact that 'the employer gets less and the employee more'. [1] In the later years of the depression the rate

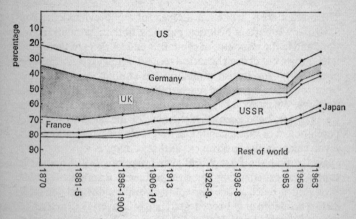

Figure 1. Shares of world manufacturing output 1870–1963
Source: See Table 2.1.

of profit rose again. But capitalists had learned from the experience that they could not permit their wage costs to rise above those of their overseas rivals. This 'acted as an externally imposed constraint upon any given wage negotiation'. Wages could rise faster if productivity rose; otherwise profit margins would be hit. The employers' resistance to wage claims varied 'with the ability of their foreign competitors to undersell them'. [2]

From 1870 the relations of capital and labour[2] had been in-

[1] The *national income* is the total of wages, salaries and profits earned in the country in the course of production, and it therefore equals the total value of production.

[2] Often we refer to the workers as a whole as *labour*; by analogy *capital* refers to the whole capitalist class.

creasingly strained by the growth in power and organization of the working class. In the 1870s unionism had spread among skilled workers. In the late 1880s the growth of mass unskilled unionism began. In 1890 Britain, with 8 per cent of its industrial workers in unions, had by far the most organized labour force of any major capitalist country. Trade-union membership rose from 2 million in 1906 to over 4 million (27 per cent of all industrial workers) in 1914. At the same time the foundation of the Social Democratic Federa-

Table 2.1. Shares of World Output of Manufactured Goods (percentages)

	United States	Germany	U.K.	France	U.S.S.R.	Japan
1870	23	13	32	10	4	—
1881/5	29	14	27	9	3	—
1896/1900	30	17	20	7	5	1
1906/10	35	16	15	6	5	1
1913	36	16	14	6	6	1
1926/9	42	12	9	7	4	3
1936/8	32	11	9	5	19	3
1953	41	6	6	3	14	2
1958	31	7	5	3	18	3
1963	28	6	4	2	20	4

Sources: League of Nations, *Industrialisation and Foreign Trade*, p. 13, Table 1.

I. Patel, 'Rates of Industrial Growth in the Last Century', in B. Supple (ed.), *The Experience of Economic Growth*, p. 77, Table 3.

U.N., *The Growth of World Industry*, 1968 edition.

U.N., *Patterns of Industrial Growth 1938–58*.

tion in 1884, the Independent Labour Party in 1893 and the Labour Party in parliament in 1906 had helped to spread socialist ideas and politics among workers. Of course there were setbacks. And in the years before the First World War the working class was under attack on many fronts: from the employers directly, through resistance to workers' rights and wage increases, from the courts and from growing unemployment.

In 1908 British industry was swept by a tidal wave of labour militancy. More than 10 million days were lost through strikes in

1908, 1910 and 1911; more than 40 million in 1912. The strikes were partly a response to the capitalist attack. Many were protests of rank and file workers as much against their own leaders as against their bosses. But an influence on nearly all the struggles was the slow growth of wages.

Throughout Britain's industrialization the wages of most workers had been very low even by earlier standards. Between the fifteenth and eighteenth centuries real wages[1] had probably fallen

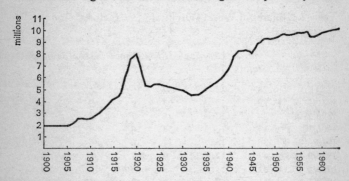

Figure 2. Trade-union membership 1900–1964
Source: British Labour Statistics, Table 196.

a good deal. The limited information available suggests that only after the Napoleonic wars did the level of real wages 'take off on the path of climb that was to take it by the end of the nineteenth century to levels never reached before. In the course of that climb it regained for the first time the level of the fifteenth century plateau . . . in 1880'. [3] The drop in imported food prices and increases in money wages kept real wages rising up to 1895. Between then and 1913 real wages actually fell.

The fall in real wages from 1900 was one of the causes of labour militancy, which in turn contributed to the slow growth of productivity. In Britain more than other countries the period was marked

[1] *Real wages* means the purchasing power of wages. If prices of the things workers buy rise on average by the same proportion as the rise in *money wages* then real wages are unchanged; if prices rise more than money wages, real wages fall, and vice versa.

by a major change 'in the will and power of organized labour to resist management' which included 'resistance to changes in methods and the use to the full of labour-saving equipment'. [4]

But productivity had failed to rise mainly because British industrial capitalists were unable to maintain an adequate level of investment. In the decade before the First World War net investment[1] at home probably fell to no more than 5 per cent of the national income, compared with over 8 per cent in 1870. Except for a few years around the end of the nineteenth century, the amount of capital equipment per worker in Britain remained constant between 1870 and 1913, while in Germany and to a lesser extent in the United States it was rising very fast. There was no rise in the productivity of capital or of labour from 1900 onwards. Hence profit margins in industry and real wages were both hit.

British capitalists were increasingly investing overseas. From 1905 to 1914 they invested about 7 per cent of the national income abroad – markedly more than was invested at home. The real value of British-owned capital abroad in 1913 was probably greater than the total American capital abroad today. Britain's foreign investment was done in the main not by industry but by finance capitalists. In contrast to Germany and France, finance and industry in Britain were particularly distinct.

The earnings from the growing stock of British overseas assets built up with extraordinary speed. In 1870 it was £35m. (about one eighth of total industrial and financial profits); by 1913 it had reached £200m. – about 9 per cent of the national income and more than one third of total profits. In addition there was a substantial profit element in the £168m. 'invisible' income from shipping, financial services in trade, banking and insurance.[2]

Because this income was growing so rapidly and increasingly becoming essential to the balance of payments equilibrium,[3] the

---

[1] *Investment* (accumulation of capital) is expenditure on factories, machines and so forth for use in future production. *Net investment* is expenditure on additional capital equipment over and above expenditure on replacing capital equipment worn out during the year (gross investment includes this replacement expenditure).

[2] *Invisible income* is receipts for services rather than goods.

[3] A country's *balance of payments* is the balance of what it pays to foreigners for imports and for assets (foreign investment) less what it

finance capitalists[1] gained a strategic position in relation to the government and began wielding a political influence which was out of all proportion to their share of the national income. On the eve of the First World War, financial capital, unlike industrial capital, was at the peak of its success. Britain still had unchallenged leadership in foreign investment and in international transport and financial services. The pound sterling was the prime international currency. This situation was not to last.

2. The First World War and the inter-war crises

The war was fought very largely because of the conflicts to which the international expansion of capitalism and imperialism was leading. Ironically, though, the war proved something of a disaster for financial capitalists. Some of their assets were destroyed in the hostilities, became unprofitable because of lost markets, or were sold by the government to finance the war effort. Others were lost in revolutionary upheavals, especially in Russia after 1917.

For industrial capital the effects of the war were mixed. Some industries welcomed it and the *Daily Telegraph* (19 August 1914) spoke for them: 'This war provides our businessmen with such an opportunity as has never come their way before. . . . There is no reason why we should not permanently seize for this country a large proportion of Germany's export trade.' Indeed, the war temporarily restored the profitability of large sections of capital. There was practically no control of profits, and there was a sudden huge demand for the output of many industries (in particular those producing clothing, munitions, engineering or transport equip-

[1] *Finance capitalists*, like commercial, merchant and investment banks, or insurance companies, make their profits out of owning financial assets – stocks, shares, government bonds (the national debt) – or performing financial services like insurance. The profits of industrial capital on the other hand come from making commodities. We sometimes refer to the two kinds of capital as finance and industry.

receives from foreigners for exports and for assets sold to foreigners. The balance of payments is in equilibrium if payments to foreigners and receipts from foreigners cancel out; it is in deficit if payments to foreigners are in excess of receipts from them.

Table 2.2. British Overseas Investments 1854–1930

	Total £m.	PERCENTAGES IN					PERCENTAGES IN					
		British Empire	United States	Latin America	Europe	Rest of world	Govt. & Municipal	Railways	Public utilities	Commerce & industry	Raw materials	Banks and finance
1854	210											
1880	1,300											
1885	1,302											
1895	1,600											
1905	2,025											
1909	2,332											
1913	3,763	47	20	20	6	7	30	41	5	6	10	8
1930	3,726	59	5	21	8	7	42	24	5	8	13	7
Rate of return in 1930 (%)							4·5	4·9	6·0	7·0	9·0	6·2

Source: Royal Institute of International Affairs, *The Problem of International Investment*, pp. 119, 121–2, 142–4, 154.

ment). Moreover, the nature of the war economy was such as to virtually eliminate international competition. Before government control was imposed there was a vast amount of profiteering, especially in shipping and coal, where profits in 1916 (the year they were restricted) were three times the average of the five pre-war years. But because of the demands of war expenditure there was very little investment in new plant and machinery or in new industries. So by the end of the war the amount of capital equipment per person in Britain was almost certainly well below what it had been in 1870. This left British industry even more vulnerable to competition, especially from the United States.

To a large extent the war was financed at the expense of the working class: up to 1917 workers allowed 'the value of their real wages to be whittled away by the creeping inflation',[1] [5] which the government spending caused. Real average wage rates[2] are estimated to have dropped by about one fifth in the first three years of the war. In other words they were back to their old level of the 1880s (and the fifteenth century!). Real actual earnings did not fall so much since there was a lot of overtime working, night-time work and bonuses. But in the long run the real wage rate was what counted since bonuses and overtime could not be relied on for ever.

The decline in wages occurred partly because so many of the trade-union leaders gave up the class struggle and joined the government, did war work of some kind or led the working class into agreements such as the Treasury Agreement of 1915 (later in the year incorporated in the Munitions of War Act) in which they voluntarily renounced the strike weapon for the duration of the war. For a time, therefore, the working class was disarmed.

But there were strikes, in South Wales and on the Clyde, for instance. And an economic historian has described how by 1917 'feelings of patriotism and self-sacrifice were giving way to disillusionment at the sight of the uninhibited profiteering and luxury spending of the rich, when it contrasted with the food shortages and queues, and occasional complete breakdowns in supplies of

---

[1]*Inflation* means rising prices.

[2]*Wage rates* means centrally negotiated rates for jobs, which may be supplemented by overtime, or employers paying more than the minimum so that earnings are greater.

tea, sugar, meat, fats or potatoes in the working class quarters'.[6]
The response to this was another enormous increase during the war
in the membership of the trade unions – from about 4 million in
1913 to over 8 million in 1919. Although the leadership of the
movement had emasculated itself by joining the war effort, the
fight to halt the erosion of rights and to improve material conditions of the workers was taken up all over the country through the
growth of the shop stewards' movement.

In the last year of the war, to the great alarm of the government,
industrial unrest, under the leadership of the shop stewards, grew
fast, especially after the Russian revolution in March. A special

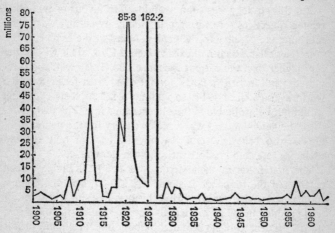

Figure 3. Working days lost due to industrial disputes 1900–1964
Source: British Labour Statistics, Table 197.

Ministry of Labour was established and the workers received a
number of concessions in the form of improved unemployment
insurance. At the same time the voluntary restrictions of wage
demands broke down. There was a major campaign for an eight-
hour working day with no loss of pay, and here, as on other questions, 'the rank and file membership appeared to be far more
militant than their leadership'.[7] The number of working days
lost through strikes rose from about 2½ million in 1915 and 1916 to

over 5 million in 1917 and 1918. But the real struggle was to break out when the war was over.

The end of the war allowed the pent-up demand both for consumer goods and investment goods to be satisfied, and the post-war boom was sudden and devastating. In spite of demobilization, full employment was achieved within a few months. Because of the lack of investment during the war (and the years before it) industrial output did not reach the 1913 figure during the 1919–20 boom. To some extent the boom was engineered by the government to avoid intensified social conflict resulting from demobilization followed by unemployment.

But this strategy was soon abandoned in favour of two other related objectives – restoring profitability by cutting wages and returning the country to the gold standard at the exchange rate with the dollar which had existed before 1914.[1] This was 10 per cent higher than the current exchange rate. This revaluation[2] required a fall in British costs, for they had risen faster than the world average since 1914; so without a fall in costs exporting would not be profitable at the old exchange rate. The plan to restore the gold standard was a major victory for the financial interests who believed, somewhat mystically, that only the old exchange rate could restore their pre-war dominance.

The first fruits of their victory was the 1920 Budget which engineered the tremendous slump of 1920–21, one of the most sudden and catastrophic in British history. In a single year industrial production fell by more than a quarter; unemployment rose from 2 per cent to 18 per cent of the labour force; company profits fell by more than half. Mining, railways, metals, vehicles and cotton were worst hit. If they were to compete in world markets and still make a profit the industrial capitalists would clearly have to cut their costs. In the circumstances, unemployment was a major

[1] Under the *gold standard* the government guaranteed to buy and sell gold in exchange for pounds at a particular rate. Given that other currencies were also fixed in terms of gold this implied particular rates at which for example pounds and dollars could be exchanged – the 'exchange rate'.

[2] *Revaluation* of a currency means that it becomes more expensive in terms of other currencies (the opposite of devaluation). Thus when the pound was revalued the dollar prices of British goods would rise, unless the sterling price of these goods could be reduced.

weapon of the industrialists against the bargaining strength of the workers, and throughout the 1920s it never fell significantly below 10 per cent of the working population.

The end of the war saw a huge increase in strikes. In 1919 in the major trades 35 million working days were lost (compared with 10 million in 1970). Between 1919 and 1926 (excluding the General Strike) the average number of working days lost was about 40 million a year. Clearly, the social climate and the relationship of the ruling and the working classes had been irrevocably changed by the war. There was a 'growing determination of Labour to challenge the whole existing structure of capitalist industry'.[8] But then, as today, the ruling class was more conscious than labour of the really critical nature of the situation. From 1919 to 1921 the Cabinet was haunted by the possibility that continued strikes, especially from the Triple Alliance of miners, railwaymen and transport workers, would lead to coups in major cities. Lloyd George feared a 'Soviet government' if the miners won their proposed strike of 1921.

The most conflict-ridden industries were those whose profitability had been most damaged – the railways* and the traditional exporting industries. Worst of all was the coal industry, which had to be given a government subsidy – 'the issue at stake in the British mining dispute in 1919 was not so much an industrial question as it was the government's role in the total economy and on whose behalf government powers should be used'.[9] The government rejected outright some sort of nationalization, which was what a majority of the official Sankey Committee, and the mining workers' union, had been demanding. This left the owners to find a solution when government control of the mines was ended in 1921, though the government was prepared to give all the political and military support which they required. The mine owners lost their guaranteed profit and they demanded massive wage cuts, which provoked the miners' strikes of April 1921. The Triple Alliance issued a call for a sympathy strike on 15 April. A statement proposing regional settlements made by Hodges, the miners' general secretary, on the

---

*The railways were in such straits that the owners' leader, Sir Herbert Walker, described the government's implementation of the 8-hour day as 'perhaps the most wicked thing that had ever been perpetrated on a community'.

14th was repudiated the next day by the N.U.M. executive. But Hodges' retreat gave Thomas, the N.U.R. leader, the excuse he wanted to withdraw the Triple Alliance support. This was Black Friday.

By 1921 wage-cutting and efforts to lengthen the working week were becoming central to the capitalists' strategy. Baldwin believed that 'all the workers in this country have got to take a reduction in wages to help put industry on its feet'.[10] Money wages in fact fell 38 per cent between the winter of 1920–21 and the winter of 1923–4; and many of these cuts were not secured without the most fierce class struggle.*

The wage cuts were needed partly because industrial capitalists were experiencing a dramatic growth in international competition. Some idea of this can be seen by comparing Britain's growth of industrial output with that of other countries. World manufacturing output had grown by a fifth between 1913 and 1925 while Britain's had fallen by 14 per cent. Industrial output had more than doubled in Japan, risen by 40 per cent in Italy and the U.S.A. and was around its pre-war level in France and Germany. Only Russia, among major countries, fared worse than Britain.

By 1925 the exchange rate with the dollar had risen to its pre-war level and the gold standard was restored. This worsened the competitive situation of British industry: and there was 'no room for doubt that British prices were too high'.[11] The financiers' hope for some restoration of their pre-war international position as a result of the restoration of the Gold Standard was vain. During the war, income earned from overseas investment had fallen in relation to the total size of imports. New capital investment was restricted by political instability abroad, low profitability at home and the emergence of New York as an easier capital market than London. In many ways the effects of the war were decisive in allowing the United States to become the premier capitalist and imperialist country.†

---

* Real wages fell less, because 55 per cent of the wage reductions in 1921 and 38 per cent in 1922 were the result of sliding-scale agreements by which money wages varied with the cost of living.

† America changed from a net long-term debtor of $1·9 billion in 1914 to a long-term creditor of $8·4 million in 1930.

Financiers, however, had benefited from the growth of the national debt on which they received the interest payments.[1] Although it meant heavier taxes, this was one of the ways in which the personal income of the bourgeoisie[2] was maintained at a time of economic crisis.*

Meanwhile the working class had from 1921 been suffering crushing defeats at the hands of capital and the government. Trade-union membership was down again to $5\frac{1}{2}$ million. Real wages fell. From 1922 to 1926 the strikes were more defensive: they were much fewer in number than in the years immediately after the war, but they lasted much longer. That was an index of the intransigence of capital as much as that of labour. Many of the days lost were through lock-outs. The prolonged engineering lock-out of 1922 ended with a return to work on the employers' terms, which included a disputes procedure which the unions only renounced in 1971. The embattled mining industry continued to be the centre of dispute. After 'Black Friday', the miners struck for three months but were forced to return on the owners' terms. In 1924, in response to a threat by the Labour government to introduce a new minimum wage for miners, the owners raised wages. Their position was eased by the French occupation of the Ruhr which reduced foreign competition. But in 1925 a worsening of the economic prospects of the industry and the return of a Tory government stimulated the mine owners to demand further wage cuts. Conflict was staved off

---

[1] *Interest* paid on the *national debt* (the government's accumulated borrowings) is financed by taxes which reduce the spending power of the incomes earned in the course of production.

[2] By *capitalist class* (*bourgeoisie*) we mean those who live off investment incomes or who manage companies on behalf of the owners. We usually use 'capitalists' when members of their class are acting in the productive process. So we talk of 'capitalists' putting up prices, but of the 'bourgeoisie' receiving profits.

*'Compared with the pre-war position, the national debt increased from 1/40 to 1/4 of the total private property in the country; the annual interest payments, negligible before the war, rose to over 40 per cent of the budget, and as prices fell in the early 1920s, the real burden of the debt, both on the budget and in more general terms, as a payment from the mainly active part of the population to the mainly inactive, became distinctly heavier.' (S. Pollard, *The Development of the British Economy, 1914–1967*, p. 201.)

by a temporary subsidy from the government ('Red Friday'), and the Samuel Commission was appointed. The T.U.C. meanwhile pledged its support for the miners.

At the end of April 1926 the subsidy expired and the miners were locked out. The T.U.C. called a general strike for 3 May. They had had nine months since Red Friday to prepare, but they had done nothing; and they would not step up their political demands. The government, on the other hand, had mobilized its strike-breaking forces with care. After nine days the struggle was decisively lost when the T.U.C. leaders, with appalling irresponsibility but evident relief, called off the strike and abandoned the miners to their fate.* The miners held out for a further six months before capitulating. The catastrophe of the General Strike led the Labour movement to a period of unprecedented weakness. One sign of this was that the average number of working days lost through strikes fell from 40 million a year from 1919 to 1926 to about 3 million a year from 1927 to 1938. By 1934 trade-union membership was down to $4\frac{1}{2}$ million.

In the late 1920s, with the exchange rate stabilized and relative industrial peace reigning, the British economy shared a little of the world-wide boom in economic conditions. For those with jobs real wages rose considerably up to 1931, and the profit situation was also easier.

But from 1929 world capitalism entered the most serious crisis of its history. 'For the first time since industrialization began the growth of production in all the industrial powers faltered.'[12]

---

*Trotsky's fears of March 1926 were, in the event, well borne out: 'In Great Britain, more than in all the rest of Europe, the consciousness of the working masses, particularly of the leading strata, lags behind the objective economic situation. In this direction the main difficulties and dangers now lie. All shades of leaders of the British Labour movement fear action, because the historic hopelessness of British capitalism directly confronts any important problem of the British labour movement. This particularly concerns the mining industry ... Great Britain is entering an entire historic phase of great upheavals. It is only the conservative British trade unionists who can wait for an 'economic' solution of the problems ... the British trade unionists are directing their efforts towards an 'economic' (i.e. peaceful, compromising, conservative) solution of the problem (i.e. are going counter to the historic process) ...' (letter 5 March 1926, quoted in *International Socialism*, p. 48).

But Britain suffered less than most other countries. Between 1929 and 1932 industrial production in the U.S. fell 54 per cent; in Germany it fell by 42 per cent; but in Britain by only 17 per cent. Construction and electricity production actually increased.

In Britain, Germany and the U.S. profit rates had climbed a little during the twenties. During the depth of the slump they collapsed into losses for about three years in both Germany and the U.S., whereas in Britain the rate of profit did not even fall back to its level of the early 1920s. Total profits fell by nearly one quarter between 1929 and 1932, which was less than in the single year 1920–21. British capitalism was less damaged for two reasons: firstly, it had become adjusted to slump conditions throughout the 1920s and secondly, the weakening of the working-class organizations during the 1920s made it easier to force down wages, though 'money wages fell very little in heavily unionized industries. Money wages in manufacturing fell much less than in service industries (where unions were in general weak), and within manufacturing money wages fell less in industries where unions were strong than in other industries.'[13] Real wages for those in employment rose even in the worst years of the depression mainly because of the collapse of prices in international commodity markets. Everywhere it was the millions without jobs who suffered most. Unemployment at its peak reached 14 million in the U.S., 6 million in Germany and nearly 3 million in Britain (22 per cent of the labour force); many towns in South Wales had three quarters of their men out of work.

There was a marked rise in national income, investment and profits between 1932 and 1934, but the rest of the recovery of the thirties was slow and there was little direct help from the government. The basic problems of the industries which had been in trouble in the 1920s were hardly touched. There was a marked shift in the structure of manufacturing industries towards those new industries – vehicles, electronics, electricity, non-ferrous metals and metal goods – which had already been built up in the other major capitalist countries during the boom years of the 1920s which Britain never experienced. These new industries were based to a greater extent on the home market than the old industries had been, and the share of exports in the national product fell from 33 per cent in 1907 to 27 per cent in 1924 and only 15 per cent in 1938.

After 1931 an attempt was made to recoup some of Britain's share of world trade by trading agreements with individual countries and by devaluation[1] (going off the gold standard). The latter policy only had an effect for about two years, since other countries, including the U.S., followed suit. Another line of policy was 'to try to keep up the rate of profit in some industries by lending support to monopolistic arrangements: coal, cotton, iron and steel, railways, agriculture and shipbuilding';[14] this was so important that '. . . in 1914 Britain was perhaps the least concentrated[2] of the great industrial economies, and in 1939 one of the most'.[15]

Although Ramsay Macdonald's National (basically Conservative) government in 1931 imposed the domestic policies which the bankers had been advocating (cuts in unemployment and other social benefits), in other ways the reaction to the financial crisis which followed the slump was a major defeat for the financial interests in Britain. The Gold Standard had gone and so had free trade, for new protective tariffs were imposed on most industrial products. The emergency in which industrial capital found itself was so pressing that it had to be dealt with even at the cost of sacrificing the interests of the City. The City and the banks reacted by involving themselves in moves, mainly through cartelization,[3] to rescue industry.

But in the 1930s industry still did not find finance to meet its needs from the banks. At times when profits fell, undistributed profits fell even more since firms felt obliged 'to maintain their dividend payments[4] in adverse trading conditions'.[16] Although 'firms were . . . preferring to rely primarily on internal sources of

---

[1] *Devaluation* meaning lowering the value of the pound in terms of foreign currencies.

[2] *Concentration* measures the degree to which industry is monopolized, i.e. the degree to which it is dominated by a few large firms. Concentration takes place mainly by firms merging.

[3] *Cartels* are groups of independent firms who agree to fix prices. If the arrangement covers a whole industry it acts, therefore, like a monopoly which does not have to worry about competitors.

[4] *Dividends* are that part of profits (after fixed interest payments have been made) which are paid out to shareholders rather than retained by the company and reinvested.

funds', investment was not as badly hit as might be expected since many firms had accumulated reserves and 'their general liquidity[1] positions were strong'.[17] This was also the reason why more firms did not collapse in the slump. But some investment trusts and hire purchase companies did manage to grow during the 1930s' recovery in close alliance with the banks, and consequently established a closer link between finance and industry. And heavy industry, steel and coalmining, for instance, made their monopolistic arrangements 'inspired by the banks, with strong support

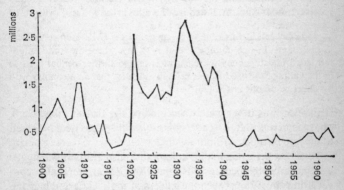

Figure 4. Unemployment 1900–1964
Source: The British Economy Key Statistics, 1900–64, Table C.

from the government'.[18] In cotton many firms 'were heavily loaded with bank debts contracted in the speculative boom after the First World War'.[19] The banks were not anxious to be further involved and encouraged mergers.

The working class was severely weakened by the high level of unemployment – over 15 per cent from 1930 to 1935 – and by the treason of its leaders – those of the trade unions in 1926, those of the Labour Party in 1931. After 1934 union membership began to

[1] The *liquidity position* of a firm is good when its reserves of cash are large relative to the debts which it may be called on to settle immediately.

rise quite fast again as unemployment fell. The number of working days lost through strikes remained at 5 million or more each year between 1929 and 1932 during the depths of the slump, as workers tried (usually vainly) to fight redundancies and wage cutting; but thereafter it fell sharply and never again approached 5 million for the rest of the 1930s. After 1934 there was no national strike in any industry for 20 years.

Capital was able to secure a steady increase in the profit share in industry and in the rate of profit from 1932 onwards. In this respect the defeat which the working class suffered during the inter-war period is comparable to that which the German working class received under Nazism: the share of wages in the value of output[1] of

... industry fell at this time in Sweden and the U.K. even more than in Germany. In two countries, that is to say, where the trade unions remained intact, money wage earnings lagged farther behind the rise in the value of the product per head in industry, than in a country with no effective unions at all. [20]

If Fascism was never widely accepted by the British ruling class, one reason was that the leaders of the working class were prepared to give up so much without a fight.

This was evidence of the collaborationist attitude which the leaders had developed towards capitalism. For instance, after conversations in 1928 between the leaders of the T.U.C. and a group of 20 employers headed by Sir Alfred Mond, founder-chairman of I.C.I., 'Mondism' was born. This was the tendency (in the words of the T.U.C. General Council) 'for the trade-union movement to say boldly that not only is it concerned with the prosperity of industry but it is going to have a voice in the way industry is carried on. ... The unions can use their power to promote and guide the scientific reorganization of industry.'[21] An addendum to the Macmillan Report of 1931 signed among others by Sir T. Allen of the Co-operative Movement and Ernest Bevin of the T.G.W.U. and T.U.C., was another example: 'A readiness to

[1] The *share of wages* in this case is total wages in industry expressed as a proportion of the value of industrial output. Sometimes the share of wages in the national income is referred to: it is the total of all wages expressed as a proportion of national income. It is the counterpart of the share of profits.

accept the fact that the value of incomes is something which must be accommodated to changing circumstances is, indeed, an essential of the sound working of the economic system.'[22]

Such collaboration by the official Labour movement had its effect on real wages, which at best remained stationary in the 1930s. This conclusion depends a lot on the accuracy of the cost of living estimate, which is disputed, and even more on the exclusion of unemployment. If allowance is made for unemployment in the estimate in order to get some idea of the average living standards for the working class as a whole, then the real wages of 1913 were not attained again until 1930, and the post-war peak of 1937 was only 5 per cent above the real wage of 1913. Because there was stagnation before the war, this represents a figure only 5 per cent above that for 1900; or to be a bit more fanciful, about a quarter above the level that had been reached in the fifteenth century!

The most militant sections of the labour movement after the early 1920s were the least official. The militants in a number of unions had come together, largely under Communist leadership, in the years 1923–4 to form minority movements and eventually, in 1924, the National Minority Movement, which rejected the class collaboration of the union leaders and the peaceful transition from capitalism to socialism. At its peak in 1926 the N.M.M. represented almost one million workers. But the movement was compromised, confused and in effect disarmed by its links with Stalinism – initially by the Moscow support of the 'left' leaders who betrayed the General Strike, and then in 1928 by the new line coming from Stalin. Instead of using the slogan 'compel the leaders to fight', revolutionary trade unionists were to 'oust the reformists, to lead the strikes that arise spontaneously, and direct them against the bourgeoisie and against the trade-union apparatus'.[23] These were, as Trotsky remarked, 'fatal excesses . . . No better favour could be done for the trade-union bureaucracy.'[24] After the new line some efforts were made to form separate revolutionary unions, but they were failures; so was a campaign for a Workers' Charter. In the end the union bureaucracies were able to crush the M.M.s: '. . . the irrelevance of the new line, and the demoralization, division and confusion which followed its imposition, prevented the

M.M. from taking full advantage of the slump and the failure of the Labour Government in 1929–31'.[25]

In the early 1930s new militant movements sprang up which were unconnected with the M.M. or the Communist Party: the London Busmen's Rank and File Movement, the Railwaymen's Vigilance Movement, the Members' Rights Movement in the A.E.U. and the Building Workers' Rank and File Movement. The National Unemployed Workers' Committee Movement waged a continuous fight against reductions in public benefits. It was by no means impotent, but all the same it was greatly weakened by its isolation from the potential strength of the organized working class. On their own the unemployed had no economic leverage, and the union bureaucracies had no strategy against unemployment.

Between the wars there were tremendous swings of fortune for capital and labour. In 20 years of crisis, profits and real wages always moved in contrary directions (see Table 2.3). In this turbulence the working class had for the time being suffered a severe defeat and capital had managed to change many aspects of its structure. It was rescued from its long instability by a new war.

Table 2.3. Percentage Shifts in Profits and Real Wages, 1920–38

	1920–21	1921–5	1925–6	1926–9	1929–32	1932–7	1937–8
Profits*	−33·4	+27·3	−6·9	−13·7	−25·2	+64·6	−4·5
Real incomes of wage earners	+3·0	−2·9	0·0	+6·0	+7·8	0·0	+2·6

* Industry, manufacturing, construction, public utilities, transport and distribution, but *not* finance and the professions.

Source: Aldcroft, *The Inter-war Economy*, p. 34.

3. The Second World War and the post-war expansion

Rearmament and then the war eliminated unemployment by 1941. The war also brought a slightly ambiguous pledge from the government that full employment would be maintained in future peacetime as a matter of policy. This was of course part of a deal designed to ensure the cooperation of the working class in the war. The membership of trade unions shot up and had passed 8 million by 1943. However, strikes were declared illegal, and the Minister of Labour had powers to refer all disputes to compulsory arbitration. The trade unions cooperated even with anti-strike legislation, wage restraint and direction of labour. A number of the union leaders (especially Bevin as Minister of Labour) were intimately occupied in the administration after the Labour Party joined Churchill's coalition government in 1940.

So 'wartime strikes were short, small and unofficial'.[26] In 1944 over $3\frac{1}{2}$ million working days were lost through strikes but in other years it was much less. Wage rates during the war failed to keep pace with the increases in prices, although 'regular hours of work if not overtime, night shifts and weekend work, together with much piecework and up-grading of workers, raised actual earnings a good deal more than wage rates'.[27] From 1938 to 1945 prices rose 48 per cent, wage rates only 43 per cent, but earnings went up 80 per cent. At the same time profit and rent restriction were enforced with far more rigour than in the First World War. The result was a marked shift in the distribution of income towards labour. By 1949 the share of labour in the total output of manufacturing industry, which in 1938 had stood at 64 per cent, had risen to 79 per cent.

The most dramatic change produced by the war was in the international position of British capitalism. The United States invested quite heavily in new equipment, while in Britain net investment was negative throughout the war; the value of capital equipment fell by about 12 per cent of the national income each year. 'At the end of the war less than 2 per cent of the labour force was engaged on exports, compared with 9·5 per cent before the war.'[28] The war was partially financed by forced borrowing by the British government from a number of Commonwealth countries such as India, Burma and Australia. The loans constituted a new debt for the British government which became known as the sterling balances. By 1945 these amounted to about £3,500 million, and they were destined to restrict the British government's latitude in economic policy in the years following the war.

The explosive political sequel to the First World War did not follow the Second. 1945 saw a Labour government, committed to a wide range of reforms, returned with an enormous majority. The working class gained from better schooling and subsidized school food, a general free health service, improved unemployment benefit and pensions and, perhaps most important of all, early full employment. Apart from a brief rise to 3 per cent in 1947, unemployment stayed below 2 per cent for most of the Labour government's term of office.

The government altered the structure of capitalism by nationalizing a number of basic industries. Some of these had already been under public ownership and others had been publicly controlled during the war. Many of the nationalizations had been recommended by the Tory-dominated committees. But nationalization meant a bit more than legalizing an existing situation. It brought up to 20 per cent of industry under public ownership, though usually under the same management as before.

Nationalization created an important economic and political difference from the situation which arose after the First World War. The coal industry and the railways were no more capable of making profits in the forties than they had been in the twenties. The profitability of the industries which were nationalized had been on average about one third that of the rest of private industry before the war. But the workers' demand for nationalization, which had been politically explosive after the First World War, was now carried out. So the pressure on the miners was for a short time lifted; nationalization, which could endure long periods of unprofitability, ended for the time being the threat to jobs and wage levels which existed in the 1920s.

Nationalization also took some of the pressure off the capitalists. Most of the owners of the mines, railways and other industries were happy with their compensation, described for some industries as 'generous beyond the dreams of avarice'.[29]* In other industries some of the pressure of costs on profitability was re-

---

* Lenin shrewdly remarked that 'a state monopoly in capitalist society is nothing more than a means of increasing and guaranteeing the income of millionaires in one branch of industry or another who are on the verge of bankruptcy'.

lieved by obtaining supplies of basic industrial commodities (fuel and transport) from the nationalized industries at prices which were lower than they would have needed to be under private ownership struggling for profitability. So the nationalized sector bore the brunt of the fall in the rate of profit over the war and this eased for a time the economic and political pressure which would otherwise have resulted.

There were other ways in which the Labour government broke new ground in its relations with private industry. It gave large grants for re-equipment, and set up councils on productivity which aimed to help the modernization of private industry. More than any previous administration the Labour government felt itself responsible for the prosperity of British industry. There were widespread controls, but much of the price fixing was administered by businessmen, and in fact kept profits up and real wages down. There was no effective anti-monopoly policy, but there were Development Councils for industries (on which management, unions and government were represented) which aimed to promote rationalization and efficiency.

The government also formed new relations with the working class. The trade-union leadership was incorporated into the structure of government. Their cooperation was asked for and received over numerous issues, the most dramatic being the wage freeze of 1948. They also accepted the drop in living standards implied by the devaluation of 1949. The wage restraint practised by the unions held the growth of real disposable income down to virtually zero over the five years of Labour rule. Most important of all, the union leaders agreed to the continuation until 1950 of the National Arbitration Order which made all strikes illegal and they supported some partial direction of labour to particular jobs from 1947. Over the five years 1945–50 the number of working days lost never rose above 2½ million a year and the strikes were all unofficial.

The result of all this was the growth of dissatisfaction at the rank-and-file level among the trade unions, a sign of which was the General Council's defeat at the 1950 T.U.C. over the continuation of wage restraint. The nationalizations, the efforts to increase productivity, the devaluation and the wage restraint all served to strengthen the position of British capital after the war, and up to

1950 the workers' share of the product in industry fell significantly.

However, the underlying condition of British capitalism was critical. Aside from two brief periods at the end of the twenties and the end of the thirties, there had been nearly fifty years of very low or negative investment in manufacturing industry. The result of this did not show so much in the first five years after the war: controls on trade and the destruction of industrial capacity in Germany and Japan allowed British capitalists a brief prominence on the world stage. Only the U.S. was obviously ahead. But the fifties ushered in a very different period.

The inflation caused by the Korean War, and the election of a Conservative government in 1951 which remained in office until 1964, saw the end of effective wage control. Also, the dismantling of trade controls began a new era of rapidly growing international trade in which British capital faced increasingly fierce competition from Germany, Japan and Italy, whose economic recovery after 1950 was astonishingly rapid. Devaluation was ruled out as an instrument of policy. Though no one admitted it, this implied that full employment might have to be sacrificed in order to reduce imports by controlling demand.

There were some marked similarities between the fifties and the era before the outbreak of the First World War. British capitalism faced increasing competition in world markets; it was continuously losing part of its share of world output and exports. Its level of investment and economic growth was low by international standards. This lack of competitiveness, combined with unwillingness to devalue the exchange rate, led to repeated crises in the balance of payments which were always answered by restrictions on home demand, further checking the rate of growth. British capital once more turned to overseas investment as a source of profit. The outflow of private long-term investment averaged £180 million between 1952 and 1955. In 1961–4 the average had risen to £320 million. The income from British investment abroad had reached about £500 million a year by the early 1960s. But this investment was very much less significant than that before the First World War. Another major difference was that the phenomenal growth in the capitalist world market during the period from 1950 to 1964 could hardly fail to involve Britain to some extent. While the economy fared worse in Britain than in most other major capitalist countries, it still experienced its fastest sustained rate of growth since the middle of the nineteenth century. Real wages in Britain also grew at an unprecedented rate, about twice the average increase over the previous century and faster than in other periods of similar length. Again, this was much slower than in Germany, Italy or Japan.

The union leadership was often as eager to cooperate with a Conservative administration as it had been with a Labour one; 'Wage moderation', declared the General Council, 'is more than a political matter, to be used discriminately to help one government or another.'[30] The pressures of militancy which had built up during the years after the war were less easy to control after the Labour government had gone. The result was an increase, though not a very great one, in the number of strikes during the 1950s. After 1953 at least 2 million working days were lost every year; in 1957 over 8 million days were lost, mostly in the shipbuilding and engineering industries, and in 1959 and 1962 over 5 million. The average length of strikes was much lower than it had been before the war. It was in the motor industry especially that the strikes, mostly unofficial, became common. This had a lot to do with the power and strength of the shop stewards' movement in the industry and the constant re-negotiation at local level of wages and conditions.

Trade unions tended to push hard for wage increases and, as the period wore on, the annual wage claim became more and more of an institution. By the end of the 1950s the unprecedented growth of wages had badly damaged the position of capital (see chapter 3). The government began to institute various forms of wages policy (see chapter 8). Given the growing rank and file pressures it was, however, difficult for a Tory government to maintain the cooperation of the trade-union leadership.

Throughout the period from 1950 to 1964 capital was once again subject to two pressures – one from the trade unions on the wages front and in resistance to measures which might have increased productivity; the other from the growing competition of other capitalist countries. The high level of demand[1] compared with the

[1] *Demand* is the total of expenditure on goods and services by private

Table 2.4. Average Rates of Growth of Incomes, 1946–64
(1963 prices, average for the population)

Between the years ...	per cent a year 1946–51	1951–64
... average personal incomes before tax grew by ...	0·0	3·1
... but tax payments on income rose or fell by ...	−4·3	3·4
... and national insurance contributions grew by ...	14·5	5·7
So personal disposable income only went up by ...	0·1	2·9
Out of this average, consumers' spending increased by ...	0·7	2·4
... leaving savings changing by ...	−19·9	17·4

Source: Incomes Data Report 92, p. 31.

Table 2.5. Average Days Lost per Worker on Strike, 1914–64

1914–18	8·4
1919–26	32·2
1927–38	10·6
1953–64	3·3

Source: T. Cliff, *International Socialism*, p. 48.

inter-war period could not check the joint result of these pressures: a steady shift in the distribution of income away from capital towards labour, and a reduction in the rate of profit (see chapter 3). These changes heralded the acute crisis of profitability which was to build up in the 1960s. They escaped the notice of much of the

consumers, by the government (e.g. building, schools), by private companies when they carry out investment, and by foreigners when they buy exports. The government can expand demand by spending more itself (public expenditure) or by cutting taxes or relaxing credit controls in order to increase private consumption or investment.

bourgeoisie partly because taxes on property income fell for the post-war period as a whole and bourgeois living standards were not hit along with capital's share of the national income. A new and critical situation was slowly but unmistakably developing.

4. Historical origins of the crisis

The history of British capitalism over the last hundred years has thrown up some recurring themes. One of these is the problem of the international competitiveness of industry. This first became a cause for alarm in the 1880s, when Britain's industrial monopoly was challenged. It became even more obvious in the years before the First World War. After the war some of the basic exporting industries were in terrible trouble and many firms were forced out of existence. The growth of protection and the change in industrial structure of the 1930s made the problem less acute; but since the Second World War it has become prominent again.

One cause of competitive weakness was the relatively low level of investment in industrial capacity, especially since 1900. This led to a slower growth of productivity than in rival countries. One of the major reasons for this low investment was low profitability. Profitability was not always higher in other industrial countries, but German and American industry has never relied as much as British on the supply of finance from its own resources often instead borrowing from banks and outside investors. This exposes another of the recurrent themes: the comparative separation of industrial from financial capital.

There have been many examples of the rivalry of finance and industry at work. At times finance has preferred free trade (because it coexisted with free movement of capital) when protection would have been beneficial for industry. This was certainly true in the years between 1880 and 1913 and again after the First World War. Finance favoured a high exchange rate when industry needed devaluation, and this was true not only in the years after 1920 when the rate was forced up to an absurd level and held there until 1931, but again from the late 1950s, until 1967 at least. Finance has pressed for high interest rates to attract foreign funds and maintain

41

the reserves while industry has wanted low interest rates to cheapen the finance of investment: again the 1920s were such a time, and so were the 'stop' phases of the cycles of the 1950s and 1960s. Finally, finance has opposed increases in government spending to avoid shaking international confidence in the currency at times when industry undoubtedly needed a higher level of demand: 1931 provides the most obvious example of this, though fewer industrialists realized it at the time than when it happened again in 1966. Of course, this conflict is not absolute: now and again the interests of the banks and of large sections of industry, especially the large exporters, have coincided.

However, over the years the divergence has grown bigger. It first became substantial in the years of imperialism before the First World War. It grew again over the period from 1930 to 1950, during which time industry was re-structured to rely much less on foreign and more on the home market than in the nineteenth century. For a time after the Second World War their interests seemed to merge over the Sterling Area,[1] which formed a protected market for exports of goods and capital and for financial services. But as trade liberalization was extended and the competitive position deteriorated, the Sterling Area was of less and less benefit to industry. The financiers nevertheless believed in the importance of sterling's world-currency role in maintaining London's position as a financial centre; and they resolutely opposed all talk of devaluation, which, it was correctly thought, would end the reserve role of sterling by confirming the worst fears of those whose confidence in it was waning.

This important contradiction in the structure of capitalism in Britain seems itself to be the result of two things. One of these is the uneven pace of development of industrial capitalism in different countries during the nineteenth century; the other is the basic contradiction between capital and labour. The appearance of the division between industry and finance coincided with the accentuation of foreign competition for British industry. To face this competition vast new investments in modern industrial plant had to be

[1] The *Sterling Area* was the group of countries (mainly colonies and ex-colonies) which held their reserves in London and cooperated on monetary and trading policies.

financed; that would have required in Britain the same integration of industry and finance as existed in Germany, France and America. This did not happen and the alternative structural change in capitalism which did take place was that financial capital decided to look outwards and invest abroad. By this route capitalism in Britain became imperialism.*

The banks and the City did not want to involve themselves directly in domestic industry because they evidently expected larger – or at least more secure – profits outside England. And it is very likely that one of the underlying reasons for this was the realization that the growing strength of the working class would make the profitability of industrial investment at home increasingly precarious. And on the whole, although the advantage in the class struggle has shifted back and forth, they have proved to be right.

One thing that emerges quite clearly from the best recent work on economic history is a trend towards labour taking a growing share of the national income, though in a few periods it has been temporarily reversed. C. Feinstein writes that

the evidence suggests clearly that from immediately before World War I to the present time there has been a secular upward trend in labour's share. It increased very markedly between 1910–14 and 1921–4; was steady between the wars; rose again very weakly, during or immediately after World War II; and has continued to creep upwards in the post-war period. [31]

P. Deane and W. Cole share this opinion:

For employment incomes as a whole the trend since 1914 has been so unmistakably upwards as to suggest to those who see little significance in the distinction between wages and salaries a strong presumption in favour of an increase in the share of labour.[32]

These judgements, which now seem to be established beyond all reasonable doubt, are in marked disagreement with what has become standard received opinion, a cherished myth of economists, both bourgeois and Marxist. The general opinion that the share of labour in the national income has been constant is clearly false.

The opinion has been based on the wrong figures. It is true that

*The other capitalist countries, of course, also became imperialist, but in response to rather different pressures.

over a long period of time the share of wages (as opposed to wages and salaries) have been a remarkably constant share of the national income. This constancy seems to be a coincidence. Progressively, salaried job categories (clerical and administrative, research workers, and so on) have expanded relative to wage-earning jobs.

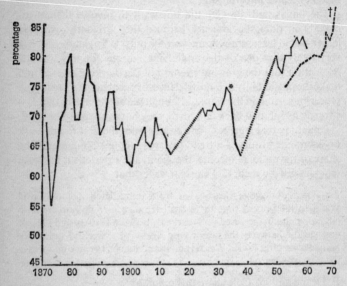

Figure 5. Changes in the share of wages in output 1870–1970
Sources: * Ratio of wages to the value of output in industry – E. H. Phelps-Brown and M. Brown, *A Century of Pay*, Appendix 3.
† Share of wages and salaries in net output (net of stock appreciation) in company sector – see Appendix C, Table C1.

At the same time many jobs have been transferred from wage-earning to salary-earning categories with no real change in their nature. The number of wage earners (that is, weekly paid workers) has not changed a great deal, while the number of salary earners has risen fast.* These salary earners have not ceased to be members

*In 1924 there were 13 million wage earners and 2·9 million salary earners; in 1961 there were 16·2 million wage earners and 7·1 million salary earners.

of the working class. Their relation to the means of production remains almost identical, though they may be entitled to more notice than wage earners when they are sacked. Although figures for salaries include the high incomes paid to company directors and the like – obviously not members of the working class – their average level relative to wages has been falling, and it is clerks and administrators, not company directors, who increasingly dominate the salary figures.* So the share of wages and salaries together is a little higher than the share of labour. But the share of wages alone is much lower than the share of labour, and the constant share of wages in income, combined with the falling share of wage earners in employment, implies that the position of labour as a whole has been improving relative to that of capital.

It is clear that within the capitalist system of a single country or firm there is a complicated interaction between the level of wages, the ability of firms to raise their prices (depending on the state of competition) and the share of wages in the total product. This relation is well explained by a major recent study of wages:

It remains for us to allow with any given level or course of the capital/output ratio [productivity of capital] it was always possible for the shares of pay and profit to rise and fall at one another's expense. Whether a general rise in wages, the outcome it may be of a wave of trade union militancy, would raise their share of pay, seems to have depended on the market environment of the time. If that environment was soft, firms generally would be able to edge prices up so as to maintain the same profit margin as before over the now higher unit wage cost. Only in the hard market environment, when there was no escape route through higher prices, were trade unions when they bargained about wages also bargaining about their share in the product.[33]

In addition, the productivity of capital is itself partly determined in the class struggle. It is part of what labour and capital are bargaining about when they debate manning, productivity, the speed of the line, the introduction of new equipment and so on.

The slow growth of labour productivity in British industry and the related low productivity of capital, combined with the frequent

* The average salary fell from 3 times the average wage in 1911 to only one third above it in 1961.

periods in the history of the last one hundred years of intense and growing international competition between capitals, means that the British working class have often had to bargain about their share of the national product. It is not very often that they have realized that this is what they were doing, except perhaps in retrospect, and by implication from the militancy of capital. But over the long run the working-class movement should have built up an awareness of what it has done in terms of increasing its share of the total product, and what the consequences of this are for the capitalist system. Without this awareness, and the political conclusions to be drawn from it, the working-class movement is weakened because it fails to understand the logic of its own strategy.

The consequence of a strategy which attempts to obtain wage increases or to resist wage cuts in a period when capital faces increasing competition, is that capitalists find it harder and harder to meet these demands and to remain profitable at the same time. Sometimes, therefore, capital and labour are bargaining not only about wages, nor even the division of the national income, but about the survival of the capitalist system. The leaders of the British working class have too often failed to realize this, or have realized it and retreated before its political implications. Times of crisis for capitalism are, therefore, times of choice for the working class – between revolution and collaboration.

In the past capitalism has sometimes managed to adapt itself to the working-class demands which it could not defeat. This adaptation has had a variety of forms. After 1880 it took the form of imperialism and the growth of foreign investment, and this has been a partial way out on other occasions. But in the 1920s there was no such answer and the re-structuring was more forcible and painful, taking the form of two decades of low investment, high unemployment and a good deal of monopolization and rationalization of the least profitable parts of industry. After the Second World War nationalization was a weapon of re-structuring which averted the situation which had arisen in the 1920s. At various times great merger movements have developed: one of these periods was between 1890 and 1914; another was in the 1930s; and another began in 1964. But there is a limit to the structural changes of which capitalism is capable.

Table 2.6. The Components of Real Wage Increases, 1871–1959

On average in the years – industrial productivity grew each year by — per cent and the	worker's share of output rose (+) or fell (−) by — per cent. The	purchasing power of his share rose (+) or fell (−) by — per cent so his real wages changed by — per cent.	
1871–95	2·06	−0·15	0·05	1·94
1895–1913	0·03	−0·32	0·16	−0·11
1924–38	1·79	−0·63	0·49	1·68
1949–59	2·07	+0·13	−0·92	2·16

Source: E. H. Phelps Brown and M. Browne, *A Century of Pay*, pp. 170, 263, 312.

The type of re-structuring which is possible, and the kind of first aid and emergency assistance which is available, depend a lot on the position taken by the government. The extent to which financial capital has controlled British government policy has meant at various times that industrial capital has been severely damaged by state policy, and forced into otherwise avoidable conflict with the working class. The state has not of course left it to fend for itself. On the contrary, it has often intervened in the class struggle on the side of capital. This has involved a great variety of policies. In extreme cases the whole military power of the state has been mobilized against the working class, as it was in a number of the struggles of the 1920s and especially during the General Strike. At other times legislation has been tried. The rights of the trade unions have been restricted in wartime by the ban on strikes between 1915 and 1918 and between 1940 and 1950; and in peacetime by the Taff Vale and Osborne judgments,[1] by the Trade Disputes Act of 1927,[2] and once again by the Industrial Relations Act of 1971. A more common method has been the attempt to incorporate the leadership of the working class into the apparatus of the state. This occurred in the 1930s, when the trade unions were particularly weak, during both world wars, and especially during the post-war Labour administration of 1945, when the unions were potentially very strong. It has to some extent become habitual.

The state has also tried to regulate the more specifically economic aspects of this struggle. Most important, it has tried to control or influence wages. This occurred during both world wars, and in the 1920s the government used all its influence to support the employers' demands for wage cuts. In the period after the last war the trade unions were induced to accept wage restraint and one period of complete wage freeze. The Tory government of 1951–64 revived wages policy in the last years of its rule, though not with very much success. The Wilson Labour government which succeeded it made continuous efforts during its term of office to implement various forms of wages policy (see chapter 8).

But some sections of capital cannot be saved by these methods alone. Hence the need sometimes for subsidies to capital which serve two purposes: first, they save it from bankruptcy or major decline; second, they alleviate for a time the immediate cause of class struggle in those industries. For both these reasons subsidies were granted to the failing coal industry in the post-First World War period, and again in the nine months before the General Strike. In the second case they were used to allow the state to prepare its administrative and military reaction to the General Strike. Since the Second World War subsidies have taken the form of taxation and investment allowances. Large government handouts

[1] The *Taff Vale judgment* established that the funds of a trade union were liable for damages done by its officials. The *Osborne judgment* banned political contributions by trade unions to the Labour Party. They were largely reversed in 1906 and 1913 respectively.

[2] This outlawed political strikes and strikes in sympathy with other workers and split off the unions in the government service from the T.U.C. It was repealed by the Labour government after the war.

to failing industries have also become more common, especially in the shipbuilding and aerospace industries (see chapter 8). When subsidies are not enough there is always the possibility of nationalization or direct state management of industries; this the Labour party has implemented during its two post-war governments, and even the Tory government was forced to do the same in the case of Rolls-Royce in 1971. It appears that the need for all these measures or some combination of them has grown more or less continuously over the past 70 years.

The state has not always intervened directly on the side of capital, however. On occasions the threat from the working class has compelled the state to act in its defence, if only as the best way of stemming the pressure towards revolution. This was what lay behind the permitting of wage increases in the later years of the First World War. It was fears of revolution which prompted the government to suspend wage-cutting for six months in 1919. At other times the interests of the working class have been furthered in a limited way by Labour governments. The fact that these have been simultaneous with actions in defence of capital merely reflects the contradictions of a Labour party intent on introducing reforms on behalf of the working class without ever remotely threatening the capitalist system.

All the methods of state interference on behalf of capitalism contain their contradictions. And this is especially true of those which involve intervention directly against the working class in the class struggle. For these are bound to arouse the political consciousness of the working class and stimulate actions to defend its interests and rights. And even the periods in which the leadership of the working class has been absorbed into the apparatus of the state have also been times when the rank and file and the shop stewards have grown in power and strength. It now looks as though these developments may be irreversible.

Chapter 3
The Profitability Crisis of British Capitalism

British capitalism has an imperative need for profits, and it has been finding it more and more difficult to obtain them. That, essentially, is the nature of the economic crisis. The rest of the book is based on our discussion of this in the chapter which now follows. We argue firstly that there have been no major changes in the division between the capitalist and working classes in Britain, or in capital's requirement for profits as the condition of its survival. And yet, as we show next, profits in recent years have greatly shrunk in relation to the national income as a whole. We spend some time assessing the relative strength of the three possible causes of this dramatic development: the push for higher wages, the slow growth of the economy and the growing strength of world competition. Next, we look at this decline of profitability from another angle – the falling rate of profit, both overall and for particular industries. Finally, we ask why it is that British capital has faced such a particularly sharp growth of competition at the international level.

Falling profitability is the link between rising wages and prices on the one hand and unemployment and slow growth on the other. This is not as widely understood as it should be because the figures which prove the drop in profitability can only be obtained from rather complex calculations. They are not published in a simple and accessible form like those for the rate of growth; nor are they obvious from daily observation, like rapid wage and price increases or high unemployment. But they are just as significant.

1. Wealth, profits and exploitation in modern capitalism

Some people claim that the analysis of British society which sees it divided into classes of capitalists and workers is no longer applicable. They argue that the huge size of modern business, and a trend towards greater equality in the distribution of wealth, means that individual companies have large numbers of shareholders. This implies that the managers of a company, who will themselves own only a few of its shares, are free to operate in a quite different way from the nineteenth-century factory owners who ground down their work force. Thus, one prominent economist has written:

No longer the agent of proprietorship seeking to maximize return on investment, management sees itself as responsible to stockholders, employees, customers, the general public and, most importantly, the firm as an institution ... The modern corporation is a soulful corporation.[1]

Reasonable profits are necessary, so the argument goes, to reward initiative and provide finance for investment; but since share ownership is no longer concentrated in a few hands these profits should not be regarded as the product of exploitation of one class by another. With so many people both owning capital and working there are no clearly distinct classes of capitalists and workers. The Conservative Political Centre once even produced a pamphlet called *Everyman a Capitalist* pointing out the advantages of the 'closer association of wage earners and other small savers with the financing of business'.

But this picture is contradicted both by the facts on wealth ownership and by the reality of how capitalist corporations are compelled to operate. In 1960 the richest 1 per cent of Britain's population owned 42 per cent of personal wealth (shares, cash, land, houses, etc.) and the richest 5 per cent owned 75 per cent.*[2]

---

* Data in *Inland Revenue Statistics 1971*, Table 130 imply some fall in the inequality of the distribution of wealth since 1960 – the share of the richest 1 per cent of wealth owners falling from 28 per cent in 1960 to 21·5 per cent in 1969. But the data are seriously incomplete in that discretionary trusts, increasingly used by the rich to minimize death duties, are omitted from these figures.

The only real difference between 1960 and the pre-war years was that the very very rich (top 1 per cent) had lost some ground to the very rich (top 5 per cent), for the share of the top 5 per cent had fallen by only 4 points (i.e. from 79 per cent). But the ownership of companies is even more concentrated than the ownership of wealth as a whole. Death-duty statistics for 1967–8 show that shares accounted for less than 5 per cent of the average estate under £5,000 but that the proportion rose steadily with bigger estates, reaching about 50 per cent for those in excess of £75,000. Thus, while around 2 million people in Britain own some shares, under 10 per cent of these shareholders – less than $\frac{1}{2}$ per cent of the adult population – own about two thirds of total personal holdings of shares.*

Even though companies taken as a whole are owned by a tiny minority of the population, it is true that fewer and fewer giant corporations are effectively owned by individual tycoons or small family groups.† However, the professional managers who now control the majority of large companies have to worry about profits just as much as the traditional tycoon. They are obliged to keep dividends growing in order to keep up the share price of the firm, or else risk the sack if the firm is taken over. Even if they are subjectively interested not in profits but in the growth of the firm and the power and prestige which this brings them, profits are still essential to secure this growth. Profits provide directly much of the finance for growth; but they are also necessary for raising extra funds from outside. Even if managers have the power to dispose of some funds in ways which the shareholders would not approve,

---

*This leaves out of account shares held by pension funds and life-assurance funds on behalf of individuals. Although these holdings are becoming increasingly important, by the end of 1969 they comprised less than a quarter of private U.K. holdings of ordinary shares (see Table 4.2 in John Moyle, *The Pattern of Ordinary Share Ownership, 1957–70*, Cambridge University Press, 1971). In any case benefit from them is very unequally spread, though less so than personal holdings. Holdings in unit and investment trusts are included in our figures; those by discretionary trusts, which are even more unequally distributed than personal holdings, are omitted.

†Even so, one calculation suggested that a third of the largest 120 companies in the U.K. were so owned and controlled (M. Barratt Brown in K. Coates (ed.), *Can the Workers Control Industry?*, Sphere, London, 1969).

such as by building prestige office blocks, this power cannot be exercised without the profits which provide the funds. The promotion of junior managers within firms depends on their being able to impress top management with their abilities; generally they will do this by producing a dramatic rise in sales or reduction in costs. Either way, profits grow.

Table 3.1. Ownership of Shares

On average during 1964–69 — per cent of the total number of shareholders,	which means — per cent of the adult population,	held — per cent of total value of shares	in holdings of shares worth — £.
53·8	2·6	2·5	Less than £1000
37·6	1·9	29·5	Between £1000 and £20,000
8·6	0·4	68·0	Over £20,000
2·6	0·13	38·5	Over £50,000

Source: Inland Revenue Statistics 1971, Table 131. Figures refer to total quoted shares (ordinary and preference) and debentures.

The professional manager is thus unavoidably committed to the development of capitalist production; that is, production for profit. And this, as Marx wrote of the capitalist of his day, 'compels him to keep constantly extending his capital in order to preserve it, but extend it he cannot, except by means of progressive accumulation'.[3] The so-called 'managerial revolution' has changed nothing of the fundamental nature of capitalism. Rather, the manager-controlled company is only a result of the fact that as time goes on larger and larger concentrations of capital are required for competitive production, and that small, personal businesses are no longer viable.

2. The story of the profits squeeze since 1950

A. The collapse of the share of profits

Profits can be compared to total national income (wages and pro-fits) to show the *share of profits*; this is the outcome of the process or struggle by which the national income is distributed between classes. From the point of view of capitalists the important thing is not so much the relationship of profits to wages, but rather the relation of profits to the amount of capital they have invested – *the rate of profit*. The rate of profit depends both on the profit share and on the amount of capital used to produce the output – the capital intensity of production.*

How to measure the share of profits

The share of profits is the ratio of total profits to total incomes. But, given that there are alternative ways of measuring both profits and incomes, which of these is it correct to use? Which of them presents the truest picture of the condition of capitalism? Before presenting the startling results of our calculations we have to answer these questions and explain briefly in turn how we have dealt with a number of awkward problems of definition and measurement. Some of these merely result from the form in which official figures are published; but others are real questions about what should be measured.

The key point is that we are concerned only with those incomes paid directly out of the proceeds of the production of goods and services – what economists call factor incomes. Taking a country as a whole, if wages are taken away from the net money value of production (that is, the value after the cost of materials is sub-tracted),† the remainder is total profits generated in production;

---

* Writing P for profits, Y for income and K for the value of the capital stock (all in current prices) the share of profits is P/Y and the rate of profit P/K. Obviously $P/Y = P/K \times K/Y$ where K/Y is the capital/output ratio – a measure of capital intensity.

† Some of the proceeds of the sales of an individual firm will not, of course, be used to pay wages or be left over as profits, but will go to buy materials, fuel, etc. from other firms. But the value of output of these sup-

and it is the relation of these profits to national income (the sum of all factor incomes – wages and profits) which fundamentally determines the profitability of capitalist production. For the individual firm an increase in the wage bill will reduce profits unless the proceeds of production can be increased by stepping up output or raising prices, and the same mechanism applies for the whole economy when the operations of all the firms are added up.

To get a true estimate of incomes from production it is important to distinguish between two components of the capitalist's wealth. On the one hand through shares in, and fixed interest loans to, companies[1] he owns *productive capital* – factories, machine tools and other things used in the actual production of goods and services. It is the dividends and interest paid by these companies, and the earnings they retain for reinvestment, that we are counting as profits.

On the other hand a lot of private wealth is in the form of loans to the government and to other private individuals.* Now, although interest earned on these loans is part of the capitalist's income, it would be wrong to take it into account in calculating the share of profits. Since these loans do not finance the accumulation of productive capital the interest on them is not part of the proceeds of production. Rather, these interest payments are what economists call *transfer incomes*; they lead to a distribution of

[1] *Fixed-interest loans* to a company entitle the lender to interest at the fixed rate provided the company has profits enough to pay it. *Shares* in a company entitle the owner to all the profits of the company after the fixed-interest payments have been met. Some of these residual profits are customarily *retained* in the company; the rest paid out as *dividends*.

*To an increasing extent this component is now handled through the 'intermediation' of financial institutions such as banks, building societies and HP companies which borrow from individuals and lend to other individuals or the government. Productive capital may also be owned indirectly through loans to a bank which in turn lends to a company.

pliers in turn consists of wages, profits and 'bought-in' materials. Ultimately the value of all sales to final consumers can be broken down into wages and profits earned in the country (value added) and imports (which in turn represent wages and profits earned elsewhere in the world). Since we are concerned with distribution of income within a country we can ignore imports and concentrate on value added by the country (its national income).

purchasing power which is different from the distribution of the national income between wages and profits. Some of the proceeds of production get redistributed away from the people who receive them in the production process to another group.* In the case of interest on the national debt the interest is ultimately paid by the taxpayer out of what he earns in the productive process. But interest on the national debt or on consumer debt is in no way *tied to* the profitability of *production*; nor can it *affect* the profitability of production.

A concrete example may help to clarify this distinction between factor and non-factor incomes. Imagine that an HP debt is incurred to buy a car. The interest paid on this is quite independent of whether or not it is profitable to produce cars. At any one time the total amount of such interest being paid is the result of past sales of cars. Nor is the increase in these interest payments (resulting from additional car sales) dependent on the profitability of new production; it is dependent only on the sale of the cars by the dealers, on the *consumption* of cars. But, it might be objected, suppose it is British Leyland which owns the finance company which provides HP facilities for those who buy British Leyland cars; surely then the interest on this HP lending represents part of the overall profitability of British Leyland's production of cars. This is incorrect, however, for all the HP interest shows is that it is profitable for British Leyland to finance the consumption of cars. If British Leyland could not produce cars profitably – if competitive pressures kept prices too low – then it would be forced to cease production. Financing consumption might remain perfectly profitable, though; so it could live on as a HP company financing the purchase of Japanese cars.† During its period of decline its profits on HP finance might help to keep the production of cars going; but in trying to measure the profitability of production they should

---

* The redistribution is not necessarily from one class to another. For example, capitalists may borrow from other capitalists to finance consumption, and they do furnish some taxes to pay interest on the national debt.

† Interest on HP debt is directly parasitic on consumption; of course consumption presupposes production *somewhere*, but not necessarily where the consumption takes place.

clearly be excluded. This is why we must focus our attention on the most fundamental question: how is the income generated by production shared between capitalists and workers?

The remaining problems of measurement can be dealt with more simply. To be perfectly accurate, we ought to reckon the salaries of people like company directors as part of the capitalist's share in the income generated by production. Unfortunately the relevant facts are not known. But in any case they would not affect our calculations much, since they constitute a very small proportion of total wages and salaries.*

We are concerned specifically with capitalism in the U.K., so our figures do not include the profits of capital owned by U.K. citizens but operating overseas. On the other hand, for the same reason we do include profits earned by foreign capitalist concerns, such as Ford, operating in the U.K. as they are part of the system of production in the U.K. We will focus our attention in the U.K. on the *company sector* (that is, on corporations like I.C.I. rather than on the local corner shop) since this is the sector where the bulk of private capital operates.

We have reckoned financial institutions like banks and investment trusts as part of the company sector because part of their function is to service industrial and commercial companies. But this does not mean that all the interest received by these is included in company profits. As we have already explained, we only include profits earned in production. (Financial companies are discussed in more detail in appendix C.)

We have deducted stock appreciation from what accountants reckon as profits. Stock appreciation is that part of profits which derives from the fact that stocks of raw materials and finished goods have gone up in value due to price rises. It is thus only a nominal profit; output is no greater and the firm has earned nothing which can be used to buy new capital, or to distribute to shareholders. Stock appreciation thus distorts profits figures upwards and (as we show in appendix C) it has been of increasing

---

*In 1967/8 all the *earned* income of those with total incomes (earned income and income from investments) over £5,000 p.a. constituted about 3 per cent of total earned income in the country. (*Inland Revenue Statistics 1970*, Table 2.)

importance, so the deduction makes an important difference to the figures.

We have also, as is usual, deducted capital consumption from profits. This is that part of company profits which must be set aside to make good the wear and tear (depreciation) of the capital stock as a result of the year's production and general obsolescence.

How much has the share of profits fallen?

Now that we have explained exactly what has gone into our figures and what has been taken out, we can present the astonishing results which we eventually arrived at. These are in our opinion the truest obtainable measure of the crisis in British capitalism.

Between 1964 and 1970 the share of profits was almost halved. A steady downward trend had existed since the early fifties – the share fell from 25·2 per cent in 1950–54 to 21·0 per cent in 1960–64. But since then the steady fall has become an avalanche. The share of profits has fallen from 21·2 per cent in 1964 to 12·1 per cent in 1970. And the share was about the same in the middle of 1971* as it had been during 1970, despite all the efforts to raise it which we describe in chapters 7 and 8. If the share had been the same in 1970 as it was in 1964 then the average worker would have had about £2 a week less than he did.

Table 3.2. Share of Profits in Company Net Output,[1] 1950–70 (per cent)

1950–54		1955–9		1960–64		1965–9
25·2		22·8		21·0		17·4

1964	1965	1966	1967	1968	1969	1970
21·2	20·2	17·6	18·1	16·8	14·2	12·1

1. Company profits as a proportion of profits and wages paid.
Source: See appendix C.

Explaining the fall in the share of profits

Various factors may have influenced this enormous relative decline in profits: they include wage pressure, economic stagnation and

* We give some quarterly figures in appendix, Table C.1.

international competition. If we are to analyse future prospects it is obviously vital to know which ones have been important. We made

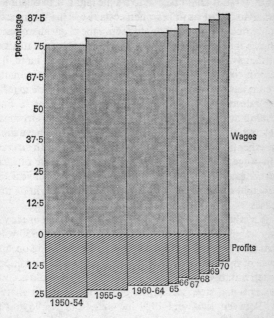

Figure 6. Share of wages and profits in company output 1950–70
Source: See appendix C, Table C.1.

an attempt to find out by a statistical model which makes it possible to measure the amount of correlation between falling profitability and these possible explanatory factors or variables.*

[a] The effect of wage increases on profits. There is a significant

*If the correlation between these is strong we can say that a significant proportion of the variation in the share of profits is in a statistical sense 'explained' by changes in these variables. If it is possible to think of a good reason why one of these variables might in theory cause changes in the share of profits, rather than vice versa, then a strong correlation in practice does something to confirm the causal link, as well as giving an estimate of its strength. Some further technical detail is given in appendix D.

correlation between falls in the share of profits and abnormal rises in money wages. On the face of it two explanations of this are possible. First, it could be due to a time lag: a firm might simply *take time* to adjust its prices when costs rise. This 'historical cost effect'* would not recur. It might reduce the profit share once, but as long as the rate of wage increase did not rise even further, the profit share would not fall any further. On the other hand, if firms are *unable* to put up their prices for fear of losing the market to their competitors, then the profit share would *continue to fall* if the higher rate of increase in wages persisted. In order to find out whether to attribute the fall in the profit share to this 'competitive effect' or to the 'historical cost effect', therefore, we have simply to see whether falls in the profit share are correlated with an *acceleration* in wage increases or simply with a higher *rate* of increase. When we examined changes in the profit share from year to year we saw that it was very little affected by any *acceleration* of wage increases.

In fact, the important thing was simply the *rate of increase* in money wages. We drew the conclusion that since 1950 wage increases have been an important cause of the declining profit share because of their effect on U.K. capital's competitive position. The next step was to see if the growth of money wages could account for the exceptional steepness of the plunge in the profit share since 1964. Between 1964 and 1969 incomes from employment rose annually by 6·9 per cent per head as compared with a rise of 6·1 per cent over the decade 1954–64. In 1970 they rose 11·2 per cent. So, with this exception the growth of wages was not all that much higher after 1964 than before; at first sight, then, it seems implausible to attribute such important effects to wage increases.

But in fact we found that as the period went on increases in money wages came to have a bigger and bigger effect in reducing the profit share.† Our explanation is that in the early fifties, when

---

*So called because prices are appropriate to some previous period's costs. A very good example of this view is the statement by C. W. McMahon of the Bank of England that companies have been 'culpably slow in adjusting to the rate of inflation', quoted by John Plender (*Investors Chronicle*, 17 September 1971).

† More specifically, our estimates suggest that, other things being equal, in the early fifties a rise in the rate of growth of money wages of 1 per cent

international competition was weak, increases in money wages could be easily passed on in higher prices, whereas by the middle and late sixties only a much smaller proportion of wage increases could be passed on. This was despite the reduction in domestic competition resulting from the increasing concentration of U.K. industry.

[b] The effect of economic stagnation on profits. Stagnation of output along with rising unemployment has been one of the most obvious features of recent years; it is often claimed that the collapse in the share of profits must be the direct result of this stagnation. We do not believe this is true to any very great extent, and since it is a point of considerable importance we must take time to argue it fully. Before considering the evidence we need to make some remarks about the theory behind this claim.

The first is that there is no obvious reason why a slow growth of output should affect the *share* of profits at all. If firms are producing at less than full use of capacity[1] then certainly the mass of profits is less. This reduces the rate of profit on capital invested; but why should it also mean that capital takes a smaller proportion of the product? It can only have this result if the lower level of output leads to either lower prices or higher labour costs. Can it in fact lead to either of these?

First, on the question of prices, it is generally agreed that in modern capitalist markets, dominated by a few large firms which are well aware of their rivals' reactions, competition takes the form of advertising and product innovation rather than price-cutting. If demand is slack, then cutting prices in the hopes of increasing sales makes sense only if the rise in sales is substantial enough to more than make up for the lower profit margin. But if competitors follow the price cut, as they must, the firm that began the price war gains less in terms of sales than it loses through lower margins. It is

[1] A firm's *capacity* is the amount of output it can produce, given its capital equipment and available labour force. The same concept may be applied to the economy as a whole.

would tend to reduce the profit share by, very roughly, 0·1 percentage points each year, but by the end of the period the effect of this would be about 0·5 percentage points.

suicidal for firms operating in a market to begin a price war when demand is weak. But a firm not already selling in that market may spoil this tacit understanding to maintain prices by moving in and undercutting established firms. Because it was not in the market in the first place, it has nothing to lose from falling profit margins and everything to gain if it can grab some of the market. Such invasions of the market will, in the main, come not from other industries in the country which is stagnating but rather from foreign firms in the same industry which have not yet got a foothold in the market. These will be impelled to invade not by low demand in the market they are invading, but rather because low demand in their own present markets leaves them with excess capacity. Thus if stagnation affected U.K. prices it would be because world-wide stagnation was making international competition more intense rather than because low demand in the U.K. itself was pulling prices down.

Second, stagnation does increase labour costs per unit of output. When output falls, or does not rise as much as usual, firms usually fail to reduce their labour force in proportion to the reduction in output. This is partly a technical matter. Some labour, such as office staff, is 'overhead labour' and has to be employed regardless of the level of output; and firms may actually hoard labour if they believe that the slack demand is temporary. Hence a slow growth of output leads to a slow growth of productivity,[1] which in turn means that costs are higher than would be the case at full utilization of capacity.* Firms evidently cannot raise their prices to compensate for this kind of cost increase, for we did find, on examining the period since 1950, that there was a significant correlation between falls in productivity (or exceptionally slow rates of in-

[1] By productivity we mean output per man. Clearly, if output falls by a percentage greater than the number of men employed then productivity falls. If wages are unaffected, wage costs per unit of output rise.

* We are ignoring any effect which low demand, and thus unemployment, has on costs by means of its impact on wage increases. We have already discussed wage increases. Whether they would have been faster or slower had there been less stagnation is a matter of debate, and unverifiable. But from the point of view of the future, the effect on wage increases is different from that on productivity because it is not reversible. The wage increases happened and must be lived with; unlike productivity, there is no 'trend' wage level which can be returned to by suitable manipulation of demand.

crease) and falls in the profit share. The reason is presumably the fear that competitors or potential competitors will not follow a price rise; even if the established firms in the market could be relied on to behave 'sensibly' and raise prices, there is always the chance of invasion of the market by foreign firms.

Turning now to the facts, it is plain that a slower rate of growth of productivity resulting from economic stagnation can have had little to do with the steepening of the downward trend in the profit share since 1964. Output per person employed actually grew faster over the five years 1964–9 (2·7 per cent p.a.) than in the previous decade (2·3 per cent); and even in 1970 there was a productivity increase of almost 2 per cent. This fact seems surprising given the argument that productivity fluctuates in accordance with the boom and slump of the economic cycle. But one explanation of it is that the very depth and persistence of the recession since 1965 has forced firms to reduce their labour forces as far as possible – there is no point in hoarding labour if there is little prospect of demand picking up again. Also, many of the less efficient and lower productivity firms have stopped production altogether.

All the same, it seems certain that productivity would have been a bit higher in 1970 had productive capacity been used, say, to the same extent as it was in 1964. A generous estimate of this 'missing' productivity would be 3 per cent;* and even then not all this extra productivity would be reflected in a higher profit share. Some of it would come from longer hours of work which have to be paid for (and at overtime and bonus rates at that), and so it would not increase the profit share.†

*F. W. Paish in *The Rise and Fall of Incomes Policy*, Institute for Economic Affairs, London, 1971, estimates that in 1970 capacity utilization was 6 per cent below the 1964 level and this is on a fairly optimistic estimate of capacity. Normally an increase of 6 per cent in output would be accompanied by a 3 per cent rise in employment and a 3 per cent rise in productivity (see J. R. Shepherd, *Economic Trends*, August 1968); though the recent shake-out of labour suggests that the rise in employment might be more and the rise in productivity less. Thus 3 per cent potential productivity increase might well be on the high side.

†Our statistical results suggest that when output per man-year rises 1 per cent faster than usual the profit share gains by about 0·4 per cent. It seems probable that not all of this discrepancy can be explained by increased hours of work. In the past firms have probably taken advantage of some

Our results suggest that, if output had in fact expanded in 1970 up to the point at which capacity utilization was at the same level as in 1964, then the profit share would have been increased by about 1½ points.* This is only about one sixth of the amount by which the profit share fell since 1964, and in our view establishes that the very slow growth of the economy has been of relatively small importance in explaining the collapse of the profit share.

[c] The effects of international competition on profits. If the capitalists could cover their increasing costs by putting up their prices, their profit margins would never need to suffer. But if they are to retain their markets, they can only put up their prices by the extent to which competing firms from other countries are raising theirs. So, not surprisingly, there is a clear tendency for the share of profits to rise (or for its falls to be moderated) when there are abnormal rises in world export prices of manufactured goods. Thus the very substantial rise in world export prices in 1970 (6 per cent as compared with increases of 1 per cent a year over the period 1954–64 and 2 per cent a year between 1964 and 1969) certainly helped to moderate the fall in the share of profits that would otherwise have resulted from the wage explosion.

If the profit share had reacted to export-price changes in the same way as it had done up to 1964, devaluation, by increasing[1] world export prices in sterling by 17 per cent, should have allowed a substantial increase in the profit share in 1968. But in fact the profit share fell somewhat in 1968.

This is explicable if we see the increase in 'world export prices'

[1] *Devaluation* (explained in the footnote to p. 30) in effect raises the prices of all other countries when these are converted into the devalued currency.

*This incorporates both the effect of productivity discussed above and the fact that, had output been higher, depreciation would have been spread over more output and would have taken a smaller share of the product – a point we discuss further in appendix C, and which turns out to be of pretty negligible importance.

part of any growth in productivity to moderate their price increases, rather than to increase profit margins; but if productivity rose in the present profits situation they might well find it more urgent to use all the extra productivity to swell their profit margins to the maximum extent.

after a devaluation as being rather different from the usual type of price increase. Because of the big boost to U.K. competitiveness, other countries were forced to reduce their (dollar) prices somewhat in markets where the U.K. is an important competitor (most notably in the U.K. domestic market, of course). Thus the *average* rise in world export prices expressed in terms of sterling is not a good index of the ability of U.K. firms to improve their profits by raising *their* sterling prices. Firms were expected to take advantage of devaluation by increasing their profit margins on exports, but, as the National Institute put it, 'the price rise in response to devaluation was very much less than had been anticipated'. This experience of the 1967 devaluation seems to us strongly to confirm our hypothesis about the importance of international competition in determining the profit share.

[d] The overall explanation. Finally, we put together the various factors that we thought might have accounted for the falling share of profits. Leaving aside the post-devaluation year of 1968, the *faster* fall between 1964 and 1970 can be almost entirely explained by the combination of changes in wages and world export prices and the continuation of the tendency for the wages increase to have a greater and greater effect as international competition intensified. Stagnation had relatively little to do with it. We conclude that the basic reason for the decline in the profit share was the squeezing of profit margins between money wage increases on the one hand and progressively more severe international competition on the other.

B. The falling rate of profit[1]

To examine how the rate of profit fell as the profit share declined we calculated, both before and after tax, the rate of profit earned by quoted companies[2] in the industrial and commercial sector. These figures, which were based on company accounts, were adjusted by deducting our estimates of the stock appreciation occur-

[1] See definition on p. 15.
[2] *Quoted companies* whose shares are bought and sold regularly on the Stock Exchange. Virtually all the major companies in the U.K. are quoted.

ing in each year in this sector. The result was that up to 1967 the pre-tax rate of profit fell in very much the same way as the share of profits.*

Table 3.3. Rates of Profit[1] on Net Assets of Industrial and Commercial Companies, 1950–70 (per cent)

	1950–54		1955–9		1960–64		1965–9
Pre-tax	16·5		14·7		13·0		11·7
Post-tax	6·7		7·0		7·0		5·3[2]

	1964	1965	1966	1967	1968	1969	1970
Pre-tax	13·7	12·8	11·3	11·7	11·6	11·1	9·7
Post-tax	7·1	7·8	4·9	6·1	5·2	4·7	4·1

1. After deducting stock appreciation.
2. 1967–9.

Source: See appendix E.

But between 1967 and 1969, to judge by these figures, the rate of profit before tax, unlike the share of profits, hardly fell at all. But this is very misleading, one reason for it being that these figures include earnings from overseas subsidiaries. Even though we excluded companies operating mainly overseas (such as mining and oil companies), some of the quoted companies had overseas subsidiaries whose profits rose very fast in 1968 and 1969. This helped to offset the fall in the rate of profit on their home operations. Moreover, as inflation speeded up, the amount by which the company accounts were undervaluing capital actually increased. This means that the real fall in the profit rate was greater than the fall we measured, and this is true particularly for 1970, when a marked fall shows up even in these figures.

If we now consider the profits of the whole company sector, *excluding* those earned overseas, while valuing capital at current prices, we find that the rate of profit fell from 11 per cent in 1964 to 8·8 per cent in 1967, 6·8 per cent in 1969 and 5·8 per cent in 1970.†

* As we explain in appendix E, the fall in the profit rate from 16·5 per cent in 1950–54 to 11·7 per cent in 1967 may possibly be a bit exaggerated as a result of the way in which capital employed is valued.

† This rate-of-profit figure is comparable to the share-of-profits figure calculated earlier; it falls rather faster between 1964 and 1970 because of a

This shows very clearly that the rate of profit before tax has in fact fallen enormously since 1967, and just how misleading are the figures from company accounts if not interpreted carefully.

The next step is to look at the profit rate *after* tax. Company accounts indicate that the rate of profit after tax in quoted industrial and commercial companies fell from 7·1 per cent to 4·1 per cent between 1964 and 1970. So the fall in the rate of profit after tax is much greater than the fall in the pre-tax rates. This is partly because the period saw considerable increases in tax rates and reductions in investment incentives.* But as well as this, the great rise in stock appreciation (which is not part of true profits) was counted as taxable profits and thus inflated the tax bill. This extra taxation must be paid out of true profits. Thus rising stock appreciation actually *reduces* real profitability. If we counted stock appreciation as profit, then the rate would fall much less – from 7·8 per cent to 6·3 per cent. On the other hand, if companies had cut their investment in line with the fall in the rate of profit, their tax bill would have increased even more, since they receive tax concessions on the profits which they plough back into investment.

Our calculation of a drop in the rate of profit after tax from 7·1 per cent to 4·1 per cent between 1964 and 1970 is, like the figures for pre-tax profits from company accounts, a considerable underestimate of the true fall. The reasons for this – undervaluation of

---

*This is the opposite of what happened over the fifties and early sixties, when falls in tax rates and increased investment incentives allowed the post-tax rate of profit to be maintained despite the fall in the pre-tax rate. We argue in appendix F that the faster fall in the measured post-tax profit rate does reflect a genuine increase in the tax burden in the sixties, though this tax burden is consistently *underestimated* by the reduction in the tax bill caused by incentives on net investment.

---

rise in the capital intensity of production (the ratio of capital employed to output) part of which appears to be due to under-use of capacity rather than to a significant shift in the techniques of production. See appendix C, section on capital consumption, and appendix E where the alternative calculations are explained along with the general problem of undervaluation of capital in a time of inflation. We also point out there that the estimates we use for stock appreciation for the industrial quoted companies are probably on the low side and this also understates the fall in the rate of profit in that sector in 1969 and 1970 when stock appreciation was very heavy.

capital, overseas operations and under-estimates of stock appreciation – were explained in connection with the pre-tax rate of profit. Unlike the case of pre-tax profitability, however, we cannot quantify these factors properly, since we do not have an alternative set of figures which get round these problems. On the other hand, some people might have suspicions that our figures are too high. For instance, there might be systematic dishonest under-reporting of profits. We feel quite confident that this possible source of error can be discounted, since it would require a quite unbelievable *increase* in such under-reporting to cause such a large *fall* in the observed rate of profit. The Inland Revenue are unlikely to be so deceived; and anyway, more importantly, under-reporting of profits spoils the company's standing in the stock market and thus reduces its access to new capital.*

Taking into account the various possible sources of error, which all lead to our figures understating the real fall in post-tax profitability that has occurred, we can conclude that since 1964 the rate of profit in the U.K. has collapsed.

The rate of profit in different industries

Our analysis of profitability dealt with British capital as a whole. To repeat the analysis for each industry, let alone firm, is beyond the scope of this book. But it is possible to get an idea of the range of firms affected by the collapse of profitability by studying the following list of major companies† whose stated profit rate was less than 5 per cent in 1970:

Whitbreads, British Match, British Leyland, J. Lyons, Alfred Herbert (leading machine-tool firm), Vickers, Guest Keen & Nettlefolds, Dunlop, Associated Portland Cement, Bowater Paper, Booker McConnell, English Calico, Hawker Siddeley, Rediffusion, John Laing (builders).

* A good example of this is provided by the large Dutch company, N. V. Philips, which aimed to *reduce over-reporting* of profits by reckoning depreciation at replacement cost and which has since been complaining about how its stock-market rating has suffered (*Sunday Times*, 10 February 1971). Accountants are increasingly worried about over-reporting and have recently suggested a scheme for how this should be overcome (*Accountancy*, September 1971).

† We give in appendix E data for industries and individual large firms which we use in the analysis presented here.

Obviously it was not only small, inefficient firms which had become unprofitable.* Moreover, these calculations are made before deducting stock appreciation, which in some industries, particularly engineering, artificially pushes up the measured rate of profit by 2 to 3 per cent. Since these estimates for individual firms are also biased upwards by the undervaluation of capital in company accounts it is quite clear that the true rate of profit was minute in many important companies.† Very few major companies had an increase in the stated rate of profit large enough to offset the growing exaggeration of true profits produced by stock appreciation and undervaluation of capital. Firms in the chemical industry did manage to keep up profit rates at least until 1969 but in 1970 the profit situation even there deteriorated seriously with increasing international competition; this was also true of paper and textiles, which had remained more or less unscathed up to 1969.‡ By 1970 profits had totally evaporated in metal manufacture, ships, planes and cars, where foreign competition was particularly intense and in which British firms were neither particularly strong (as was I.C.I. in the chemicals industry) nor heavily protected (like textiles).§ In most other manufacturing industries the stated profit rate had fallen by at least a third between 1964 and 1970, and outside manufacturing profitability fell a lot in wholesale distribution and transport.

* In fact unquoted companies (which tend to be smaller) appear to have done better than quoted companies perhaps because they have a niche in small specialized markets where international competition is less important.

† The distortions in the measured rate of return must vary a lot between firms, but the bias is *always* upwards, so while all the companies in our list certainly had very low rates of return, probably many others with higher reported rates of profit in fact were just as badly off.

‡ The Chairman of Courtauld's said in his annual report for 1970 that for the second year in succession 'Your company was squeezed between rising costs and constant selling prices.' Chairmen of foreign chemical companies have been making similar complaints (John Trafford, *Financial Times*, 9 August 1971).

§ In a letter to the *Economist* (9 September 1967) the chairman of a Lancashire cotton firm wrote, 'When this day (the abolition of protection) arrives, then our country could be held to ransom at any time by the cheap importing countries, many of which are dominated by Communist influences.'

3. The impact of world competition on British capital

We have argued that the decline in the share of profits and rate of profit in the U.K. has resulted from the combination of international competition and wage pressure. The U.K.'s perennial balance-of-payments problem has the same cause. The U.K. declined as an exporter between 1954 and 1970; its share of world exports of manufactures was cut in half. Up to 1961 the U.K., and the U.S., lost 5 per cent of the world market. Germany benefited most, though Italy and Japan also substantially increased their shares. Since 1961 Germany and France more or less maintained their shares, as did the U.S.A. until about 1969. Italy increased her share a little, and Japan increased hers by 5 per cent. The U.K. lost a further 6 per cent; its share of world exports of manufactured goods now stands at 10½ per cent, below that of Japan (11½ per cent), the U.S.A. (19 per cent) and Germany (almost 20 per cent). U.K. companies have also suffered badly from foreign competition at home. Between 1958 and 1968 imports of manufactured goods almost quadrupled, whereas their output (all in current prices) less than doubled. Although a similar tendency for imports to rise faster than home production is found in almost all countries, one recent study found that Britain showed up as relatively 'import-prone with respect to finished goods and perhaps with respect to semi-manufactures also'. [4] The overall growth of competition from imports in the late sixties is well demonstrated in the same study. For while in the late fifties and early sixties imports of finished goods tended, taking an average of the industrialized countries, to rise about twice as fast as expenditure on finished goods, between 1965/6 and 1968 imports tended to rise about three times as fast as expenditure.

It has been suggested that the U.K. has suffered from having its trade after the war concentrated in commodities for which demand had grown slowly. But this theory is refuted by a recent study. This suggests that over the last few years British exports were in fact concentrated in the dynamic sectors, though Britain 'did suffer, apparently, the worst setbacks in the 1960s in some of the fastest growing and most important commodity groups in world trade'. [5]

British companies' concentration on exporting to the sterling area and underdeveloped countries has probably been disadvantageous: Japan and the U.S. are increasingly dominating these markets. On the other hand, in the continental countries 'which mainly trade amongst themselves Japanese competition was in general only barely significant'. [6] The success of American exporters in the sterling area has been ascribed mainly to the tying of American aid,[1] to the exports which result from direct investment by American corporations, and to the ending of discrimination in many countries against dollar goods.

The obvious reason for the poor British performance in world trade is its high or rapidly rising prices. A recent study showed that in most metal-using and -producing industries British price competitiveness was more or less maintained over the period 1953–64, but it deteriorated in electrical machinery; and the highly competitive position in transport equipment (cars, aeroplanes, etc.) disappeared. The biggest fall in the British share of the market was in electrical machinery – from 28 per cent to just over 13 per cent during this period.

This study further points out that for non-electrical machinery 'there was a striking similarity between the price changes in the different countries'. [7] The implication is that in this industry firms cannot offset an abnormal rise in costs by raising their prices. Over the period 1954–64 unit cost increases in manufacturing, after allowing for changes in exchange rates, grew at comparable rates (about 3 per cent p.a.) in the U.K., Germany and France, but much slower elsewhere – only around 1 per cent in Italy and the U.S. and $\frac{1}{2}$ per cent in Japan. This in turn suggests that the tendency for British exporters to raise prices more than their competitors is almost certainly the result of an attempt to offset part of the effect of rising costs on their already inadequate profit margins. Other countries either had a slower growth of wage costs or had fatter profit margins in the first place and so were more willing to cut them in order to increase their share of the market.*

[1] Aid is tied when it is conditional on being used to buy goods from the donor country.

*A government survey carried out in 1966 found that on average the profitability of exports was substantially less than that on home sales. Ninety per cent of the products cost as much or more to supply abroad than at

Of course the loss of exports is not entirely the result of uncompetitive prices, but it is the most important factor. The matter of price was also important in explaining the increased buying of imported manufactures, though in the case of capital goods 'technical performance emerged from the users' views as the decisive reason'. [8]

It seems probable that Britain has faced even stiffer international competition since 1964. Up to the devaluation at the end of 1967 British costs rose faster than elsewhere, and the differential was greater than in the fifties and early sixties. The U.K.'s share in its markets fell a good deal faster over the period 1964–8 than during the previous ten years. [9] For a short time devaluation helped Britain's competitiveness, and in 1969 her share in world manufactured exports remained more or less stable for the first time since 1961. But in 1970 the fall in the share resumed as wage costs grew faster in Britain than in any other major exporter except Italy, and as British export prices again grew faster than the average. The reduction in the growth of home demand in many countries (particularly Germany, the U.S. and Italy) during 1970 also added to competitive pressures as firms strove to make up for low orders at home by stepping up their sales efforts abroad.

There is scarcely any chance that this competition will evaporate and leave British capital freer to push up prices and restore profit margins. As we argue in Chapter 4, the problems facing British capitalists are facing capitalists in other countries too. And so the struggle for world markets is likely to become more rather than less intense.

---

home whereas almost 60 per cent of the products were sold at lower prices overseas than on the home market. When the firms were approached again in 1968, after the devaluation of the pound, there was a 5 per cent fall in the number of products sold more cheaply abroad and the proportion of firms which considered their export margins 'unacceptable' had fallen from 40 per cent to one quarter. Although the extent of the lower profitability of exports was reduced, on average it remained quite substantial. (J. D. Gribbin, *The Profitability of UK Exports*, H.M.S.O., 1971). This suggests that a further reason for the failure of the profit share to rise after devaluation (see page 64) was that there was a diversion of sales by British firms from the home market, which was being curtailed by tax increases, to the (still) less profitable export market and that this acted to offset the effect on the profit share of export sales becoming more profitable.

Chapter 4
World Capitalism in Crisis

The crisis is not confined to Britain. It is essential to look at its international context. This is partly because British capitalism is linked through trade and investment with the world capitalist system. What happens in the rest of that system has an important bearing on the British crisis. In particular the condition of capitalism in other countries affects the international competition which British capitalists face. Similarly, what happens in Britain has some influence on other countries. The result is a complex interaction between what occurs in particular countries and what is happening to the capitalist system as a whole.

As foreign trade gathered pace and labour markets grew tighter in the late fifties and early sixties, the tendency for the profit share to be squeezed between the pressure of wages and international competition emerged as a clearly observable trend in more and more countries. The tightness of the actual squeeze varied between countries; in some it was offset by particularly rapid productivity growth or by restraint in demands for higher wages. Differences between countries may be explained by different stages of development of capitalist production. Britain, as the 'maturest' capitalist country, is both the weakest part of the system and gives an example of the path which other capitalist economies might quite rapidly follow. The profit share is being maintained in the strongest countries while it falls elsewhere; and the rate of fall depends on competitiveness and wage pressure. As the process continues it is quite likely that the profit share will fall everywhere.

As it has become more difficult to maintain a high level of private investment, government spending has almost everywhere become more necessary to maintain high levels of demand and employment; but this does not solve the profitability problem. In one

73

country after another these developments are marking the end of the long post-war capitalist expansion.

1. Critical changes in wages and profits

In 1950 the proportion of the product of the company sector in the United States going to profits was very similar to that in Britain. It fell quite sharply in the depressed years of the late fifties and early sixties. Since then it has climbed again, though not as far as its 1950 level. The overall fall in these two decades, 1950–70, is from around 29 per cent to 27 per cent,* which is much less than the fall experienced by British capital.

In other countries it is more difficult to get reliable information on the change in the share of profits for the period since 1950 as a whole. We discuss the problem in appendix G, where we conclude that there has been a marked fall in the profit share in Belgium, Italy and the Netherlands; that in Canada, France and Germany there probably has not been much change; but that in Japan there has been a strong upward shift in the profit share since 1950.

We have also made a statistical analysis of profits in other countries which is similar to the one for the U.K. described in the previous chapter. And we have looked at the extent to which year-to-year changes in the profit share were associated with wage changes, productivity changes and world export price changes. For the econometrically-minded we give our results in table G3 of appendix G, the conclusions of which are summarized below.

(*a*) In every capitalist country that we examined a relatively rapid increase in money wages was found to lead to a setback for the share of profits. The effect of a faster rate of growth of money wages is not just a once-and-for-all reduction in the profit share as prices lag behind wages: if the faster growth of money wages is maintained, then the profit share will go on falling. In two countries (France and Belgium) there did seem to be a once-and-for-all effect as well; but in other countries (the U.S. and Japan) wage

---

*These figures are before deduction of capital consumption, comparable estimates for which are not available for different countries. Data in appendix, Table G1.

pressure appears to have a cumulative effect – a high rate of increase in money wages lowers the profit share *more* if there was a rapid increase in the previous year.

On the whole, wage pressure has a bigger effect on the profit share in the manufacturing sector than in the rest of the economy. This fits in with our emphasis on international competition, to which the manufacturing sector is most exposed. But the same increase in the annual rise of wages has different effects in different countries. For example, wage rises appear to have relatively small effects in France. And even where the effects appear similar, as they do in the U.S. and the U.K., the underlying situation may be different – in this case the U.K. is more affected by international competition than the U.S.

(*b*) As in the U.K., the profit share in other countries fluctuates with the alternation of boom and slump, rising as productivity increases and falling in recessions. The main exception to this is France.

(*c*) As with the U.K., we found that the profit share in other capitalist countries tends to rise when world export prices rise fast. However, as far as we could tell from our crude figures, the effect is not necessarily most significant in the countries or sectors most exposed to international competition, or where wage pressure is most important. But there is indeed some quite strong evidence that it is the rise in domestic costs *relative to world prices* which affects the profit share, rather than just the rise in domestic costs themselves; a point which underlines the crucial importance of international competition.

Thus we find that the profit share has indeed been under pressure from wages and international competition in all the major capitalist countries, as in the U.K. Moreover, even in those countries where the profit share has not declined over the period as a whole, capital's position has deteriorated markedly since the late fifties. In Europe especially the first years of the sixties saw the emergence of important trends which had dramatic results at the end of the decade. In the rest of this section we try to locate the critical moments at which the changes in the profit share began or intensified in the major capitalist countries.

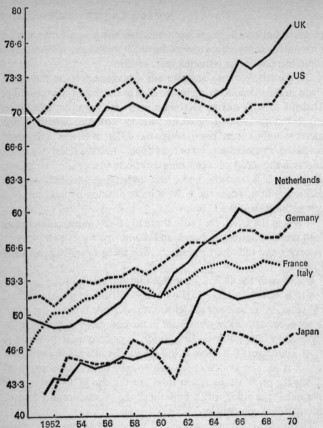

Figure 7. Shares of wages and salaries in total income in different countries 1950–70
Note: Comparison between countries and overtime is complicated (except for the U.S. and the U.K.) by the inclusion of self-employed incomes in the total. See text p. 74 and appendix G.
Source: See appendix G, Table G1.

The Netherlands

The Netherlands is of interest because it is very exposed to international competition and because it has tried more consistently and for longer than any other country to control wages through an incomes policy. Between 1950 and 1960 the profit share almost certainly rose. But from 1959 the government steadily gave up interfering with wage bargaining, and in 1961–3 there came a turning point. Wages grew quite rapidly, and this culminated in a wage explosion in 1964 with increases averaging 15 per cent. The Organization for Economic Cooperation and Development,* after a hard search for an explanation (in the course of which it suggested 'over-full employment' as well as the low wages in Holland compared with other Common Market countries) was forced to conclude:

> The change in attitude of the unions, from relative moderation and acceptance of the centrally established 'norms' or 'guidelines' up to 1962, to massive demands in 1963 and 1964, may have reflected tensions between rank and file and union leadership, which eventually forced the leaders to change their attitude. [1]

The militancy evidently had a startling effect on the ratio of wages to total incomes (the 'wage ratio') which rose from 51·4 per cent in 1960 to 60·1 per cent in 1966. No doubt this was partly due to the 5 per cent revaluation of the guilder in 1961: international competition forced Dutch exporters to cut their export prices (in guilders) by 4½ per cent in the year following revaluation and this squeezed profit from one side while the growing wage pressure squeezed it from the other. To begin with, declining profitability did not reduce private investment much, but firms were forced to finance much more of their investment from external sources.

In May 1966 the government reverted to a more interventionist policy: price controls and a temporary wage freeze succeeded in moderating wage claims. The effect was short-lived. Price increases had accelerated by 1969 to 7½ per cent a year, which O.E.C.D. explained thus:

> Anticipating the additional wage costs and knowing that most prices would have to rise anyway as a result of the value-added tax,[1] many

[1] The *value-added tax* is a general tax on goods and services.
* Virtually all the capitalist countries are members of O.E.C.D., and the organization conducts an enormous amount of research on the economies of member countries. Much of the data in this chapter comes from O.E.C.D. and we frequently quote their analysis of developments in particular countries, which is often very revealing.

producers and traders probably concluded that this would produce a climate in which they could correct old price lags and redress the income balance in their favour. [2]

As a result of this the real earnings of the average worker rose by only 0·7 per cent in 1969, as compared with average increases of 4 per cent p.a. in previous years. So the profit share gained a little. Such was the climate which led the workers to launch a new offensive. After some important unofficial strikes, beginning with one in the Rotterdam docks in August 1970, rather large wage increases were granted. In the middle of 1971 *The Times* correspondent was writing that:

In 1970 wages rose by 12½ per cent and despite statutory wage limitations in the first six months of this year Dutch economists expect wages in 1971 to increase by at least as much as in 1970. Industry has been feeling the pinch as mounting overheads made it all the harder to remain competitive. Wage rises for a time could be offset through price increases but time is now running out and corporate profits are slipping badly ... What disturbs Dutch economists is that falling profits will lead to serious corporate investment cut backs ... [3]

Despite some rise in unemployment no let-up in wage and price increases is forecast for 1972 and statutory wage and price controls have been abandoned. Output growth is expected to slow down to 3 per cent p.a. and industrial investment to fall by 5 per cent, reflecting the profit squeeze. The Planning Bureau forecast a 7½ per cent increase in labour's share between 1967 and 1972.

Italy

In the 1950s the Italian economy was caught in an exceptionally 'virtuous circle' from a capitalist point of view, as an O.E.C.D. report described:

The low initial level of wages increased rather moderately because of the pressure of unemployment; with the expansion of total demand, which was helped by public policy, and was sustained by the growth of exports, the volume of profits rose considerably and allowed an increased rate of investment; this in turn resulted in higher output per man-hour and thus in increased rates of profit. Particular incentives for higher industrial investment have come initially from the urgent needs of modernization in important branches like the steel industry; then from the need to meet competition both with imports and in foreign markets the importance of which was growing for Italian industry: finally the mechanism of feedback between high profits, high investment and rapid growth of productivity came into full swing. [4]

The share of profits increased particularly in the late fifties.

In 1962 and 1963 the 'miracle' ended with the first wage explosion. Wage increases accelerated from around 7 or 8 per cent p.a. to 14 per cent in 1962 and 19 per cent in 1963. The O.E.C.D. attributes this to a fall in unemployment from around 1·8 million in 1956 to around 600,000 in 1962, together with what it delicately calls 'a changing social and political climate'. [5] Profits suffered drastically: the wage ratio in manufacturing rose from 58·5 per cent in 1961 to 65 per cent in 1963. Not surprisingly, industrial investment collapsed; in 1964 it fell by 20 per cent.

An essential reason for this turn-round in private investment was the squeeze on profits; its effects were reinforced by factors not directly connected with the course of final demand or costs* which led to a general deterioration of business expectations, to massive capital flights abroad and to a depressed capital market ... The increasing integration of the Italian economy with foreign markets prevented industry from passing on to prices a greater share of the increase in wages, because competing imports expanded rapidly. The gains in productivity only offset part of the rise in wages and industrial profits must have fallen considerably. This meant both lower possibilities of self finance at a time when external sources of finance were shrinking, and a decrease in the attractiveness of new investment projects. [6]

The authorities responded by cutting demand even further, and before growth was resumed unemployment had risen from 400,000 to 700,000. Despite quite a rapid expansion up to 1969, with only moderate wage increases which allowed some restoration of profit margins, annual industrial investment never regained its previous peak. Then came the 'hot autumn' of 1969 – a massive wave of strikes involving some 12 million workers and leading to the loss of about 2 per cent of annual output – in turn leading to another wage explosion with increases of 30–35 per cent over $2\frac{1}{2}$–3 years. It was expected that once more the profit share would take a knock

*Including nationalization of the electricity industry (our footnote).

similar to that caused by the previous wage explosion and the 2 per cent rise in the wage ratio in 1970 suggests that this is likely to be the case. Output stagnated and the rate of inflation increased to about 5 per cent a year.

Following the widespread strikes of late 1969, the recovery in output in 1970 was much weaker than expected. . . . An important reason was the persistence of work stoppages and other forms of labour unrest. The direct and indirect effects of these developments on incomes, precautionary savings and business confidence may partly explain why, one year after Italy's latest 'wage explosion', there have been increasing signs of deficient domestic demand . . . [7]

But currently prospects for a repeat of the relatively successful expansion of 1965–9 seem remote. In the autumn of 1971 the government announced massive increases in public investment in an attempt to get the economy out of its depressed state while private industry prepared for the re-negotiations of the 1969 wage deals at the end of 1972. Meanwhile labour militancy grew as unemployment reached 1 million and prices continued to rise rapidly. The workers are increasingly demanding not only higher wages but also better conditions and more control. In 1971 the three major trade union federations advanced towards unity. Signor Lombardi, the president of the Italian employers' federation, talked of 'the most serious crisis which Italy has suffered'.

Japan

By the late fifties Japan had a phenomenal rate of capital accumulation: total investment was absorbing about one third of total output, compared with about one quarter in the main continental countries and well under one fifth in the U.S. and U.K. The basic cause of this was the very high level and rate of growth of profits. Between 1953 and 1962 the wage ratio in manufacturing fell by about 12 per cent and the profit share rose to a level unparalleled in the rest of the capitalist world. The rise in real hourly earnings of $3\frac{1}{2}$ per cent p.a. was less than half the rise in productivity. A relatively slow rate of growth of money wages (around $6\frac{1}{2}$ per cent p.a.) and rapid productivity growth (10 per cent p.a.) made Japan more competitive than ever in world markets, while the domestic market was heavily protected.

In 1960 things began to change and wage increases accelerated. They averaged 14 per cent over the period 1961–4, fell again until 1968, although never below 10 per cent, and then rose to 15 per cent in 1969 and even higher in 1970 and 1971. So far this has done no more than just stabilize the profit share, and accumulation has been able to continue at a very rapid rate. Real private investment actually doubled in the boom of 1965–9. Despite increasing inflation (prices rising by 8 per cent in 1970) Japan's balance-of-payments position has been getting stronger and stronger; for the first time restrictive measures, which halted growth in 1970, were taken for domestic rather than balance-of-payments reasons. Japanese capital in 1971 was facing a combination of quite sharply increasing costs and (under American pressure) a sizeable revaluation of the yen, which would reduce profit margins since exporters would have to lower yen prices in an effort to keep their markets.* In 1971 private investment actually fell and is expected barely to increase in 1972.

France

From 1938 to 1953 real hourly wages in France fell. The O.E.C.D. Survey of France for 1953 argued that further rises in money wages would only increase real wages 'if measures are taken to reduce excess profit margins by restoring external and internal competition'. Up till the middle of 1957 little was done to restore competition and there was probably a slight further fall in labour's share of the national income, though quite rapid economic growth allowed some rise in real earnings. In mid-1957 the government gave up its policy of stabilizing the cost of living with subsidies and the competitive advantage of a 20 per cent devaluation was wiped out as prices and wages rose by around 18 per cent in the year. A further devaluation of $17\frac{1}{2}$ per cent in 1958 allowed French firms to keep up prices (in francs) and thus profit margins despite

---

*The *Financial Times*, 25 August 1971, reports that the shipbuilders have hinted they might sue the government for losses on fixed-price contracts.

the intensification of competition as the welter of trade restrictions was dismantled. The ensuing export-led boom took place, therefore, at the expense of the working class: the purchasing power of average hourly earnings fell by $1\frac{1}{2}$ per cent between 1957 and 1959 while productivity per hour rose by $5\frac{1}{2}$ per cent – labour's share falling by more than $1\frac{1}{2}$ per cent. Not surprisingly, investment grew by one half between 1957 and 1961 – practically double the rate of increase of the previous few years.

The expansion led to increasing wage pressure. O.E.C.D., writing in its 1962 Survey, announced:

> Over the last year there have been clearer signs of a spontaneous wage push with the result that the increase in real wages is tending to outstrip that in productivity . . . if it were to get any stronger it might well endanger the possibility of financing the investment essential to future growth.

Growth was, in fact, slowed down by the 'Stabilization Plan' at the end of 1963 which by 1968 had caused nearly a trebling of unemployment. The growth of real wages slowed from roughly 6 per cent p.a. to 3 per cent p.a., with the preceding gains in labour's share of income being partly lost.

This was the economic background to the largest strikes in the history of any country in May/June 1968, resulting in the loss of 750 million hours of work (3 per cent of annual hours). The 'Protocole de Grenelle' which ended the strikes gave the workers a 10 per cent increase in wages, reduced their working hours and improved fringe benefits. The government attempted to neutralize these gains: it expanded demand rapidly in order to absorb the wage increases in higher productivity, reduced company taxation, and organized cheap credit to help firms meet the higher wage bills. This policy was spectacularly successful. Productivity rose very rapidly, so wage costs rose by less than 2 per cent and firms were able to keep their promise to hold price increases down to 3 per cent between April and December 1968 without endangering their profit margins. There was only a fractional rise in labour's share in 1968 ($\frac{1}{2}$ per cent) and none at all in 1969.

The government's policy of expansion had to be moderated at the end of 1968 'first and foremost to restore confidence in the franc which had been severely shaken'. [8] The balance of payments continued to deteriorate as money wage increases were less and less offset by productivity growth, and in August 1969 there was yet another devaluation of 11 per cent – the possibility of which had been implicit in the policy of expansion. However, 'Given the buoyancy of foreign demand many exporters did not feel called on to reduce their prices in foreign currencies'; [9] that is, they used the devaluation to increase their profits. As in 1958, devaluation allowed French firms to push up prices and this was a useful weapon for redistributing income from labour to capital. Continued wage pressure, however, probably prevented the redistribution from being very large since real wages seem to have risen by more than 5 per cent in 1970, with prices going up by about the same, even though unemployment was also rising quite fast.

But this situation is unlikely to last. Early in 1971 there were some widely publicized wage settlements in the public sector which implied the acceptance of a fall in labour's share.* The conditions for a further wage offensive have been established. With unemployment rising from 230,000 early in 1970 to 380,000 by the end of 1971 as growth slowed down, all the major unions were opposing the new wage deals on which the government's incomes policy relied. Meanwhile employers complained that the price controls were reducing their profits and hampering their investment.

Germany

Memories of the catastrophic inflation of 1920–23 and the end of the Second World War have enabled the German authorities con-

---

*In coalmining, for example, it was announced that there would be a basic increase of $6\frac{1}{2}$ per cent, full cost-of-living compensation for price increases over 4 per cent, and an additional bonus of half the increase in national output over 5·4 per cent. Assuming inflation continues at more than 4 per cent and real output grows by $5\frac{1}{2}$ per cent, then real wages under this agreement will rise by only $2\frac{1}{2}$ per cent – less than half the increase in production and a good deal less than productivity. Similar deals were being signed late in 1971.

stantly to invoke the bogey of inflation to oppose wage claims. The President of the Central Bank, in a speech in 1950, said:

As long as I remain in this position I shall do everything to justify and strengthen confidence in our D-Mark . . . It is we who must see to it that the German housewife is able to get by with her household money, that price increases do not make a shambles of her tiny budget, that the pensions of our war wounded remain intact . . . in the inflation which preceded the currency reform a street car conductor could not even buy a pound of butter with his entire month's wages. Let us not forget this! [10]

Germany has experienced less inflation since the war than most other capitalist countries. Until 1969 prices had not risen more than about 3 per cent p.a. and there had been periods of near price stability. These periods, however, have recently been getting shorter and rarer, and have been bought at the cost of increasingly severe restrictions on demand.

In many ways 1960 was a turning point. Nearly full employment was achieved, being greeted by a wage explosion in which money wages increased by 15 per cent in a year. The immediate effect on profits was limited as it was accompanied by a very rapid increase in productivity; but in the next year this counteracting factor was much smaller. The 5 per cent revaluation of the D-Mark in 1961 automatically pushed up the dollar prices of German exports; and this meant German capitalists could not raise prices to protect their profits. The ratio of wages to total income in the manufacturing sector, having drifted downwards for several years, rose from about 59 per cent in 1960 to almost 63 per cent in 1962.

In the previous year's report the Central Bank had analysed the implications of successful wage pressure with exceptional clarity:

Attention must finally be drawn to the consequences which the present trend of costs might produce on the country's investment. The great cost increases which trade and industry have had to face during recent years have, as is known, been passed on only partly in prices. In future their passing on in full may become still more difficult . . . Above all the growing foreign competition just mentioned sets a limit to price rises . . . It would be a mistake to assume that this creates an opportunity for decisively improving the position of wage and salary earners, that is of rapidly 'redistributing' the national income, without causing harm to the economy as a whole. Cost increases which cannot be passed on in the price will detract from profits ... profit margins largely determine the propensity to invest, just as the ability to find fresh finance for capital expenditure depends on them; there is, therefore, always a danger that abrupt cuts in profits may cause undesired repercussions on total investment and hence may impair or even suspend economic growth ... What after all is the use of a greater share in the national income if at the same time the growth of the national income is impaired, and if price rises reduce the real value of that greater share? [11]

The Central Bank's argument was implemented by a squeeze, and wage increases were effectively restrained. The number of unemployed climbed from 125,000 to 600,000 by the end of 1967 and wage increases slipped from 10 per cent p.a. to 3 per cent p.a.; the result was a substantial fall in labour's share during the next economic upswing. With the wages share of output in manufacturing dropping in 1968 from $63\frac{1}{2}$ per cent to $60\frac{1}{2}$ per cent, the 1969 level of manufacturing investment was well above its 1961 peak.

But then suddenly, as O.E.C.D. put it, 'the relatively peaceful wage climate changed dramatically in September (1969) when a wave of wildcat strikes led to pay increases', [12] part of the reason for which was to be found in the preceding profits boom:

The rapid increase in profits seemed to violate the principle of fair shares in income growth and the 'social symmetry' on which the Government had promised to base its incomes policy. This created a social climate unfavourable to orderly corrections of the distortions which had occurred. [13]

By 1970 the government's 'Concerted Action' meetings with employers and unions, which had had some success in moderating wage claims in 1967–8, were 'under increasing strain because of sharp inflationary pressures and an upsurge of rank and file militancy'. [14] Earnings increases in early 1971 easily exceeded the government's guidelines, which themselves allowed for some increase in labour's share. In 1970, under the pressure of earnings increases of almost 17 per cent, the overall wage ratio had risen by $1\frac{1}{2}$ per cent. The D-Mark revaluation at the end of 1969 had certainly helped to achieve this increase:

The decrease in import prices of manufactured goods closely competitive with domestic production probably acted as a brake on domestic price increases; in particular it would seem that the relatively stable trend of prices in the chemical and automobile industries reflected the impact of foreign price competition. [15]

Not surprisingly, German capital had opposed revaluation in 1961 with what was described as 'terroristic propaganda'. [16] Its attitude was not softened by the experience of the 1969 revaluation. When the 1971 currency crisis threatened another revaluation there was a new 'desperate and determined campaign' [17] against it, with Volkswagen producing figures to show that a 4 per cent revaluation would wipe out their profits (down 42 per cent in 1970), and a leading chemical company, Bayer (profits down 26 per cent in 1970), arguing that a 9 per cent revaluation would wipe out theirs.

But it is very difficult for a government to avert revaluation in conditions of crisis: the mere expectation of a revaluation leads to an inflow of speculative funds from abroad.* In exchange for incoming funds (e.g. dollars) the Central Bank pays out D-Marks and so the domestic money supply becomes impossible to control. Fear that an expanding money supply may raise domestic demand and worsen inflation makes an adjustment of the exchange rate to stop the inflow of funds almost inevitable. This is so even when, as O.E.C.D. argued was the case in May 1971, the surplus on the underlying balance of payments does not point to a 'fundamental disequilibrium'. [18]

1971 saw very slow growth and inflation spreading up to 7 per cent. Investment was expected to be stagnant as a result of the 'profit squeeze of unprecedented severity resulting from the continued rapid rise in wage costs and the 1969 revaluation'. [19] In the autumn of 1971 forecasts for 1972 were for negligible growth and a 7 per cent fall in industrial investment. Warnings of dividend cuts by many major firms, such as Volkswagen, underlined how fiercely profits were being squeezed by rising wage costs and the upward floating of the D-Mark. The German economic 'miracle' appeared to be at an end.

---

*These inflows can reach huge proportions – reportedly more than 1 billion dollars in an hour in May 1971.

The United States

After the doldrums of the middle and late fifties the U.S. economy began to move. This expansion was associated with a large increase in the share of profits in company income – from 27·7 per cent in 1961 to 30·9 per cent in 1965. To a great extent this can be attributed to the cyclical productivity increases; but our estimates suggest that the very small rate of increase of wages was another factor – money wages going up about 4 per cent p.a., real wages 3 per cent. But after 1965 productivity gains slackened off and money-wage increases rose; so that by 1968 the profit share had fallen by more than 1 per cent. With consumer prices rising by 6 per cent in 1969, the administration clamped down on demand in an attempt to reduce wage increases. The Council of Economic Advisers, while rejecting 'a sharp and prolonged rise in unemployment', argued that the 'best hope of curbing inflation and restricting the rise in unemployment to a relatively small and temporary increase rests with a policy of firm and persistent restraint on the expansion in the demand for goods and services'. This was somehow supposed to 'produce high employment with much less inflation than we have recently experienced'. [20]

In the event, unemployment practically doubled to more than 6 per cent at the end of 1970 and the continued pressure of wage increases together with sluggish productivity led to a gain of a further 3 per cent in labour's share between 1968 and 1970.* Business investment grew from 9·8 per cent of national income in 1955–60 to 10·9 per cent in 1966 and it proved to be 'highly resistant to the deterioration in business conditions in 1969', [21] but nevertheless fell by around 2 per cent in real terms in 1970 as pressure on liquidity intensified.

* In 'Notes and Numbers on the Profit Squeeze' (*Brookings Papers on Economic Activity*, No. 3, 1970) Okun and Perry also find that a substantial part of the fall in the profit share cannot be explained by slow productivity growth, but they offer no alternative explanation. The decline in the profit share is even greater if capital consumption is deducted, for then the fall is from 22·9 per cent in 1964 to 17·5 per cent in 1970; even then it appears that the official estimates of capital consumption lead to a slight underestimate in the true fall in the profit share. It seems that no general recovery in profitability took place in 1971.

In August 1971, with the Presidential election little more than a year away, the failure of rising unemployment to check inflation and the sudden worsening of the American balance of payments precipitated the most dramatic reversal of economic policy since the war. Nixon, the prophet of the free-market economy, instituted a 90-day wage and price freeze and took some measures to reduce unemployment by cutting taxes and increasing incentives on investment inside the United States. At the same time he suspended the convertibility of the dollar into gold, attempted to force other countries to upvalue their currencies (so devaluing the dollar) and imposed a 10-per-cent surcharge on all imports to the United States.

These measures led first to the most severe and prolonged monetary crisis of the post-war period as other capitalist countries tried to resist the forced revaluation of their currencies which would lead to a decline in competitiveness and profitability of their capital. They led also to a sharp deterioration in the relations between the U.S. government and the American labour movement. One official union leader contrasted the 'bonanzas' granted to 'coupon-clippers and money-lenders' with the requirement that workers should 'sacrifice their opportunities for economic gain in the name of reducing inflation'.

The Nixon government's successful attempts in 1971 to impose 'voluntary' restrictions on exports of textiles to the U.S. from Japan and a large number of underdeveloped countries as well as the 10-per-cent surcharge gave a considerable boost to protectionist forces inside the United States. At the end of the year a bill was before Congress which would restrict the level of American imports to the average in the years 1965–9, a measure which was so protectionist that in the words of the *New York Times* it made the protectionist legislation of the 1930s 'look as if it might have been written by Adam Smith'. This bill was supported by the A.F.L.–C.I.O., the central federation of the American labour movement.

After Nixon's measures of August 1971 the stock market initially rose in the expectation of higher profits as U.S. competitiveness was increased by the surcharge and the forced revaluations. But by the end of the year these gains had been lost and fears grew of a more fierce international trade war and, in the face of Nixon's attempt to activate Phase II of his wage control policy, of a rise in labour militancy. Meanwhile, in spite of economists' predictions of a boom election year for the economy, the unemployment rate showed no sign at all of improving.

2. Trade, competition and the dollar

We saw in the last chapter how Britain's competitive position deteriorated in the fifties and sixties. In fact all the O.E.C.D. countries have faced growing competition in their own home markets. The volume of imports has generally been growing one and a half or more times as fast as output. But while some countries have expanded their exports of manufactures as much as twice as fast as their manufacturing output, in the U.S. and U.K. output and exports have expanded at nearly the same rate. The poor performance of the U.K. is shown very clearly by the fact that since the mid-fifties her exports of manufactures have grown only one third as fast as those of Italy and Japan. An interesting feature of the expansion of trade has been that the socialist and under-developed countries have not been an important *net* source of demand for exports from capitalist countries. The amount the capitalist world sold to them, less what it bought, grew to only 0·2 per cent of output of the O.E.C.D. countries in 1968.

But domestic producers have been facing more and more competition from foreign subsidiaries, so trade does not tell the whole story of increasing international competition. More than 80 per cent of the expansion of U.S. firms' sales to foreigners over the period 1958–65 has been in the sales of subsidiaries, many of which are located in industrialized countries. Several U.S. electronics companies have recently set up manufacturing facilities in low-wage countries and their products are then exported back to the U.S. For the U.K. as well, the value of sales of subsidiaries has grown more than that of exports. [22]

Even when account is taken of manufactured imports and sales of foreign subsidiaries inside the U.S. economy, American capital still expanded its net sales of manufactures to foreigners by some $27 thousand million between 1957 and 1967. This compares with increases of net sales of about $6 thousand million for Japan and Germany, $1½ thousand million for U.K. and little change in Italy and France (where imports and setting up of foreign subsidiaries just about offset rapid increases in exports). This net expansion of U.S. sales and therefore of U.S. capital was double that of her five main competitors combined. Consequently, it may seem hard to reconcile this with the U.S.'s notorious balance-of-payments deficit.

The explanation is simply that sales of U.S. subsidiaries overseas do not count as U.S. exports since they do not directly earn foreign exchange for the U.S. The only balance of payments gain is the remission of profits back to the U.S. from these subsidiaries and this may easily be outweighed by extra investment coming from the U.S. and increasing the capacity of the subsidiaries. Apart from the severe deterioration in the last three years, the U.S. ran a sizeable current account surplus throughout the sixties. However, the current account balance-of-payments surplus was quite inadequate to finance the growing outflow of long-term capital; direct investment abroad (acquisition of factories, etc.) and government grants and loans were both running at about $4 thousand million a year by 1970. In the face of this rising outflow of long-term capital the current account was actually worsening and was increasingly in deficit from 1969 onwards. Military expenditure abroad rose from around $3 thousand million in the early sixties to $5 thousand million a year in 1969. The overall deficit was paid for by running down the U.S. gold stock and short-term borrowing from foreigners.* Over the period 1955 to 1970 the reserve assets of the U.S. (mainly gold) fell from $23 thousand million (40 per cent of the 'free world' reserves) to $14½ thousand million (well under 20 per cent); and net short-term borrowing rose by almost $15 thousand million. The liquidity ratio (reserve assets of the U.S. divided by dollars accumulated abroad) fell from almost 3 to around ⅔.

The international money crises since 1969 are a result of this

* This short-term borrowing took the form of paying foreigners in dollars which they then held on to (investing them in New York, say). Although individuals did not owe these dollars, they represented a general claim on U.S. resources.

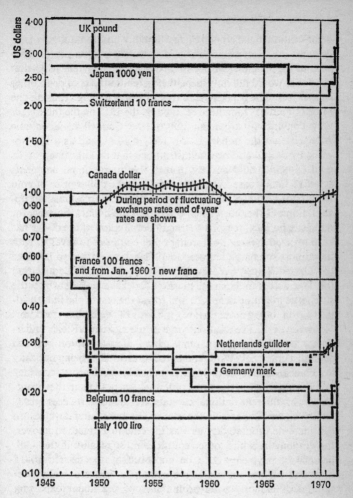

Figure 8. How parities have changed
Source: The Times, 21 December 1971.

deterioration in the United States' liquidity position. Initially U.S. deficits were welcomed as a way of spreading reserves more evenly around the capitalist world. But as U.S. liquidity fell, fears that the dollar would fall in value, either in relation to gold or to other currencies, caused periodic waves of dollar-selling. Raising the price of gold has long been rejected by the U.S. on the (no longer very convincing) argument put by the Council of Economic Advisers that the dollar 'is so widely held abroad as a store of value by official and private institutions that an adjustment in its gold content would gravely disturb the international payments system'. In any case a straight increase in the dollar price of gold would not help U.S. competitiveness unless it occasioned an up-valuation of other currencies in terms of the dollar. Probably for domestic political reasons a straight devaluation of the dollar has been rejected in favour of forcing other countries to revalue, with the import surcharge imposed in 1971 being retained to improve the United States' bargaining strength over trade liberalization (i.e. free access to Japanese markets 'in exchange' for which the surcharge might be dropped) and to get the rest of the industrialized world to pay more towards the costs of 'defending freedom'.

Whatever the eventual outcome of the current crisis, it underlines most clearly the anarchic nature of competition between capitalist countries. While sometimes presented as being basically a technical matter involving irresponsible speculators, currency crises always affect the vital interests, in particular the profitability, of different national capitals. Revaluation reduces profitability, as we have seen in the case of Germany; and devaluation can increase profitability, as was the case in France. Moreover, the amount by which other countries must revalue if the U.S. balance of payments is to be improved by the desired 10–15 thousand million dollars is big enough to make a really substantial difference to the profitability of the major exporting industries in Europe and Japan. It would be preferable for European capital if the U.S. took sterner measures to restrict the outflow of American capital to Europe. Not only would this reduce the size of the revaluation and loss of competitiveness, but also it would stem the growth of competition which the invasion of American capital into Europe has caused. Reductions in U.S.

expenditure overseas would also be preferable to revaluation; even a major increase in the European contribution to N.A.T.O. might, from European capital's point of view, be a preferable solution, particularly if it was financed by higher taxation of working-class incomes.

The realities of the situation were well expressed, after Nixon's attempt to force the revaluation of the yen in 1971, by the fall on the Tokyo Stock Exchange (reflecting worsened profitability prospects) and the contrasting rise on Wall Street. That one capitalist country cannot go its own way alone is clearly demonstrated by the example of Germany. The profitability of German capital encouraged U.S. investment in Germany, which in turn exacerbated the balance-of-payments deficit in the U.S. and the surplus in Germany. This made revaluation in Germany, and thus reduction in profitability, inevitable.

The recent intensification of international competition is affecting all the major capitalist countries by limiting the capitalists' ability to raise prices in response to cost increases. For each country, therefore, it is one cause of a tendency for profit margins to be squeezed. At the same time the difficulty of maintaining high profitability, which has been experienced by all the capitalist countries, has led to more determined efforts to enter new markets and increase sales. This is particularly the case when the government's reaction to the wage pressure is to deflate demand. This adds excess capacity to low profitability as a force impelling firms to look to new markets. Low profitability has, therefore, intensified international competition even further. And it would be wrong to think that in international competition one capital's loss of profits is another capital's gain. On the whole, the opposite is true: international competition harms everyone's profits, though at a rate which will depend on the competitive strength of the country. But relative weakness in international competition tends to be self-reinforcing, since falls in profitability inhibit capital accumulation. This slows down productivity growth and also increases pressure for higher money wages as real wage increases are impaired. At the level of an individual country, international competition is a *cause* of a squeeze of profits; at the level of the capitalist system as a whole it is an *effect*.

3. Capitalist reality and bourgeois explanations

In a major report issued at the end of 1970 entitled *Inflation: the Present Problem*, the O.E.C.D. pointed to what it saw as the social and political consequences of inflation:

> ... under inflationary conditions, income gains and the accumulation of wealth often appear to result not so much from work or sacrifice, but rather from ingenuity and the exercise of economic and political power and influence. Resentment against inflation is incoherent and diffused throughout the community. It therefore tends to strengthen other forces making for disenchantment with government and existing political parties ...
>
> To sum up, the essence of the problem today is that the cumulative economic, social and political consequences of inflation, which up to now some may have regarded as tolerable, could begin to build up rather quickly. Further the relation between inflation as the cause and its effects – growing distortion, friction and discontent – may not be either clearly or immediately apparent to large sections of public opinion. [23]

This analysis is exceptionally revealing. Inflation is seen as undesirable because it causes resentment against income gains that result from the exercise of political and economic power. But inflation is an essential part of capitalist reality. It is not so much a *cause* of 'distortion, friction and discontent' as an *effect*, because capital puts up prices in response to labour's call for higher wages. And it is mere wishful thinking on the part of the O.E.C.D. that makes them see nothing but 'a succession of somewhat heterogeneous developments' in the major capitalist countries. The most striking thing, in fact, is the *homogeneity* of recent developments. The wage explosions in different countries all reflect working-class successes in the class struggle, and they have all elicited similar deflationary responses.

But, as the O.E.C.D. recognizes, deflation, or the creation of unemployment, may have contradictory effects:

> The hardest line is taken by those who believe that inflation can only be checked by recreating fear of a real recession ...

Apart from concern about the social and political implications of

Table 4.1. Unemployment, Inflation and Growth of Production in Major Countries, 1960–71

	Unemployment rates (per cent)			Rates of inflation (per cent a year)			Rates of growth of industrial production (per cent a year)		
	1961–5	1966–70	1971	1960–65	1965–70	1971	1960–65	1965–70	1971
U.S.	5·5	3·9	6·0	1·3	4·2	4·2	5·7	4·0	−1·5
Japan	1·3	1·2	1·5	6·2	5·5	8·4	11·4	16·7	5·5
U.K.	2·6	3·5	5·6*	3·6	4·6	9·9	3·2	2·2	1·0
France	1·9	2·8	4·2	3·8	4·2	5·7	5·3	6·4	4·0
Germany	0·4	0·8	0·9	2·8	2·7	5·9	5·3	6·3	1·9
Italy	3·3	3·8	3·5	4·9	2·9	4·9	5·9	7·2	−3·3

Sources: Unemployment: *National Institute Economic Review*, May 1971, p. 67, November 1971, p. 22. The figures are of registered unemployed, adjusted to secure comparability with U.S. definitions (see May 1971 reference). 1971 refers to the third quarter.

Inflation: Rates of increase of consumer prices from O.E.C.D. *Main Economic Indicators*. 1971 figure refers to increase between September 1970 and September 1971.

Production: Rates of increase of industrial production from O.E.C.D. *Main Economic Indicators*. 1971 figure refers to average of first three quarters of 1971 as compared with corresponding quarters of 1970.

*Excluding Northern Ireland.

such a policy, critics may be doubtful whether it is really possible to turn the clock back in this way. People's reaction to going bankrupt or being thrown out of a job may have been different in the 1930s when it could be thought that this was the result of a natural disaster. But today, a serious recession would be clearly recognized to be the result of a deliberate policy being followed by the government. The experience of those few countries which, at one time or another during the 1960s, fell short of their potential growth rates for some period of time, suggests that the undercurrents of social and political discontent thus generated may eventually have violent repercussions in the form of wage explosions which are difficult to foresee or control.

... Circumstances vary considerably from country to country but the fundamental problem is how to get people to exercise the moderation that they would do if they believed that a major recession was possible, without having to administer the lesson. [24]

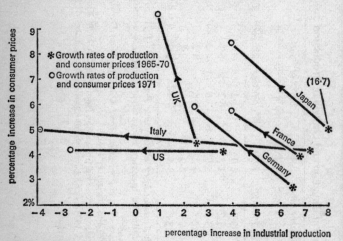

Figure 9. Stagnating production and accelerating inflation
Source: See Table 4.1.

In other words, according to the O.E.C.D., the working class must be bluffed into believing that, unless wage demands are not moderated, a major recession will result. But as long as the working class react politically and quickly enough to mass unemployment this *can* only be a bluff. The admission that capitalism can only work by fostering an intense feeling of insecurity in the working class is a good sign of its present weakness. Incomes policy may be tried, of course, but

... The major problem encountered in trying to build up a prices and incomes policy is obviously the heavy burden of responsibility it imposes on the *social partners*. They are called on to exercise moderation in the pursuit of their legitimate interests. Viewed from the top the proposition that if money incomes and profits rise faster than national productivity the consequence will not be higher real incomes and profits is impeccable. But it is not true when applied to individual groups or enterprises. It is thus all too easy for leaders on both sides to be persuaded into accepting over-ambitious commitments on behalf of their members [our emphasis]. [25]

O.E.C.D.'s assumption is that the demand for higher wages cannot increase labour's share at all but can only re-distribute income as between different sections of the working class. But the facts we have presented show decisively that this theory is false. And indeed the capitalists know this. They resist wage pressure precisely because it *does* tend to increase labour's share and to threaten profitability.

The O.E.C.D. also stresses other 'Positive Price Policies through the whole Range of Government Activities'. Along with 'efficient' public expenditure and social policies, their suggestions include liberalizing international trade and decreasing protection for uncompetitive sectors and industries. The virtue of trade liberalization, according to them, is that

... The rapid growth of international trade has contributed to holding down prices, both by providing low cost substitutes for domestic products, and through its effects on productivity and price policy in domestic sectors exposed to international competition. [26]

Of course it is true that this will curb inflation and probably moderate money wage claims too, since real wages will then be greater. But it will also curb profits and thereby threaten the system; and the real aim of other capitalist anti-inflationary policies is to maintain the profit share. The common belief in the efficacy of competition to cure capitalism's current problems seems to be based on the myth that under competitive capitalism conflicts of interest are solved harmoniously (and to mutual advantage) in the market place. The fact is that greater competition between national capitalist economies can only damage profitability. The only competition which is really in the interests of the capitalists is competition in the labour market: in other words the promotion of unemployment and the weakening of working class organization.

4. The end of the long boom

The output of all the O.E.C.D. countries taken together (that is, most of the developed capitalist world) grew at $4\frac{1}{2}$ per cent p.a. between 1950 and 1968. At this rate of growth, output doubles every 16 years. Productivity has been doubling every 10 years in Japan, every 15 years or so in the major Common Market countries, and about every 30 years in the U.S. and U.K. The downward trends in profitability which we have just described are already affecting the prospects for maintaining this tremendous expansion in output.

Profitability is connected with the expansion of output through its effect on the rate of accumulation of capital (investment), which in turn is important in determining the rate at which productivity increases. We find that Japan, in the late fifties, devoted much the highest proportion of output to private investment (about 25 per cent), with the Common Market countries investing a good deal less (around 20 per cent), and the U.K. and U.S. a bit less than 15 per cent.*

And countries are ranked in almost exactly the same order in terms of profitability, though inadequate data make it difficult to compare profit shares accurately. Japan has by far the highest profit share; in the E.E.C. it is lower and in Britain and the U.S. lowest of all.

It is striking that in the 1950s the three countries which were best able to maintain high profit shares – Japan, Italy and Germany – were those in which fascist governments had ruled before and during the war. Their destruction of independent labour movements enabled capital to impose in the post-war years, before the

*For rough figures of *total* investment see p. 80.

labour movements could recover, a very high share of profits. In Italy, where the labour movement was rebuilt most rapidly, the economic miracle first came to an end; and it has lasted longest in Japan, where the labour movement has remained weakest.

The reaction of investment to *changes* in profitability is particularly clear when the experience of the main E.E.C. countries in the 1960s is compared. Italy had the sharpest reduction in the profit share, and the share of investment fell; Germany had a substantial reduction in profitability, and the share of investment stopped growing; France virtually avoided the profit squeeze, and the investment share continued to grow. In Japan the rate of increase in the investment share was much reduced in the sixties around the same time as the rise in the profit share was halted; and in the U.K., when the fall in the profit share speeded up in the middle sixties, and was no longer offset by tax reductions, the investment share stopped rising from its low level.

To some extent the setbacks suffered by profits and investment in the sixties reflected a tightening labour market. The decline in agricultural employment and employment in small family businesses, which was most important in Japan but still very large in the continental countries, was becoming a less plentiful source of industrial workers. So were the unemployed (important in Italy and Germany in the fifties) and inflows of refugees (especially into Germany in the fifties). A plentiful supply of industrial workers will tend to keep up a high profit share and thus encourage investment because it puts workers in a weak bargaining position and may also increase the difficulty of union organization. But it also encourages investment directly since the investment will tend to be more profitable if it is used to equip new recruits to the industrial labour force with capital, rather than merely to increase the amount of capital used by the existing labour force. The slow rise in money wages and the rapid gain in productivity which results from the high level of investment will keep up both competitiveness and the profit share. At the same time, demand for this expanding output will be sustained by the expansion of exports which competitiveness brings (e.g. Germany and Italy in the fifties, Japan in the fifties and sixties).

The relationship between changes in profits and investment is more complicated in the case of the U.S., where the Kennedy and Johnson governments' success in getting the economy moving brought increased investment *and* profit shares.* The expansion was initially stimulated by tax cuts – between the end of 1960 and the middle of 1965 increased defence expenditure comprised less than 10 per cent of total 'expansionary actions' of the government. [27] But then expenditure in connection with the Vietnam war helped maintain expansion; defence spending provided two thirds of the government stimulus in the 2½ years up to the end of 1967. Initially business investment failed to respond to the expansion because of 'the cumulative effect upon business expectations of 5 years of persisting slack in the economy . . . left businessmen with a record of consistently . . . redundant capacity'. [28] However, in response to further tax cuts and investment incentives by the end of 1968 there had been a 40 per cent rise in the real stock of capital goods (as compared with the beginning of 1961). As we have seen, profit margins expanded considerably, helped by relatively low money-wage increases. This must have played some part, even if a subsidiary one, in keeping up the level of investment.

The growing importance of the government in maintaining demand is not unique to the U.S. Between the early and late fifties there was no increase in the share of resources directly absorbed by public expenditure[1] in the major capitalist countries. In the U.K., indeed, there was a considerable reduction. But between the late fifties and mid-sixties there were substantial increases in the share of national output devoted to public expenditure in Italy, Germany and the U.K., as the drive for capital accumulation weakened. The exception in Europe was France, where the share of public expenditure remained more or less unchanged and where, as we saw, investment remained buoyant and the profit share hardly fell at all.

[1] Expenditure by government and local authorities on armaments, hospitals, teachers and so forth, but not including transfers to supplement incomes (unemployment benefit, etc.). Such transfers help to boost demand indirectly by increasing private consumption (or investment, in the case of U.K. investment grants). Data in appendix, Table G4.

* The United States' stagnation is well shown by the fact that at the beginning of 1961 G.N.P. was estimated to be 10 per cent below its potential at the so-called full employment level (4 per cent unemployed).

In Japan there was probably some fall in the share of public expenditure in the fifties, but it rose in the sixties.

Within the whole area of public expenditure *defence spending* has played a decreasing role in maintaining demand. In all the major capitalist countries for which data is available defence spending was a substantially smaller fraction of total output by the end of the sixties than in the early fifties. Taken together, the O.E.C.D. countries' defence expenditure took 10·2 per cent of G.N.P. in 1952–3 at the height of the post-Korean war rearmament; while at the next peak, in 1967, the proportion was only 6·5 per cent. In 1968 the fall in defence expenditure elsewhere more than offset the further rise in the U.S.*

When we also take into account changes in the budget deficit[1] the general picture of the state playing an increasingly important part in keeping demand expanding is reinforced. For though budget deficits were mostly reduced in the middle and late fifties, they increased in the middle and late sixties to offset slackening private demand. This applied even to France and Japan, where there was not much expansion of public expenditure.†

Increases in government expenditure and tax cuts could always,

---

[1] The expression *budget deficit* as used here means the difference between total government expenditure (on current and capital account and including transfers) and taxation and other receipts. An increase in the deficit will magnify the effect of an increase in government expenditure on goods and services on total demand, since the lower taxation stimulates private demand.

* This is not to deny that military expenditure, in absolute terms, is an important component of demand and thus employment – particularly in the U.S., where it constitutes almost 9 per cent of G.N.P. In that country, especially, military power also plays a vital part in protecting overseas interests. For individual firms, not least those in the aerospace industry, military contracts are vital, although the tribulations of Lockheed show that they do not solve all their problems.

† Data in table G.4 in appendix G. The analysis is admittedly rather crude; in particular we neglect the fact that in some countries, such as the U.K. and Germany, there was a low level of output in the economy during part of the more recent period. This reduced tax revenue and so tended to increase the budget deficit, which makes it look as though the government is being more expansionary than it really is. The opposite is true of the U.S. where the high level of demand increased tax revenue and reduced the deficit. But a more sophisticated analysis is unlikely to contradict the results.

as Keynes showed, keep economies at full employment. But they leave unsolved the problem of profitability. For as we argue in detail in section 6 of chapter 8, securing full employment through government expenditure cannot resolve the contradiction concerning the struggle over distribution of the national income once full employment is achieved. This was quite clear in the U.S. after the government succeeded in prodding the U.S. economy back to what is called full employment. Then, as we saw earlier, wage pressure caused the Keynesian weapons to be used in reverse in order to create unemployment – a trend which is becoming more and more obvious in all the major capitalist countries. Thus the checks on investment that come from the squeeze on profitability are reinforced by government action aimed at restoring profitability in the long run; but for the capitalist system as a whole stagnation only adds to the pressures on profitability as the scramble for world markets becomes more desperate. So with the maintenance of high rates of investment becoming increasingly difficult, the foundations of the long post-war expansion have been undermined.

Part Two
The Results

Chapter 5
The Effect of the Crisis on Standards of Living

We have already seen that the distribution between capitalists and workers of income generated by production in the company sector has changed dramatically in recent years. This is a change in what can be called the *functional* distribution of income. The functional distribution of income is determined by the struggle over wages and profits at the point of production; and it also depends on the ability of capitalists to hand on their higher costs as higher prices. The functional distribution of income decides the overall prospects for individual firms and for the capitalist system as a whole.

But profits and wages are both subject to tax. And both classes receive other forms of income – interest and capital gains for the capitalist class (or bourgeoisie), certain state benefits for the workers. It is only when we take all this into account that we can see what has happened to the *personal* distribution of income – whether labour's enormous gains in terms of functional distribution have resulted in an improvement in the relative living standards of workers, and how living standards of the bourgeoisie have held up in the face of falling profitability. These changes in living standards have important effects on the economic and political attitude of the classes towards each other, and towards the system.

1. The average standard of living

Before we try to unravel the complex changes in *relative* standards of living it is important to be clear about how *average* consumption levels have changed. Consumption per head grew quite fast – 2·9 per cent per year – between 1951 and 1964. Between 1964 and 1969, however, the rate of growth fell to only 1 per cent p.a.; in fact, between the first quarter of 1966 and the last quarter of 1969 people only managed to keep their consumption growing by running down their savings as they had in the five years after the war.

Table 5.1. Average Rates of Growth of Incomes, 1964–70 (1963 prices, average for the population) per cent a year

Between the years ...	*1964–9*	*1966–9*	*1969–70*
... average personal incomes before tax grew by ...	2·0	1·6	4·1
... but tax payments on income rose by ...	8·0	6·6	8·3
... and national insurance contributions grew by ...	4·4	2·9	11·6
So personal disposable income only went up by ...	1·0	0·7	2·8
Out of this average consumers' spending increased by ...	1·1	1·0	2·4
... leaving savings changing by ...	−0·1	−2·3	9·1

Source: Incomes Data Report 92, p. 31.

The very slow rate of growth of private consumption between 1964 and 1969 was not due only to the fact that output grew relatively slowly; a further influence was that the proportion of the total increase in output which was absorbed by personal consumption fell over these years to less than one half from the previous level during 1951–64 of about two thirds. This is a reflection of the big increase in taxation which kept down the growth of personal disposable income.[1] But if consumers did not benefit much from the meagre growth in output, where did the output go?

One factor was that increases in public expenditure absorbed a higher proportion of extra output under Labour, particularly in

[1]*Personal income* consists of labour incomes, income from self-employment, dividends and interest and grants received from the government (undistributed profits are not included). Personal income less taxation and insurance contributions gives *personal disposable income*. When adjusted to take account of inflation it is called *real* personal disposable income.

1965 and 1966. But more important, a sizeable proportion of extra output went into the conversion of the balance of payments from a £400m. current deficit in 1964 to a surplus of about £400m. in 1969. By 1969 not only were all imports being paid for by higher exports, leaving less to be consumed and invested at home; but devaluation pushed up import prices so that more exports were required to meet the import bill, and this was reflected in small increases in private investment as well as consumption. By contrast between 1954 and 1964 export prices had been rising and import prices falling so that the growth of total home consumption and investment was greater than the growth of home production. This earlier pattern re-emerged in 1970 when the rise in U.K. export prices helped to pay the import bill. Thus there could be some increase in public expenditure and in private accumulation even though private consumption absorbed 90 per cent of the extra output, which brought its rate of growth up to the 1951–64 average.

Table 5.2. How the Growth in Output Was Used, 1951–70

Proportions of extra output devoted to:	*1951–64*	*1964–9*	(per cent) *1964–6*	*1966–9*	*1969–70*
Private consumption	65·6	48·9	57·0	43·8	87·9
Public expenditure (current and capital)	19·6	26·0	40·9	16·9	10·5
Private investment (and stockbuilding)	20·1	7·3	−20·2	24·1	12·1
Balance of payments (increase in exports less increase in imports)	−5·4	17·9	22·4	15·1	−10·5
Average per cent rise in output a year	3·0	2·3	2·3	2·3	2·1

Source: National Income Blue Book 1971, Tables 14 and 51.

2. Workers' living standards

The income of industry and commerce is divided into wages and salaries on the one hand and profits on the other. But wage and salary earners are obliged to make certain payments such as income tax and national insurance contributions. Some workers get further income from other sources, in particular from the government in the form of family allowances, social security benefits, family income supplement, rates or rent rebate. Changes in these things have nothing directly to do with the distribution of income between pay and profits in industry; but they do affect the relative standards of living of different classes.

Wages and salaries

Average weekly earnings in money terms rose on average by little more than 6 per cent per annum between 1951 and 1969. In 1970 they rose by 12 per cent, the highest annual figure since the wage explosion which followed the First World War. A substantial portion of these increased money earnings throughout the period have been worn away by inflation. So between 1959 and 1969 the real earnings of the average manual worker rose by just under 3 per cent. But wage increases were eroded by rising taxation and national insurance contributions as well. These increased faster than money earnings, so that a growing share of workers' incomes was taken by the government. Over the period 1959–64 real wages after tax payments grew by only 2 per cent p.a.; in the period of the Labour government from 1964 to 1969 the rise was down to a mere 1 per cent p.a.; but 1970 saw a high rate of increase of almost 3 per cent p.a. due to the wage explosion. With wages rising more slowly, and prices rather faster, in 1971 the growth of real incomes fell back again.

Table 5.3. Manual Workers' Incomes, 1959–70

	Real income before taxes grew by — per cent but taxes rose faster so net real income increased by — per cent a year	
1959–64	2·7	1·9
1964–9	2·8	1·0
1969–70	5·5	2·7

Source: H. Turner and F. Wilkinson, *New Society*, 25 February 1971.

However, the average figures conceal the predicament of certain sections of the working class.* Between 1965 and 1969 the real disposable income of council manual workers, for example, did not rise at all; that of electricity workers actually fell. And in 1970 any workers who did not receive a rise of about 9 per cent suffered a fall in their real disposable income. [1]

During the later 1960s, when an incomes policy was operating which at least nominally aimed to redistribute income to lower-paid workers, and when there was what has been called a revolt of the lower paid, the distribution of wages seems to have got worse rather than better. Between 1965 and 1969 the poorest quarter of workers (reckoned by average pay in their industries) received percentage increases in incomes which were about average. But the lowest paid 10 per cent of workers were doing worse than the average for most of the time. [2] During the wage explosion of 1969–70 several pieces of evidence point to the fact that the worst-paid industries did worse than the average (though the T.U.C.

*In April 1971 21·8 per cent of full-time male manual workers had gross weekly earnings (before tax and national insurance contributions) of more than £35, 12·9 per cent got less than £20; about 4 per cent got less than £17 and nearly 1½ per cent made less than £15. On the whole, non-manufacturing industries, where almost 18 per cent of manual workers got less than £20 p.w., were worse payers than manufacturing industries, where the proportion was less than 8 per cent, and the service industries, like distribution, were particularly bad. But the worst industry of all in respect of pay was agriculture, where almost 50 per cent of the workers received less than £20 and about 8 per cent less than £15. Among manufacturing industries the smaller-scale ones paid the least. A fifth of workers in the leather industry earned less than £20, whereas in vehicles the proportion was about 2 per cent. The average wage in 1970 was £29·4 for full-time manual workers. The lowest paid 10 per cent of all male manual workers got two thirds of the average wage or less. The highest paid 10 per cent got 47 per cent more than the average wage. And it would appear that these proportions have been amazingly constant over a very long period – perhaps since 1886 or earlier. (J. R. Thatcher, *Journal of the Royal Statistical Society*, vol. 30, part 2.) There has been a very slow relative improvement over the years in the rates of pay of women workers. But in 1969 women's wages in industry were seldom more than three quarters of those of men, and sometimes less. A further source of inequality arises from regional variations. The proportion of full-time male manual workers earning less than £20 p.w. in Scotland, East Anglia and the South-West was double the proportion in the East Midlands.

claims that the opposite was the case). [3] Within industries it seems that the lower-paid workers usually got smaller increases than the higher-paid. There is also evidence that workers in the lower-paid industries received increases with larger intervals between them than those in the better-paid industries. The incomes policy almost certainly failed to affect the overall rate of wage increases; it also did nothing to improve equality even among wage earners.

Taxes and benefits

The Prices and Incomes Board has claimed that 'the tax and social security system has provided an effective means of redistributing net income in a way which favours the low paid'. [4] This is quite untrue. In a limited way income tax *is* progressive; the rich pay proportionately higher income tax than the poor; and the very poor pay none at all. But the tax system relies heavily on excise taxes on tobacco, etc., and on national insurance contributions. Taxes on goods as a whole tend to take more or less the same proportion of income for all classes. And insurance contributions take a markedly higher proportion of the income of the poor than of the rich and so are sharply regressive.[1]

Taken as a whole the tax system is not at all progressive, except at the very lowest levels (income under £12 a week) and at really high income levels, where surtax begins to bite, since in the income range of £1,000 p.a. to £3,000 p.a. taxes take about one third of households' incomes. During the period 1964 to 1968 the proportion of all incomes taken in taxes went up from 31 per cent to 35 per cent. The tax burden was reduced only for those earning £7–11 a week and for those earning over £60 a week.

In incomes of up to £16 a week there is some progressiveness in the benefits system. This manifests itself chiefly in the various allowances, e.g. social security and supplementary benefit, rebates

---

[1] A *progressive tax* system takes a higher *proportion* of the income of the rich than the poor so that the difference between their incomes is smaller after tax than before (e.g. an income three times as great as another before tax might be twice as great after tax). A regressive tax system takes a higher proportion of the income of the poor so that the gap (in relative terms) is widened by its operation.

on rates, rent and other charges, such as school meals and prescriptions and family income supplement. But in a way the benefits system operates very unfairly, for as incomes rise from an extremely low to a very low level, people lose their eligibility for these benefits. For example, the family income supplement declines by one half of the increase in pay, and is thus for very low income families equivalent to a 50 per cent income tax.

Consequently in periods of inflation a very low-paid worker who increases his pay at the same rate as prices are rising becomes worse off. It has been calculated that, after the introduction of the family income supplement and the oddly called 'fair rent' scheme, a worker with two children and an income of £14 a week will, in order to keep pace with 8 per cent inflation, need an annual increase in wages of 22 per cent; with £12 a week to start with, he needs an increase of 38 per cent; and with £10 a week he needs a rise of 42 per cent.

Even if benefits like the family income supplement give a slight improvement when they are introduced, they are bound to be rapidly eroded. While the tax and benefits system may at any given moment be progressive at these levels of income, the combination of the tax system with inflation becomes appallingly regressive over a period unless lower-paid workers get much bigger percentage increases than others. And in fact they have been getting *smaller* increases. The alternative is for the government to act very quickly to push up the income levels at which the benefits are received (tying them to inflation); but the very notion of linking benefits to inflation is anathema to a government pretending to cope with rising prices. And of course pensioners and others who do suffer from the government's failure to control prices give it a splendid weapon with which to belabour the unions.

Poverty

The worsening position of lower-paid workers, along with the spread of unemployment and the rising rate of inflation, contributed to the growth of poverty from the late 1960s. The best recent estimates suggest that 'it would be surprising if those with incomes less than the supplementary benefit scales[1] numbered fewer than 3,500,000 at the beginning of 1971, or a million more than in 1966.'[5] Certainly, the supplementary benefit level as a proportion of average earnings had not risen during this time and in the 12 months from August 1970 it fell. The number of people in poverty rose by 10 per cent in that one year.

But why are the poor getting poorer in our advanced, mature, industrial economy? The income of the country could easily give everyone a comfortable material standard of living if it were spread more equally. The profitability crisis of British capital has led to efforts to control workers' wages. But the capitalist system permitted no method of raising the pay of lower-paid workers faster than the average. At the same time the government, when faced with an economic crisis, after 1966 drastically cut into the increases in public expenditure which had been substantial in the first two years of the Labour government. For example, 1970 public-sector spending on housing in real terms was no higher than in 1966. Capitalist reality put paid to good intentions. In conditions of declining profitability it was hard to increase taxation of capital, and the most insistent pressures for new state spending came not from the poor but from capitalist corporations faced with impending bankruptcy or with problems in financing their research or investment. It was these imperatives of the system, not old age, sickness and large families, which were the real causes of increasing poverty. 'Pauperism', as Marx said, 'forms a condition of capitalist production, and of the capitalist development of wealth.' [6]

3. The incomes of the bourgeoisie

A change in the distribution of income between wages and profits is only one of many factors determining the living standards of the bourgeoisie. Dividends and interest paid by companies out of profits generated in production are of course an important source of income, but they are not rigidly tied to profits; spending power

[1] The level of income supposedly guaranteed by the State, subject to qualifications such as earnings when in work.

may also be enhanced when share prices go up and share prices are not wholly determined by current profits. Furthermore, most of the interest paid on the national debt and on loans to consumers (HP, etc.) finds its way into the pockets of the bourgeoisie either through their direct holdings of securities or through the interest payments they receive from the financial institutions which carry out the lending operations. These interest payments are not directly linked at all to the share of profits, nor are executives' salaries and directors' fees. Finally, of course, the bourgeoisie also pays taxes.

It is easier to find information about the income of workers than about the incomes and wealth of the rich. In 1968–9 slightly over one quarter of the incomes of those with more than £3,000 p.a. comes from investments (interest and dividends, etc.).* But this includes in 'earned incomes' the trading profits and professional earnings of the sole traders and partnerships (income from self-employment). This comprised on average more than a quarter of the 'earned income' of those with net incomes in excess of £3,000 p.a. Some part of this income from self-employment will constitute a return on capital employed in the business (particularly for farmers, retail traders, etc.).

Top salaries

It is extremely difficult to get data on top salaries. A Prices and Incomes Board Report [7] gives data on the pay and fringe benefits of main Board Members and Senior Executives in a sample of large companies for 1968. While the salary levels are interesting,† more useful is an estimate that the increases in pay of main Board members and senior executives over the three years September 1965 to September 1968 were 8 per cent and 15 per cent respectively.

* For those with net incomes in excess of £10,000 p.a. in 1968–9 the average proportion coming from investments was just above three quarters. These of course are *averages* for income groups – substantial numbers of those in a particular group will have incomes almost exclusively from one source.

† The median pay of main board members and senior executives of the largest companies (assets over £250m.) were £16,480 and £9,090 respectively. The median pay of male manual workers at the same time was less than £1,200 p.a.

This compared with average pay increases for all employees of these companies of 19 per cent and for adult male manual workers of about 17 per cent over the same period. Marketing managers, company secretaries and accountants had average pay increases between September 1968 and April 1970 of just over 14 per cent, virtually the same as average manual workers; general managers and works managers appear to have had slightly greater increases, while engineers had considerably lower increases. Surveys for the year up to the middle of 1971 suggests that executive salaries rose by about 10 per cent and directors' salaries by about 8 per cent. This compares with price increases of about 10 per cent and wage increases of 11 per cent. A fair conclusion would seem to be that high salaries have probably not increased much relative to manual earnings over the last few years. But in many firms top executives are also compensated through share incentive schemes which face lower tax rates than salaries. These schemes were expanding with tremendous speed in 1971.

Self-employment incomes

There seems to be no data available on which to make an assessment of how those in the higher brackets of self-employment incomes have fared over the last few years. We do know that between 1964 and 1970 total self-employment incomes rose by 44 per cent as compared with a rise of 55 per cent for incomes of employees; and if we could deduct stock appreciation and capital consumption from the self-employment incomes the rise would be a good deal less. Since there seems to have been something of a rise in the proportion of self-employed in total employment, this suggests a definite relative fall in the earnings of the self-employed as a whole but offers little information about how higher self-employment incomes have developed. Within self-employment incomes farmers, with a rise of 36 per cent seem to have done worse than professional persons and sole traders.

Investment incomes

At first sight it is very surprising that gross receipts of rent, dividends and interest (R.D.I.) by the personal sector rose practically as fast (49 per cent) as wages and salaries (55 per cent) between 1964 and 1970.* One would have expected the drastic fall in the profit share to be reflected in a similar fall in the relative importance of investment incomes received by individuals. There are a number of reasons why this has not happened.

First, companies have been paying out as dividends a much larger proportion of their post-tax income. Between 1964 and 1970 dividend and interest payments (distributions) by industrial and commercial companies grew by 41 per cent while their retained earnings, after deducting stock appreciation and depreciation, fell to less than one fifth of their 1964 level.† Most of the rise in distributions was due to a higher level of borrowing through fixed-interest loans and from banks, together with the higher rates of interest which had to be paid; but dividends on ordinary shares still rose by 13 per cent despite the collapse in profitability. The great reluctance to cut dividends, and the consequent fall in undistributed profits, of course, aggravated companies' problems in financing investment, although it helped to maintain shareholders' incomes.

The general rise in interest rates has also helped to push up interest payments on the national debt‡ by 55 per cent between 1964 and 1970. The rise in rates has also been instrumental in increasing by 120 per cent interest paid by individuals to banks, H.P. companies and building societies, which in turn finds its way back into gross receipts of R.D.I. by the personal sector.§ A final

* Between 1959 and 1964 R.D.I. had grown much faster than employment incomes – 63 per cent as compared with 39 per cent; again this seems surprising, given some squeeze on profits. The reasons are basically the same as those discussed below, which explain why R.D.I. grew fast in 1964–70 when profits collapsed.

† If the ratio of distributions to retained earnings had stayed at its 1964 level, distributions would have been almost £1,000m. less and the rise in gross receipts of R.D.I. by individuals would have been more than halved.

‡ Higher interest rates affect different types of interest receipts with varying lags. Short-term lending to banks, building societies, etc., benefits immediately, but the existing debt of the government, companies, etc., which is not maturing is not affected. Only when existing debt is redeemed or new borrowing made will the higher interest rates come into play, as they must be paid on new borrowing.

§ If these personal payments of interest are subtracted from the figure for important element of the gross R.D.I. figure is the estimated return on house ownership (a sort of notional rent) which rose by almost 80 per cent over the past six years. Normally the rise in interest rates which has kept up investment incomes clearly works to the advantage of the lenders and to the disadvantage of the borrowers – in the case of a rise in interest on the national debt, taxes must be raised to cover it, or public expenditure reduced, or charges for public services (council-house rents, school meals, prescriptions and so on) raised.

But the times are not normal. Rising interest rates have been accompanied by, and partially caused by, a faster rate of inflation.* This rise in interest rates pushes up the real value of interest payments at first, and this is reflected in a rise in their money value relative to money incomes.† However the faster rate of inflation also means that the purchasing power of these payments is declining faster as time goes by, due to the even more rapid fall in the value of money.‡ Only if interest rates *continued to rise* could the real value of interest payments be maintained, and such a con-

---

*If there is 5 per cent inflation, an investment at an interest rate of 5 per cent yields £105 at the end of a year for £100 invested. But the real value, taking into account the decline in the value of money, of the £105 is the same as that of the £100 at the beginning of the year. The real rate of return is zero; in order to get a real rate of 5 per cent the 'nominal' rate of interest would have to be 10 per cent. Thus inflation tends to result in a higher interest rate.

†For people holding fixed interest securities the rise in interest rates has resulted in a capital loss. Thus Government fixed-interest bonds (2½ per cent Consols) fell in price from more than £40 in 1964 to about £27 in the middle of 1971. This reflects the fact that interest rates on existing long-term borrowing cannot be revised to take account of the faster inflation. The ultimate borrowers on fixed interest gain from this. The fall in bond prices shows that, given the change in interest rates, total interest payments 'ought' to have risen more if the real return on bonds was to be maintained. It is not an additional effect.

‡The higher real value at first may more or less compensate lenders for the faster fall later, depending on whether the rise in interest rates is more or less than the increase in the rate of inflation.

---

gross receipts, the increase in net R.D.I. is about 39 per cent. Still, since personal borrowing is basically (though not wholly) a redistribution from poor to rich, the gross figure gives the best picture of what is happening to the investment incomes of the rich.

tinued rise in rates is not to be expected unless there is an *acceleration* in the rate of inflation. Thus the growth in interest payments over the past few years cannot be interpreted as a continuing phenomenon which can offset the fall in the share of profits in the long run. It has had that effect up to now; but if interest rates stayed at their current level the money value of interest payments would cease to grow, except for payment on new savings, and their real value would decline. This is more or less what has happened recently. Most interest rates have been steady since 1969, and some short-term rates have even fallen. Net R.D.I. rose by only 3 per cent between 1969 and 1970, much less than both the cost of living rise and the 12 per cent increase in wages and salaries.

Share prices, despite a considerable fall in true company profits, rose an average of 25 per cent between 1964 and 1970. With little subsequent increase in profits, share prices were by early 1972 about 80 per cent above their 1964 level. Although companies have managed to increase their dividends despite the considerable fall in genuine profits, dividends have only increased by about 10 per cent, so that the discrepancy between the rise in share prices and the rise in dividends is enormous. Nevertheless the rise in share prices has, of course, increased the spending power of shareholders. It probably reflects a feeling, quite unjustified by the evidence, that somehow profits are being 'got right' and inflation brought under control. Given the levelling off of interest payments it has certainly come at a good time for receivers of investment income. But when people learn the truth about low profits and investment a substantial fall in share prices is likely.*

So, with the possible exception of some self-employed people

---

*Share prices depend not on current profits but on expectations of future profits – future prospects are capitalized. It is possible that it is not the 1972 share prices which are 'too high' but the 1964 prices which were 'too low'. However, the 1972 prices (since they have risen much more than dividends) clearly contain the expectation of a more favourable future trend than existed in 1964. Given the evidence of the past six years, such a change in expectations is amazing. Although the speed-up of inflation has no doubt encouraged the buying of shares, the slow growth of dividends over the last few years has shown that shares will *not* perform at all well as a hedge against inflation when there is a shift in the distribution of incomes towards wages.

and salary earners, the pre-tax spending power of the rich has probably continued to rise. In spite of clever accountants, some of this gain has been eroded by taxation. Since the marginal tax rate (that on an extra unit of income) is higher for most rich people than the average tax rate, disposable (post-tax) incomes have risen more slowly than pre-tax incomes.

For the rich the advantage of capital gains (the profits made on selling assets) is that they are taxed at a constant rate of 30 per cent (well below the standard rate for investment income). The introduction by Labour of the Capital Gains Tax was a blow to the rich; but its relatively low rate has still meant that there is great advantage in taking returns in the form of capital gains. The relatively big increase in share prices over the past six years must have done a good deal, therefore, to maintain substantial post-tax increases in purchasing power (including capital gains) in the face of high marginal rates of income tax. The maintenance of dividend levels in the face of falling profits had kept up share prices as well as maintaining dividend incomes. The stock market generally takes dividend cuts to imply a very bleak future and so they cause capital losses as well. This is why they are resisted so strongly – though some major firms such as Carreras, Vickers, Unilever, Bowater Paper, British Match and George Wimpey reduced theirs in 1970.

It is not possible to quantify the overall real post-tax changes in the incomes of the rich as they depend on so many factors which cannot be neatly added together to give a complete picture. Increases in real spending power have probably been small for most and nonexistent for many, particularly those with wealth concentrated in fixed-interest securities rather than shares or property. Nonetheless, in spite of the workers' growing share of the national income, the bourgeoisie has not yet suffered a relative decline in its living standards.

But the factors which have maintained its real purchasing power levels are unlikely to continue to operate. It is becoming harder for the bourgeoisie to insulate itself from the consequences of the profits squeeze. Those who have suffered recent bankruptcies, together with the unemployed graduates and executives about whom the newspapers are so concerned, are already suffering hardship like millions of workers. The ruthlessness of capitalism as a *system* is shown by the fact that the capitalist class cannot even look after its own in an emergency.

This will almost certainly lead to an intensification of effort to reverse or to neutralize labour's growing share of the product by attacking the working class. Up to now these efforts have resulted in a comparatively slow growth of real living standards for the working class. Since not all of the workers' drive for higher wages could be neutralized, the capitalist reaction has also led to a re-distribution of income within the working class which is likely to continue: a worsening of the position of lower-paid workers, the growth of unemployment and of poverty.

The mechanism of redistribution of personal incomes only accentuates the contradictions which the capitalist class is facing. Given the erosion of profits at a time of crisis, any successful effort to divert income away from the workers to maintain capitalist incomes will only intensify the bitterness and frustrations over living standards. And this must strengthen the determination be-hind the drive for higher wages which has contributed so much to the crisis.

Chapter 6
The Impact of Falling Profitability on Corporations

1. The blow to investment

In Britain, as in nearly all capitalist countries, there are signs that the tightening profits squeeze is making it increasingly difficult to finance investment and so keep economic growth going. Statistical studies show that the amount of investing done by individual companies depends a lot on their relative profitability. [1] The mechanism which brings this about has two parts. First, current profits influence expectations about the likely profitability of new investment;* and second, they are the main source for finance. However, there has not in the recent past been much correlation between year-to-year fluctuations in *total* profits and *total* investment. But this was a period of 'stop/go' cycles when firms regarded changes in their current profits as irrelevant to long-run investment decisions. We are now dealing with a completely different situation, and the unprecedented decline in total profitability can hardly have failed to influence total investment.

Until quite recently the level of investment was surprisingly high. After more than three years of stagnation from 1965 real manufacturing investment rose by about 10 per cent p.a. between the middle of 1968 and 1970. And in the chemicals industry, where profits remained quite high, investment soared. In current prices it rose by more than 70 per cent between 1968 and 1970 – and there were also increases of 40 per cent in the vehicles industry and more than 30 per cent in the engineering industries. But the vehicles industry was in a special predicament, for although firms had to

---

*Even if saving is not much affected by interest rates, the choice of assets towards which savings are directed will be influenced by relative rates of return. Thus Antony Vice wrote in *The Times* of 20 January 1971 in the context of low rates of return, 'that it will make better sense for many companies to invest their money in fixed-interest securities with no management problems and virtually no risk, rather than new factories or working capital'. Many firms will be able to invest in factories overseas as well.

invest heavily in order to keep up with their competitors, it was becoming very unprofitable. Outside manufacturing there had been an amazing rise in the fixed investment of financial companies (i.e. investment in offices, computers, etc.). It had more than trebled since 1964 and, in 1970, was more than one quarter of total manufacturing investment. This increasingly popular kind of investment does not contribute very much to economic growth.

Since the end of 1970 manufacturing investment has been falling. It fell in real terms by 10 per cent between the last quarter of 1970 and the second quarter of 1971, which makes the annual rate of decline 20 per cent. The seriousness of the collapse in confidence over recent months is shown by the rapidly changing forecasts by economists of the National Institute of Economic and Social Research of how manufacturing investment would move between the last quarter of 1970 and the last quarter of 1971. In August 1970 they said it would rise 2 per cent; six months later they were forecasting a 4-per-cent fall (despite the reflationary October budget); and in August 1971 the forecast was for a 15-per-cent fall despite two more reflationary packages in April and July which included cuts in corporation tax and increased incentives to invest. The latest figures suggest there may be an even greater fall than this and the prospects for 1972 are bleak. Machine-tool orders, for instance, in the autumn of 1971 were more than 40 per cent lower than a year earlier.

But without more investment the international competitiveness of U.K. capital can never improve. As it is, a recent survey showed that only one in five British machine tools is less than five years old, compared with one in four in Italy and one in three in Germany. Since 1966 the British engineering industry has bought less than 200,000 new machine tools, less than a quarter of the purchases by Japanese industry. U.K. capital is caught in a downward spiral of falling profitability, falling accumulation and poor competitiveness. The government, as long as its tax cuts and attempts at reflation are ineffective in reversing this, is reduced to exhortations to reckless courage, such as that of Edward Heath:

I think there's rather too great a tendency in British industry to wait until everybody is absolutely certain that they want to do it, and then all go and rush in together ... My advice to them is 'Now look, see what the possibilities are – they're bound to come – you're bound to get this growing demand. It's the way the whole Western world is moving.' [2]

(For a refutation see chapter 4.) By contrast the businessmen of the Industrial Policy Group, in a recent pamphlet entitled 'Economic Growth, Profits and Investment', laid the blame for low investment and growth on low profitability. They called for lower taxes on profits, an end to attempts to control inflation through limiting price increases and to 'the constant social denigration of profits, even in places of teaching and learning'.

2. Finance and worsening liquidity

In the fifties and early sixties companies tended to pay out an increasing proportion of their profits as dividends, and yet investment levels rose. Each of these factors made companies less and less able to finance their own investment programmes. The proportion which they themselves financed from current retained earnings* fell from more than 75 per cent in 1950–54 to under 65 per cent in 1960–64. The profits squeeze and the maintenance of dividend and investment levels seems to have led to a big acceleration in this fall: the average proportion of funds coming from within the company fell to just over 40 per cent in 1968–70. But this figure is affected by the recent takeover boom (see chapter 7).

When one company takes over another it issues shares and debentures in exchange for the shares of the company it is buying. Such issues of shares 'in exchange' have increased from around £200m. over the period 1960–64 to well over £1,000m. in 1968, and these issues of shares are shown as being an external source of finance. For a given company which is taking over another these share issues are indeed as much a source of finance as any other share issues. The factors which affect a firm's ability to issue shares

---

*That part of profits retained by the company plus what it sets aside to spend to replace capital (depreciation). Investment may also be financed by borrowing from banks; by selling 'debentures' which give the buyer a fixed sum in interest each year; or by selling more shares (equity financing) which give the buyer a share in the profits of the firm after interest is paid.

– such as a low share price resulting from low profitability – will apply to issues 'in exchange' as much as to issues for cash.

These issues 'in exchange' are only transactions *within* the company sector. No new finance is raised, so we must exclude them in order to estimate the sources of new finance for the company sector as a whole. Once this adjustment is made, the proportion of companies' finance coming from internal sources fell from 72 per cent in 1960–64 to a little over 55 per cent in 1968–70.* But this did not mean an increase in the proportion of finance coming from the issue of shares and long-term debts; in fact the proportion fell slightly.

When raising cash from outside, especially over the period 1965–7, firms were tending to issue not equity shares but fixed-interest debentures, which were encouraged by the corporation tax. But there are limits to how far companies can increase their long-term debt relative to their total assets (their 'gearing ratio'). From their own point of view failure to meet their interest obligations will involve bankruptcy, and, in a time of falling profitability, lenders will tend to be very much more cautious.

Equity financing (issues of ordinary shares) differs from other forms of finance in that a company is not obliged to pay out dividends. This is obviously an advantage, at least in the short term, for a company in difficulty. Equity financing gained popularity in 1968 as share prices on the stock market rose; but it soon subsided again, and by the end of 1971 did not seem to be reacting much to the rise in share prices. Profitability (and thus the availability of internal finance) has important effects on the possibility of raising equity finance, and so the effects of low profitability cannot be offset simply by issuing more shares. A general depression of the stock market resulting from low profitability will also inhibit share issues; and, of course, the most unprofitable companies, being those with the greatest need for outside finance, will

*There has been some rise in the absolute level of internal finance, but this is all accounted for by the increase in depreciation. By 1969 the level of retained earnings was in absolute terms about half the average level for 1960–64. This estimate excludes stock appreciation, which is a nominal capital gain and not a source of finance, but includes investment grants to make it comparable with earlier years when all investment incentives were in the form of tax concessions which bolstered retained earnings.

tend to have the lowest share prices and so will find it most difficult to raise funds in this way.

Thus the need for external finance, and the difficulty of raising it, have increased together. Companies seeking finance have resorted to 'short-term' borrowing, of which the main component is borrowing from banks. This provided about 8 per cent of total finance in 1960–64 and rose to nearly 30 per cent in 1968–70. The amount owed to banks by industrial and commercial companies doubled between 1964 and 1969 and rose a great deal further in 1970 and 1971. At the same time companies have run down to a minimum their stocks of liquid assets (cash and holdings of government securities). These assets rose over the period 1964–9 by only 11 per cent despite a much larger increase in turnover.* This reduction in liquidity (more short-term borrowing, less liquid assets) means that reserves of cash and of borrowing power are being reduced by the profits squeeze. There is a limit to the amount banks are willing to lend. This limit depends on the assets the company can offer as a security; and the value of these assets is dropping as profitability decreases. A continuation of the present low level of profitability will make further borrowing from banks and running down of liquid assets inevitable. Companies making a loss must borrow even to pay for labour and materials. More and more companies will find that they have exhausted their borrowing power and liquid assets.

We have calculated figures for net liquidity by industry groups up to the end of 1969 and there is some tendency for industries with big falls in profitability to have big reductions in liquidity, particularly if, like the vehicles, textiles and non-electrical engineering industries, they were also doing a lot of investing. In contrast the chemical industry, whose profits had not declined much by that stage, and retail distribution, whose investment was stagnant, had virtually no deterioration in their liquidity position. At the end of

* A certain amount of cash, related to the turnover of the company, is required to keep even a profitable company ticking over, since there are on occasions lags between its payments and its receipts. These balances are not available as reserves for a company making a loss. Thus since turnover (in current prices) has risen much more than holdings of liquid assets, it is reasonable to conclude that the reserves which *may* be used during periods of unprofitability have declined a good deal.

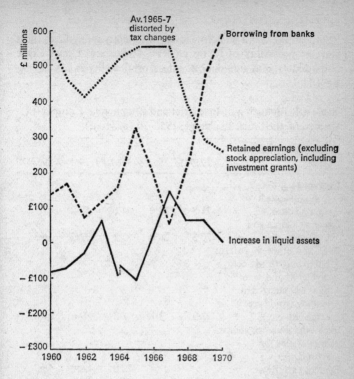

Figure 10. Finance and liquidity in industrial and commercial companies 1960–70
Source: Business Monitor, M3, 1970.

1970 a wide range of large companies had bank borrowings (less cash) equal to more than 10 per cent of their long-term assets, which is some evidence of their financial shakiness. The list includes Cadbury Schweppes, E.M.I., Hawker Siddeley, Metal Box, British Ropes, Richard Costain (construction), British Oxygen, Joseph Lucas, Carreras (tobacco), Coats Patons (textiles), Thomas Tilling (building materials), and Babcock & Wilcox (engineering). With such low levels of liquidity many firms must face the possibility of following Rolls-Royce and Upper Clyde Shipbuilders into liquidation unless profitability is rapidly restored.

Table 6.1. Financing of Industrial and Commercial Companies Quoted on the Stock Exchange, 1950–70 (per cent)

Proportions of finance from:	1950–54	1955–9	1960–64	1965–9	1968–70
Current cash flow* excluding stock appreciation	75·8	71·0	64·6	52·8	41·9
Issues of shares and long-term debt	20·3	26·0	28·2	37·5	36·3
Bank and other short-term borrowing (trade debt, dividends and taxation due) less short-term lending (trade credit extended, etc.)	3·9	3·1	7·3	9·6	21·8
Excluding issues of shares in *exchange for subsidiaries*					
Current cash flow			72·0	68·0	56·7
Issues of shares, etc.			19·9	19·5	13·9
Short-term borrowing			8·1	12·5	29·4

Source: 1950–60: *Economic Trends*, April 1962. 1960–70: *Business Monitor*, M3, 1970, 1971.

*Retained earnings and depreciation.

3. Bankruptcies

Capitalist corporations are not immortal. Under British law a company is not permitted to continue trading if it does not have the funds to pay its bills. It is the lack of liquid funds, therefore, which is always the immediate cause of bankruptcies and company failures. But illiquidity is usually the outcome of declining profitability, though even potentially profitable companies can fail.*

The need for liquidation may be hastened by bad management, as in the case of Rolls-Royce and Upper Clyde Shipbuilders. On the other hand it may be postponed by good management or by a timely government grant or loan or by a bank loan. It may, indeed, be averted altogether by permanent government financial support or nationalization.

The average number of firms which went into liquidation in Britain was 4,225 per year between 1950 and 1964; from 1964 to 1969 the average had risen to 8,723. Then the number fell a little, so that there were 7,040 liquidations in the year ending May 1971. But these figures do not mean very much, since they do not take account of the size of the firms involved. It is obvious, however, that 1971 saw a marked change in the pattern of liquidations compared with the rest of the post-war period. Before 1971 large bankruptcies had tended to be in highly speculative and rather disreputable ventures like Rolls Razor. In 1971 large and very respectable companies began to be hit: Rolls-Royce, whose shares had for decades been regarded as a 'blue chip' investment; Vehicle and General Insurance, which handled 10 per cent of British car insurance and was a member of the prestigious British Insurers' Association; and Upper Clyde Shipbuilders, in which the government owned almost half the shares. The situation produced alarm in capitalist circles. The Engineering Industries Association, for example, had to report that in 1970 'an unprecedented 117 out of

---

*Thus a company which has been unprofitable and which is therefore short of funds may be unable to keep on producing because its inflow of cash is insufficient to pay its suppliers, its wage bill and its interest payments. But if it could secure extra funds to meet these payments – extra working capital – it could be in a position to sell its production quite profitably. The problem is that it has nothing to sell until it has produced it and it is unable to find the money to finance the production. Thus it has been argued that U.C.S. was *becoming* profitable and went into liquidation because of inability to raise funds. The capital market will only supply these funds if it is *convinced* of future profitability, and a record of losses may mean that no funds will be available.

the E.I.A.'s membership of 3,200 companies' went bankrupt and that there was 'every indication that this figure will be exceeded' in 1971. [3]

There is nothing exceptional about the firms which have failed; their failures have been caused by factors affecting all branches of British capitalism. First, they have all faced tremendous competition. V. & G.'s competition was largely domestic: it was only by undercutting other companies in the increasingly competitive car-insurance business that they had managed to take such a large share of the business. Rolls-Royce faced competition from Pratt & Whitney, the American aero-engine producers, for supplying the engines for one at least of the new generation of air-bus airliners, the Lockheed Tristar.* Lockheed itself faced intense competition with the Douglas Company's DC-10 airliner. So not only was Lockheed *able* to force a hard deal on Rolls because of Pratt & Whitney: it *had* to because of Douglas. Another failure was U.C.S., which, like other British shipbuilders, faced the extraordinarily strong competition from Japan and other countries during the late 1960s. They were ill equipped to produce the sort of ships for which demand was growing most rapidly. Lines Bros., makers of Triang and Dinky Toys, could not survive the competition from the major American toy producers (including Marx) and were liquidated after the collapse of a rescue operation mounted by a tobacco firm. B.S.A. seems to have been bailed out by its bankers, at the cost of 3,000 redundancies, after an attempt to meet Japanese competition with a huge new range of motor bikes.

In this difficult competitive position each of these firms was, to some extent, affected by rising wage and other costs. For Rolls-Royce such damage from this source has been much exaggerated in reports: after all, the RB 211 contract had a flexible price clause in it such that the price could climb with rising wages. [4] So there was no truth in the story that grasping unions were solely responsible for the bankruptcy. The real problem for Rolls-Royce was that because of competition the *base* price had to be so low. As for

---

*Sir Denning Pearson, former chairman of Rolls, said that the decision to go ahead with the RB 211 was 'a considered risk of staying in business or the certainty of a catastrophic decline in the value of the company's assets and employment' (*Financial Times*, 2 December 1971).

V. & G., they were indirectly very hard hit by rising wages which led to a rapid escalation in the charges for motor repairs.

Bankruptcy, for all the disruption it causes, is in a way the natural reaction of the capitalist system, since it enables capital to be rescued from unprofitable activities. When a firm goes into liquidation the capitalists are saved from liabilities which they would otherwise have had to pay (often, of course, directly to other capitalists). Some of the fixed capital which remains may be sold off at bargain prices and become profitable again; the rest is left to rust. But widespread bankruptcies are not a sign of a healthy 'shake-out' of useless capital; they are emergency measures which will grow when the system is in crisis.

Bankruptcies are illustrations of the fundamental anarchy of the capitalist system. They are not a punishment for inefficiency. A firm may collapse because its market suddenly disappears or because of a price war. Instead of a planned re-allocation of resources when circumstances change, there are crises and confusion. Moreover, the decision to cease production is taken solely on the grounds of profitability of production without any regard to its social results, such as unemployment.

This chapter has shown how falling profitability leads either to lower investment or, if investment is maintained, to a higher level of borrowing by firms. The results – slower growth or worsening liquidity – both make bankruptcies more likely. In Britain these results of the profits squeeze are probably further advanced than in any of the other capitalist countries.

Part Three
The Responses

Chapter 7
The Capitalist Response

1. Putting up prices

Profitability of capital in any country can be restored only by finding more profitable outlets abroad or by raising prices relative to costs at home. Inflation – which means no more than rising prices – is therefore a part of the capitalists' strategy. It is unpopular for obvious reasons, so there has recently been an effort to re-define inflation to mean, in part at least, increases in wages as well. The idea was to make people extend their dislike of price rises to wage increases.

This, however, is an incorrect definition. Prices rise (inflation occurs) not because they are automatically tied to the level of wages, nor through some invisible machinery of demand and supply. By and large they go up because manufacturers and traders *put* them up for the sake of their profits. Inflation erodes wage increases; therefore it is used by the capitalists to protect the profit share.

If the share of profits in net output (wages plus profits) is to be maintained then profit margins in money terms must be widened to keep up with average wage costs. Leaving aside the cost of materials bought in from outside the firm, prices must rise at the same rate as unit wage costs if the share of profits is to remain constant. If the profit share is to increase, then prices must increase faster than wage costs. Just how much faster depends on the level of the profit share to begin with.*

*The current profit share before deducting capital consumption – the correct measure for these purposes since depreciation is a cost which must like any other be recovered in the price – is about 20 per cent. In order to get it to 21 per cent, labour's share must be reduced to 79 per cent. It might seem that this requires prices to rise 1 per cent faster than wages, but in fact the reduction in labour's share from 80 per cent to 79 per cent requires a drop in real wages not of 1 per cent but of 1/80, i.e. 1¼ per cent. Conversely, a rise in labour's share of 1 percentage point (i.e. from 80 per cent to 81 per cent) implies a real wage increase of 1¼ per cent.

But as wages are not the only cost of production, then the situation is clearly more complicated. A rough calculation* gives the following breakdown of total costs for the company sector as a whole:

Imports (and purchases from agriculture)	16·5%
Purchases from nationalized industries	7·0%
Wages	61·5%
Depreciation	5·5%
Profits	9·5% (the profit margin)
	100·0%

Thus profits depend not only on prices and wages but also on costs of imports and purchases from nationalized industries. If the proportion of profits in the final price of the product (the profit *margin*) is to be constant, the rate of price increase must be the same as the average rate of cost increase. The slower the costs of imports and products of nationalized industry rise, the less fast will prices have to increase in relation to wage costs.† The fact that companies face costs other than wages also modifies the relationship between price increases and the share of profits. Taking the other costs into account, then a 1 per cent price increase pushes up the profit *margin* from 9½ per cent to 10½ per cent, but increases the *share* of profits in the net product by 1¼ per cent. Thus, to recoup the 9 per cent fall in the profit share between 1964 and 1970, producers would require an increase in prices of slightly over 7 per cent, assuming all other costs were constant.

Not all personal expenditure is on products of the company sector. Something like a third of consumer spending goes to the government in the form of purchase taxes and payments to nationalized industries and local authorities. So a 7-per-cent in-

* Based on the 1968 Input Output table (*National Income Blue Book, 1971*, Table 19) and some debatable assumptions.

† If wage costs were rising by 7 per cent and other costs by only 5 per cent, then, on our rough figures for cost breakdown, the profit *margin* would be maintained if prices rose by about 6⅓ per cent. If wage costs were rising faster than other costs then, to keep the same proportion of profits in net output (wages plus profits), prices will have to rise a bit faster than the *average* rate of cost increase (though slower than the rate of increase of wage costs). This will allow unit profits to grow as fast as unit wage costs.

crease in the prices of company output would seem to increase average consumer prices (and thus reduce real wages on average) by only about 5 per cent. Hence it might be thought that we have exaggerated the scale of the problem; that workers would hardly notice the sacrifices they would have to make to put British capitalism back on its feet.

But this would be a misreading of the situation. While a 7-per-cent increase in *average* company prices would be enough to restore profit margins, companies cannot possibly put up their prices this much in the more competitive export markets. In fact, the price rises will virtually be confined to the domestic consumer. He will either have to pay more for the goods he consumes or pay higher taxes to cover the increased cost of the part of output which the government buys. If the 1964 profit share had been repeated in 1970, £2,500 million more profits would have been needed; and this would have meant prices rising 8 per cent more than wages. Seeing that wages went up 12 per cent in 1970, this would have meant inflation of 20 per cent in 1970 for the profit share to have been completely restored in that year.

Obviously such an increase in prices, and corresponding reduction in real wages, could not be accomplished 'at a stroke'. If we assume that productivity grows 3 per cent each year, then for the profit share to remain constant prices would need to rise at the same rate as wage costs and real wages would grow by 3 per cent (the same rate as productivity). If the 1964 profit share were to be restored over a 1-year period a 5 per cent reduction in real wages would be needed during the year (8 per cent, minus the 3 per cent growth in real wages which would have occurred anyway) – prices rising 5 per cent faster than wages. Over 3 years the profit share could be restored if there was no growth in real wages. Over 5 years a $1\frac{1}{2}$ per cent p.a. rate of increase could be allowed* – prices rising $1\frac{1}{2}$ per cent slower than wages.

Given the rate of growth of wages in the middle of 1971 (still about 11 per cent a year), and rapid increases in prices of imports of materials and the products of nationalized industries, it was a

---

*The rate of increase of real wages over N years which would restore the profit share is $(3N-8)/N$. These calculations assume other costs grow in line with wage costs.

safe prediction that there would be little or no let-up in the rate of inflation. Capitalists would evidently wish to raise prices as much as they could in order to get back on the road to profitability. It came as no surprise when the head of the C.B.I., Campbell Adamson, stated at the end of May 1971 that no measures of price restraint could be expected in the near future. [1] This was a great deal more credible than his plan six weeks later to get firms to sign a 'pledge' not to raise their prices by more than 5 per cent in the year. Without effective wage control and with average costs rising much more than 5 per cent p.a., this was in effect a pledge to accept a further *fall* in their profit margins. How then could the 5-per-cent inflation pledge be interpreted? Was it any more than a hypocritical public-relations gambit?

The C.B.I. avoided making any unconditional promise; they kept reiterating that the pledge could only be kept if it was matched by wages restraint from the unions. In a television interview Adamson said the pledge was to keep price increases down 'except in exceptional circumstances', and that firms which 'needed' to raise their prices more would get full C.B.I. support. It is surprising that 25 important firms were not willing to commit themselves this far, though one firm which did sign (Reckitt & Colman) claimed that the pledge would put pressure on margins. Some firms knew that they would not be able to raise their prices by more than 5 per cent anyway, because otherwise they would lose their customers to foreign competitors. (From mid-1970 to mid-1971 British export prices had risen by twice the world average and competitive positions were becoming dangerously eroded.) For some the pledge might have seemed like a cue for an incomes policy and wages control, which for those hardest hit by competition was the *only* available way to restore some profitability. Some individual industries did stand to gain a good deal from the commitment to keep down nationalized industry prices. If this succeeded in reducing the rate of increase of nationalized industry prices from 10 per cent to 5 per cent it would increase the profit share in the company sector by $\frac{1}{2}$ per cent. Lastly, the pledge provided the government with an occasion for a mild reflation which would help profits. The reasons for the pledge, therefore, were tactical.* The strategic

*Just how seriously firms are taking the price initiative is shown by the

pursuit of higher profits make it almost inevitable that a high rate of price increases will be resumed as soon as the pledge ends. In the meantime there is no let-up in capital's attempt to restore profitability by other means.

2. Sacking workers

Under capitalism, technological advances, low demand and failures in the competitive struggle lead to redundancies and unemployment, and the present crisis has seen these on an exceptional scale. At the beginning of 1971 *The Times* began to produce a monthly list of announced redundancies; in the whole of 1971 the total number of redundancies exceeded 335,000. Many took place in those firms which had gone into liquidation or been taken over – in Rolls-Royce, V. & G. Insurance, the *Daily Sketch*, Upper Clyde Shipbuilders, and Lines Bros. – but other companies announcing more than 1,000 redundancies included British Aircraft Corporation, National Cash Register (business machines), Alfred Herbert (engineering), Lucas (car components, hit by Rolls' failure), British Aluminium, I.C.I., British Steel Corporation, Birds Eye Foods, Reed International (paper), Dunlop (tyres), International Computers, B.S.A. (motor bikes). Redundancies were therefore spread throughout industry, although the paper, electronics and engineering industries seemed to account for more than their fair share. But even sectors whose profit record had been better, like chemicals, showed the same tendency.*

The Labour government's redundancy payments scheme has helped redundant workers a little. This compensates workers thrown out of a job with a small lump sum, its size depending on length of service. Half is paid by the employer concerned and half

* In the 12 months ending in October 1971 over 450,000 jobs in manufacturing industry vanished. Employment fell over 5 per cent in the year in several industries – metal manufacture, mechanical engineering, electrical engineering, and textiles. (*The Times*, 10 January 1972.)

case of P. B. Cow, the rubber component firm, which announced price increases of 10 per cent for January 1972 claiming that it was honouring the CBI's undertaking because customers will not be asked for another increase for a further year.

from a fund financed by the employer's contribution to the national insurance stamp.* In the first half of 1971 £45 million was paid out to 172,699 people, an average of about £280 each.† These figures were about one third more than in the first half of 1970.

But the redundancy-payments scheme was designed to assist the redeployment of workers to new jobs. In fact, however, the new jobs do not exist; in industry employment fell by almost half a million (4½ per cent) between September 1970 and September 1971. Of course, some of this 'shake-out' resulted from the changing structure of industry during economic development (for example, in vehicles the numbers in employment fell more than 100,000 in the sixties); but it became increasingly affected by the pressure of rising costs and falling profitability as well as by stagnant demand. More and more displaced workers were unable to find new jobs (see chapter 8). As a result the resistance to redundancies strengthened in 1971 (see chapter 9). So while individual firms might benefit from sacking their workers, the capitalist system as a whole cannot have been recruiting new supporters.

3. Innovations in wage bargaining

Capital made a tremendous but largely unsuccessful attempt in the 1960s to protect profitability by new forms of wage bargaining. The principal of these was the productivity deal. A productivity deal is not just an agreement that money wages should rise only as fast as productivity grows (either in the economy or in individual firms). The government had been advocating this principle for decades; since it is supposed to lead to price stability, it amounts to

* In cases of liquidation the fund guarantees the whole payment; on this score about £1 million was paid out in the first quarter and £2·3 million in the second quarter of 1971.

† Contrast this with reports in the press of golden hand-shakes to sacked managers, e.g. 'The 1971 accounts of Decca, the electronics company, show a sum of £65,000 paid out as compensation for loss of office as executive of subsidiary companies' (*The Times*, 24 September 1971). B.S.A., which in October 1971 announced 3,000 redundancies in its motor-cycles division, gave its former managing director £35,000 (*Guardian*, 2 November 1971).

accepting that labour's share of output should not be allowed to increase. A productivity deal, however, involves some specific concession by the workers about working methods or intensity or manning in exchange for an unusually large initial wage increase. Productivity deals involve an effort by management to restore some lost control over work or pay and thereby assist profit margins. The hope is that workers will be sufficiently blinded by a large pay increase to blunder into an important concession. Productivity deals are not new, but they only became prominent during the sixties after the deal at the Esso refinery in Fawley in 1960. At their peak in 1968 productivity deals applied to about 25 per cent of the work force, though what the Prices and Incomes Board (N.B.P.I.) called 'real productivity schemes', which were more than just a form of words, covered much less than this. The benefits of the deals went largely to capital. The Prices and Incomes Board reported that

... In about half the agreements, the workers receive about half the estimated benefits; in others the share varied, sometimes being more and sometimes less than half.[2]

This may sound very fair, but what it really means is that the workers who were doing all the extra work were being paid only half the extra output, which is less than their normal share of total output.

By 1970 productivity deals were dying out. Most unions (but not D.A.T.A.) had accepted productivity deals at least in principle, though only the General and Municipal Workers (G.M.W.U.) and the Electricians (E.T.U.) had sought them with enthusiasm. But it had become evident to the workers that many productivity deals only served to hold up wage increases after giving them an initial boost, and union negotiators gradually became disenchanted with such collaboration with the employers. At the same time the employers had discovered that they did not always lead to increases in productivity. When the Prices and Incomes Board was wound up in 1970 the pressure for productivity deals from government sources had ended. The Tories opted for a more direct confrontation.

One of the main changes in the capitalists' strategy on the wages front in the 1960s was that they tried to get agreements which would reduce, if not abolish, overtime working. Overtime was seen as weakening the employer's control over pay and work, and as a suitable subject for local bargaining. One of the most important schemes of this kind is *measured day work* (MDW):

The employee receives a time rate far higher than those commonly specified in industry agreements in return for an understanding that he shall sustain a specified level of performance,* often based on work study.[3]

Measured day work gives management a clear daily rate with control over production standards; and it ends shop-floor bargaining about rates as well as reduces the importance of overtime. Measured day work was introduced in Vauxhalls in 1956 and spread thereafter in several industries, including metal and cigarettes.[4] It has been a major issue in the motor industry, particularly in British Leyland. Measured day work is, in fact, an attempt to revive a system of payments by results which, by directly linking wages to output, had at one time been used by capitalists both to increase the product and to guarantee their share of it.† More recently, however, payment by results has become a source of lack of control and an excuse for local wage bargaining, and there have been successful attempts to reduce its importance. It was abolished in coalmining, for instance, in 1966, and in many other industries during the 1960s.

Employers have had some success in reducing the number of agreements under which wages automatically rose when the cost of living rose; 2½ million workers were covered by these agreements in 1966 and only 250,000 in 1970. However, increasing inflation in 1970 renewed the demand for cost-of-living clauses in agreements: they were part of the 1971 claims of both the Council manual workers and the construction workers (see chapter 9). And the T.U.C. has pressed strongly for 'threshold' agreements which

---

* Usually in terms of the number of jobs done in a day or, for groups of workers, the speed of the line (our footnote).

† The proportion of male workers paid by results rose from 5 per cent in 1886 to 50 per cent in 1927. 33 per cent of the workforce was partly covered by P.B.R. in 1961 and only 10 per cent in 1970. (H. Clegg, *The System of Industrial Relations in Great Britain*, pp. 170–71.)

would tie wages to the cost of living once a 'threshold' increase in the cost of living had been exceeded. After initial reactions of horror the government came to realize that these agreements could be used to combat inflation and real wage increases; in the autumn of 1971 they were under discussion at the National Economic Development Council.* In place of cost-of-living clauses, some unions had managed to negotiate 'reopener clauses' under which wage talks could be resumed when the rise in prices passed a certain figure. These clauses, along with the general reaction to growing inflation, led to a marked shortening of the average time between wage settlements – from more than a year in July 1969 to 10 months by July 1971.[5] This was an alarming development for employers, and some have responded by trying to stipulate in one wage settlement a minimum time before the next. The Ford agreement which followed the long strike in February 1971 contained a clause guaranteeing no further claim, and, more unusually, no strike over wages, for at least 12 months. But resistance to these aspects of the agreement by some of the rank-and-file Ford workers, and also the accelerating pace of inflation, make such clauses rather improbable in the near future. However, the effort to introduce these stipulations along with the productivity deals and MDW, involve conscious bargaining by capital about its share of the product.

* While threshold agreements guarantee real wage increases they also limit them; in circumstances where firms find it difficult to pass on wage increases in the form of higher prices the outcome of a threshold agreement may be more favourable to capital than an ordinary bargain. For example the agreements in France, described on p. 83, secured only a very small real wage increase, much less than productivity growth. When limiting real wage increases is not enough then as Sam Brittan put it 'it has been the experience of countries where cost-of-living-compensation has been the rule, that such agreements have to be suspended whenever real incomes have to be squeezed' (*Financial Times*, 4 November 1971). Threshold agreements guarantee a particular increase in real wages only from the moment at which they are introduced. They do nothing by themselves to compensate for the inflation which has eroded real wages since a previous non-threshold increase. That compensation still has to depend entirely on the size of the initial money increase and not on the threshold.

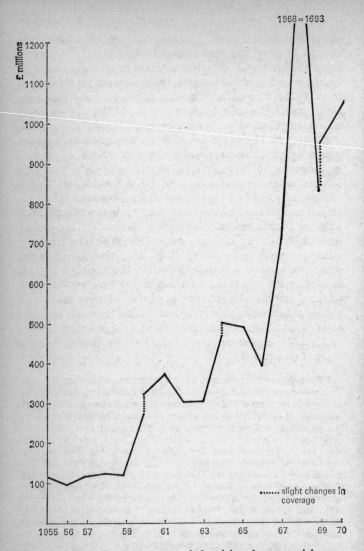

Figure 11. Expenditure on mergers industrial and commercial companies 1955–70
Sources: Economic Trends, April 1962. *Business Monitor, M3*, April 1962. *Trade and Industry*, 10 February 1971 and 19 May 1971.

4. The takeover boom

Merging with another company can represent the process of rationalization operating at the level of industry rather than at that of an individual firm. The decline in the rate of profit since 1964 has been accompanied by a merger/takeover boom which reached a peak in 1968 and remained at a very high level in 1969–70. The result was that over the four years 1967–70 expenditure on acquisitions of subsidiaries by industrial and commercial companies (treating the smaller of merging companies as being acquired by the larger) added up to almost £5,000m. – considerably greater than the total for the whole period from 1950–66. Over the period 1958–68 some 20 per cent of net assets of quoted industrial and commercial companies was acquired by other companies, and something like a further 5 per cent was taken over in 1969–70. After a lull early in 1971 the autumn saw a series of major takeover bids, the biggest being that of Beecham for Glaxo.

One effect of such mergers is the concentration of assets in the hands of large companies. The largest 10 companies at the end of 1968 owned about 24 per cent of total net assets, whereas in 1957 those same companies had owned about 13 per cent; the share of the largest 80 had increased from about 38 per cent to more than 70 per cent.*

About two thirds of the net assets transferred over the period 1958–68 were acquired by companies operating in roughly the same industry. Other acquisitions were mainly aimed at 'vertical integration'.[1]

[1] That is absorbing a firm usually in a supplying or a customer industry. Thus there were substantial cross-acquisitions between textiles and chemicals, within the metal-using industries (for example, acquisitions by car firms of electrical and mechanical engineering companies), of food companies by retail distribution companies, and of distribution companies by manufacturing companies. About 10 per cent of expenditure in 1969/70 was on subsidiaries of other company groups.

* Since a few very large companies had been taken over by other very large companies these figures tend to overestimate the increase in importance of the largest companies in 1968 as compared with the largest companies in 1957, but they do show clearly the greater relative size of those

The process of concentration by acquisition proceeded most rapidly in the electrical engineering industry, where over 40 per cent of the assets in the industry were taken over in the years 1958–68 – the most important of the mergers being G.E.C./A.E.I./ English Electric. The number of companies holding half the total assets in the industry fell from 5 to 3 between 1957 and 1968. In drink and vehicles over 30 per cent of the assets were acquired within the industry, and merging in the drink industry has continued at a high level since 1968. By 1968 the number of firms owning half the net assets in the drink industry had shrunk from 12 to 4. International competition is relatively unimportant for drink, but licensing laws make acquisition virtually the only way of expanding. In the case of textiles, over 20 per cent of assets was acquired within the industry (reducing the number of companies with half the assets from 8 to 3). Courtaulds led the way and received a good deal of government support, particularly where it could be justified as a protective response to growing danger of U.S. takeovers and competition.*

In paper, printing and publishing more than 15 per cent of assets were acquired within the industry by takeover and merger between 1958 and 1968, reducing the number of companies with half the assets from 6 to 3. Expenditure on acquisitions was again extremely high in 1970 (of the order of 10 per cent of the assets). At the end of 1970 the two giants in the industry, Reed and Bowater, began unsuccessful talks aimed at integrating their U.K. pulp and paper operations. According to *The Times* the 'principal reason

---

* The *Economist* wrote that 'Whatever sort of monopoly it produces in Lancs. the fact that Sir Frank Kearton's sudden bid for English Calico was made to forestall an American takeover is very good reason for supposing that it will get the government's blessing' (18 January 1969). In the event the Board of Trade decided to abide by the Monopolies Commission Report that Courtaulds was too monopolistic and, without any apparent authority, decided to forestall U.S. incursions by putting a stop to all mergers 'at the present time'.

---

that survived the period. Over the period there were four acquisitions/ mergers worth over £100m. and two worth between £50m. and £100m. All took place between 1966 and 1968.

given by the companies at the time of the original announcement for the merger was to combat stiffening competition in the British market from Scandinavian and North American competitors'. In shipbuilding the government exerted pressure towards amalgamation of yards on the Clyde, Tyne and Wear through withholding of subsidies and defence contracts. But (as the *Economist* argued) this did little or nothing to improve competitiveness. Amalgamation of companies does not automatically bring rationalization or economies of scale. Only the scrapping of existing yards and the construction of new ones with sufficient depth and up-to-date equipment for the new methods of construction could make U.K. prices internationally competitive.

Other manufacturing industries with around 5 or 6 firms holding 50 per cent of the assets in 1957 (metal manufacture, food, bricks, etc.) tended to have a fair amount (about 10 per cent) of assets acquired within the industry. By comparison, in industries already dominated by one or two firms (metal goods, chemicals, clothing and tobacco) merging activity within the industry was on a fairly small scale, though there were a number of cases of fairly widespread incursion into other industries for motives of diversification (tobacco into food) or vertical integration (clothing into retail distribution, chemicals into textiles).

Part of the reason for the merger boom was that capitalists wanted to strengthen and extend monopolies so that they could increase prices and so take the pressure off their profits.* But this cannot be the whole explanation, since the pressure of competition may rule out price increases anyway. The merger boom also reflected the need for larger firms as international competition stiffened, and our analysis of mergers industry by industry suggests that they have been most common in industries particularly exposed to foreign competition – electrical engineering, vehicles,

*Thus 'Britain's throwsters are looking for an early improvement in yarn prices following the establishment of Intex, I.C.I.'s new subsidiary which includes Qualitex and the fibre processing interests of Carrington Viyella. The trade has been suffering from low, and in some cases non-existent margins, but the big hope is that the establishment of a market leader, responsible for more than 35 per cent of total production, will lead to a considerable stabilization of prices'. (*Guardian*, 30 September 1971.)

shipbuilding, paper, textiles. A major reason behind the Beecham bid for Glaxo was said to be the advantage from pooling pharmaceutical research effort, which even so would be much smaller than that of the largest international companies.

The Labour government's attitude to this process of concentration was somewhat ambivalent. Under the 1965 Monopolies and Mergers Act all mergers involving the acquisition of assets worth more than £5m., or the creation of a firm controlling more than one third of the market (a 'technical monopoly'), had to be referred to the Monopolies Commission. But this legislation was not effective. Over the period 1965–8 there were 120 mergers which fell within the terms of reference of the Commission. Many of these were not in fact referred to the Commission at all, and only four proposed mergers were effectively stopped – one of them to be allowed later in a modified form. Meanwhile, the Industrial Reorganization Corporation* was rushing 'to create industrial giants (and show the flag to the voracious American subsidiaries) with an enthusiasm worthy of the buccaneers of nineteenth-century American capitalism'. They were working on a theory popular with the Labour government 'that might be caricatured as follows: in order to achieve industrial efficiency, find the most efficient firm in Britain and merge the rest of them into it'.[6]

The details of Tory policy on monopolies have yet to be spelt out, though it has been announced that the Monopolies Commission can suggest its own subjects for investigation and (a favourite diversionary tactic) can look into publicly owned enterprises. Government policy is likely to reflect the views of the Industrial Policy Group (consisting of the chairmen of some of the largest British companies) who argue that [7] 'the main pressures for reform and readjustment must, of course, come through the operation of competition and the working of market forces' and not through government control.† There could be little benefit to

* According to its former chairman, Sir Joseph Lockwood, the I.R.C. existed 'to make the capitalist system work as it is intended that it should' and not as it actually does, which is not very well. (*Guardian*, 5 August 1971.)

† The I.P.G.'s view of what constitutes competition is very broad indeed; they argue for example that bicycles face 'competition from a wide range of private and public transport'. This was in response to a statement in the House of Commons on 6 April 1970 that 'on the most recent information

profitability if the potential advantage from a merger was eroded by government control of the monopoly which resulted. The C.B.I. has objected strongly to government proposals to examine monopoly group price increases resulting from wage increases on the grounds that it could lead to effective controls on prices without corresponding influence on wages.

Rationalization of production through mergers has obviously helped profits, though it is hard to say by how much, and maybe the full benefit of rationalization has not yet been felt. But it should be remembered that other countries are undergoing a similar process. The creation of big firms does not inevitably lead to high profits; what is required is larger and more efficient units than in other countries and there is not much evidence that these are developing.

5. Investing overseas

In response to falling profitability at home British capitalists have turned increasingly to overseas investment opportunities. In the late fifties and early sixties domestic and foreign investment were about equally profitable.* The introduction of the corporation tax in 1965 may have reduced the relative profitability of foreign investment. But the rapid increase in earnings on foreign investment since 1967 (even allowing for devaluation) suggests that this fall was reversed – particularly in the vehicles industry which was doing very badly at home.

*Between 1955 and 1963 the average post-foreign-tax rate of return on manufacturing investment overseas was about 8 per cent, according to the Reddaway Report on Foreign Investment, and our comparable figures for U.K. companies as a whole (including foreign operations) was 7½ per cent. Some U.K. tax has to be paid on the foreign profits.

available to the Department it is believed that at least half the market is in the hands of one company for the 156 commodities in the appended list'. The list included a wide range of foods, chemicals, motor-vehicle components and bicycles.

Another powerful factor which lures investment overseas is the need to respond to international competition. Firms may buy up overseas rivals, or they may find that they need large distribution subsidiaries to market their products in foreign countries, or they may decide to establish production facilities abroad. For this reason the actual rate of profit on foreign operations may not be a very good indication of the true significance of these operations since the gain in monopoly power, or in ability to resist international competition, may offset otherwise falling profits on home operations. In addition, many firms which invest abroad do a certain amount of trading within the firm itself: the foreign branch may supply raw materials or semi-finished goods to the parent company; the parent company may sell capital equipment or manufactured goods or parts to its branch or subsidiary. In both directions these deals need not take place at world market prices; instead, they would take place at what are called 'transfer prices' internal to the firm. By altering its transfer prices a firm can shift its profits from one branch to another and it may well want to do this in order to reduce its total liability for taxation. There is some indication that materials producers in particular keep their transfer prices up relative to the world prices; in other words they prefer to keep their profits in the foreign country. Between 1955 and 1964 the profit rates of materials producers were nearly twice as high on sales to their parent companies as on sales to the general market.[8] This, then, is another reason why a figure for the rate of profit or for the amount of new investment financed out of unremitted profits can be misleading.

Over the last few years there has been a huge growth in foreign investment by British corporations, though it is not certain whether in response to a difference in profitability or to international competition. The total value of accumulated British direct[1] investment abroad rose from about £3,750m. in 1962 to about £6,000m. in 1968 and over £7,000m. by the end of 1970. So for the first time it has regained the level in terms of money value (though not real value) of foreign investment, mostly indirect, in 1914. A particu-

[1] Investment in factories overseas, as opposed to foreign shares (portfolio investment).

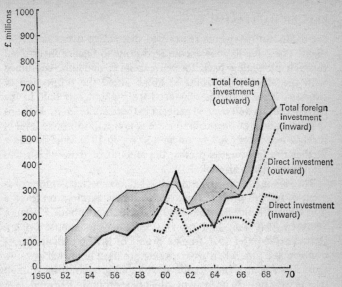

Figure 12. Foreign investment, outward and inward, 1952–69
Source: United Kingdom Balance of Payments, 1971, Table 26.

larly big surge in direct investment occurred after 1967.* After having run at around £250m. p.a. since the early sixties it suddenly rose to over £400m. in 1968 and £550m. in 1969, and this despite a strengthening of the exchange controls and regulations designed

* Over half this investment (apart from oil) is in manufacturing; about a fifth is in distribution (shops and stores as well as sales subsidiaries of manufacturing corporations), and roughly another fifth is in banking and insurance. Commonly less than a tenth is in mining and a tiny amount in agriculture. Most of the investment takes place in developed countries. At the beginning of the 1960s their share was over two thirds; by the end of the 1960s about 80 per cent of British overseas investment was being done in other developed countries. Throughout the decade the share in the United States was erratic and varied between about 5 and about 20 per cent with no visible trend. A growing part of the investment was in the Common Market countries whose share rose from under 14 per cent at the start of the decade to about 20 per cent by the end. Two other major absorbers of British capital throughout the period were Australia (one quarter falling to one fifth) and South Africa (normally 10–15 per cent).

for balance-of-payments reasons to discourage overseas invest-ment. These regulations encouraged firms to finance investment through ploughing back foreign earnings; and this, combined with the absence of profits at home, lifted the proportion of overseas investment thus financed from about one half in the early sixties to well over 60 per cent in the years 1968–70. Perhaps in consequence of the profit squeeze at home, the absolute level of foreign investment fell to under £500m. in 1970, and despite a further rise in overseas profits, the amount of these which was retained overseas also fell.

The leap in foreign investment has led to a spectacular improve-ment of foreign profits. The average annual earnings on foreign direct investment* between 1959 and 1962 were about £250m. a year; by 1970 they had risen astonishingly to almost £700m. Between 1964 and 1970 foreign profits of British capital almost doubled at a time when gross trading profits at home fell by more than 5 per cent.† But despite their rapid growth, total foreign profits were only 20 per cent of total home profits in 1970 and have been an important compensation for falling profits at home only for the large corporations which do nearly all the overseas invest-ing.

But foreign investment is no solution to domestic problems; rather, it is an escape from them. Probably, few foreign profits are used to offset the financing problems resulting from low home profitability. Some may be used to keep up dividends for com-panies doing badly at home. The possibility of higher profits abroad is more likely to reduce investment at home and this, if anything, will reduce the competitiveness of U.K. production.

* Excluding oil on which there seems to be little data. On average during 1958–64 post-tax oil profits were at least £100 million and have obviously grown since then. (Reddaway Report.)

† Since the foreign profits are after depreciation but before stock appreci-ation, we subtract capital consumption, but not stock appreciation, from domestic profits. Even excluding the effect of devaluation the rise in foreign profits was around two thirds.

6. Foreign investment in Britain

It is when we look at investment by foreign companies in the U.K. that we see how inadequate it is to explain foreign investment solely in terms of different average profit rates in various countries. After hovering just under the £200m. mark during the early sixties, foreign investment in Britain rose sharply to average just over £300m. during 1968–70, just when U.K. profitability as a whole was collapsing. Nor is there much evidence that foreign investment has escaped the overall fall in profitability. Thus, while U.S.-owned investment in Britain was much more profitable than British-owned capital in 1950, it was only slightly so in 1965, though foreign firms may have done slightly better between 1964 and 1968.

Much of this investment must be motivated not by the attraction of high profitability in Britain, but by the need to strengthen the investor's competitive position in the large British market. It is not surprising, therefore, that the inflow of capital comes overwhelmingly from the United States, where domestic investment opportunities are limited.* Between 1967 and 1969 two thirds of it was American; 14 per cent came from the Common Market countries.† The rate of profit on this investment from the E.E.C., more than half of which comes from the Netherlands, has been particularly low, perhaps because it has involved breaking into new markets.

The basic effect of foreign investment in Britain is that it increases competition for U.K. firms: after all, it represents an

* During the 1960s the direction of U.S. investment in Europe shifted decisively towards the Common Market and away from Britain. But U.S. capital is still more important in Britain than elsewhere. In 1966 U.S.-financed firms owned over 7 per cent of total company capital stock in Britain. They had over 10 per cent of all manufacturing sales and over 17 per cent of exports of manufactures in 1965. In particular industries, of course, U.S. investment was highly significant and at times dominant. In 1964 U.S. firms accounted for over 40 per cent of turnover in refined petroleum products, computers, and tractors and agricultural machinery; 50 per cent in refrigerators; over 50 per cent in cars, razor blades, safety razors and carbon black.

† West Germany and also possibly Japan have been increasing their portfolio investment in the U.K. – buying securities – but this is of little significance from the point of view of competition.

attempt by large-scale foreign enterprises to capture part of the U.K. market. It may be something of a relief for sections of capital of declining profitability to be bought out (though this constitutes only a small part of foreign investment*). But, unlike nationalization, takeovers tend not to be made on very generous terms. After a takeover American capital often adopts a more ruthless view of profitability than is politically possible for the original British owners. So foreign, like domestic, takeovers are often the cue for large-scale redundancies and rationalization. Major redundancies resulted from two particular instances of foreign investment in Britain and Europe: the Ford plant in Doncaster shut down after the 1961 takeover; and the Remington typewriter and shaver plants in Scotland were closed and the activities shifted to Europe.[9] American firms seem to be prepared to stand up to very long strikes. There are a number of examples of this at Ford (especially in 1971), and also the long strikes at Roberts Arundel in Stockport [10] and Fine Tubes in Plymouth, where, according to a government report, the 17-month-long strike might have been averted if the management had approached the unions for a meeting. But the strength of workers for international companies such as Ford is severely weakened by the threat of moving new investment projects to other countries.

The government has usually welcomed foreign investment because it improves the balance of payments in the short term; they may also hope that U.S. encroachment will help concentrate the minds of British managers. Efforts have sometimes been made by the government to alleviate or anticipate some of the problems of foreign investment. In the Chrysler/Rootes deal of 1966 and the Litton/Imperial Typewriter takeover in 1967 the Labour government sought specific assurances about the future of the firms' operations in Britain.

But in the long run all this foreign investment can only damage the profitability of British industry. Observing the twin trends towards British investment overseas and foreign investment in Britain (both of which are growing faster than British domestic

* Acquisitions of U.K. firms accounted for only about £60 million p.a. in 1969 and 1970, or one fifth of total direct investment (*Business Monitor, M7*, 1971).

industrial investment), one could speculate that the problems of British domestic industrial capital will be painlessly solved because British capital will have been internationalized out of existence. This is, in our opinion, rather a dangerous fantasy: British domestic industrial capital is still very much with us and it remains central to the economic and political life of the country. It is as well to remember that less than 10 per cent of industrial capital in Britain is foreign-owned and that British-owned investment abroad is little more than 10 per cent of British-owned capital in Britain. Even if both these figures continued to grow, it would be many decades before foreign capital was dominant in Britain or foreign-owned assets dominant in total British capital. In other advanced countries, with the single exception of American overseas investment, the proportions are a good deal smaller than they are in Britain. Capital is certainly becoming more international, but is still essentially nationally based.[11]

7. Financial operations

The historically important division between industry and finance (banks, insurance companies and so on) in Britain (see chapter 2) still to some extent survives. And several of the trends we have already described have combined very substantially to increase the profits of financial companies, as compared with total profits generated by production. First of all low industrial profitability had led to much more bank borrowing by industrial companies, and higher interest rates have meant that interest payments on this borrowing have risen even faster than the volume of borrowing. There is also a long-term trend for individuals to hold company securities indirectly through their holdings in investment and unit trusts. As a result, an increasing proportion of the payments of dividends and interest by industrial and commercial companies is channelled through financial institutions before they reach their ultimate destination – in 1964 the proportion was just under 20 per cent but by 1970 it was practically 30 per cent.*

* An important part of the process of centralization of holdings has taken place through life assurance and superannuation funds, whose receipts of

An important result of higher interest receipts is that it is those financial institutions which do not directly rely on the *profitability* of industrial capital whose income has risen most. It appears that the profits (after payment of interest to depositors) of clearing banks, of H.P. companies and of merchant banks and discount houses each rose by over 100 per cent between 1964 and 1970, while the profits of investment trusts rose by only about 25 per cent.* Of these institutions investment trusts are the only ones whose profitability is directly linked to the profits of industrial capital since they have very large holdings of ordinary shares, the return on which depends on profits. The other institutions lend to companies, as well as to the government and to the private sector, but they do so mainly on fixed interest terms and consequently do not feel the pinch of low profitability of the companies they lend to unless those companies are actually going broke (because going bankrupt means being unable to pay interest). The rise in interest rates increased their receipts from lending to industrial companies (though this is partially offset by the higher rates they had to pay on their deposits) while investment trusts only received the very modest increases in dividends on their holdings of ordinary shares.

But financial institutions lend to private individuals and to the government (by holding the national debt) as well as to industrial companies, and total payments of these types of interest payments have grown very rapidly since 1964.† Total receipts by companies

---

* These figures are calculated from the *Financial Times* analysis of company accounts and should be taken with a large pinch of salt because of notorious problems in analysing the profitability of financial institutions. The figures for commercial banks is 117 per cent, H.P. companies 106 per cent and merchant banks and discount houses 137 per cent. The profits of property companies rose by 81 per cent.

† See above, p. 115. Total debt of public authorities rose by not much more than 10 per cent between 1964 and 1970. In the sphere of personal borrowing monetary control virtually halted the growth of borrowing from banks and H.P. companies, but building-society mortgages more than

---

rent, dividends and interest as a proportion of personal receipts as a whole rose from 19 per cent to 23 per cent between 1964 and 1970. These funds are not treated as financial institutions by the national income statisticians and so are not included in the figure. They remain an enormously important channel for new personal savings.

of these types of interest rose by 115 per cent between 1964 and 1970, and virtually all of this has gone to financial companies.* Over the same period gross trading profits of all companies (i.e. income generated in production) after deduction of stock appreciation were unchanged. The ratio of total income of financial companies (including that received from industrial companies) to the total income of industrial companies rose from about 0·17 in 1964 to 0·29 in 1970.

The enormous expansion of their business has led to a boom in financial companies' fixed investment (offices, branches, etc.) and whereas in 1964 they more or less financed this investment out of their own retained profits, in 1969 and 1970 they had to raise more than £300m. per year from elsewhere. So the fact that holdings of securities are becoming more and more centralized, and lending to the government and public more profitable, has not resulted in the automatic accumulation by financial institutions of enormous quantities of finance which can be used to offset the fall in profitability of the industrial sector. The funds they channel into the industrial sector must first be raised by them from individuals. Of course, the fact that interest paid by them has risen so much does add to the potential sources of investment funds from individuals; but here we must re-emphasize that the increase in interest rates in recent years has been a once-and-for-all boost to investment incomes and therefore to potential funds for capital accumulation.

Investment incomes derived from lending to the public sector and to other individuals in the private sector have nothing to do with the profitability of capitalist production. H.P. profits or interest earned on the national debt could not, even if they increased enormously, prop up a system of production which is no longer viable in its own terms – those of profitability.

*Income from investments, including trade investments, was just over 4 per cent of gross trading profits of quoted industrial and commercial companies in 1969.

---

doubled. Since building-society mortgages are more than four times as big as H.P. and bank borrowing together, the total increase in personal borrowing from those (major) sources was around 80 per cent. Between 1964 and 1970 the book value of capital employed (net assets and bank loans) by industrial and commercial companies rose by about 35 per cent.

But as these forms of income grow, side by side with redundancies and unemployment for more and more workers, they come to demonstrate more conclusively the essentially parasitic nature of the capitalist class. They must do something therefore to undermine the strength of the capitalist system, even though they may prop up the bourgeoisie financially for the time being.

So we have now examined all the options open to British capital in the present crisis of the profit squeeze. Each of them, though it may make some contribution to profitability, also seems to contain its own contradictions. Raising prices only worsens international competitive standing, and stimulates further wage militancy; as redundancies grow they may provoke greater resistance as well as political reaction; there is an end to mergers when a whole industry becomes concentrated in one firm; more profitable investment abroad does not aid home profitability which is anyway being continually undermined by inflows of capital from outside; and financial profits do not solve the crisis in production. So it is not surprising that all these actions taken together have completely failed to reverse the decline of profitability. With such meagre resources of its own to combat the crisis, capital is forced to rely to an ever greater extent on the support of state action, especially action which will weaken the working class.

Chapter 8
The Role and Policy
of the Government

As a result of capital's relative weakness, the economic and industrial policies of the government have become a central element in capitalism's fight to survive the profits squeeze. We can separate these policies into three broad groups. The first group contains those which can directly redistribute income to capital; it includes taxation, public expenditure and the nationalized industries.

But profits are also affected by a second group of much broader government policies concerned with the overall 'management of the economy', such as policy on the exchange rate of the pound, entry into the Common Market, and the level of demand.

Both Labour and Tory governments implemented policies to undermine directly the economic strength of the working class. As well as unemployment, this third group includes incomes policy and the Industrial Relations Act, which aims to subject the labour movement to more fundamental restraint.

1. Cutting the tax burden on capital

It is the level of profits after tax which affects both the financing of investment and the return to investment; so a decrease in the taxation of company profits can offset a fall in the share of profits or rate of return before tax. In the fifties and early sixties the reduction in company taxation and the Tory government's attempt to stimulate private investment by increasing the value of investment incentives ensured that the fall in the pre-tax return on capital employed was not reflected in a similar fall after tax. By contrast, Labour added to the burden of company taxation as a politically necessary part of packages of general tax increases.

Since the Tory government was elected corporation tax has been reduced from 45 per cent to 40 per cent and Labour's investment grant system has been scrapped in favour of a return to tax allowances. This means a reduction in company taxation of about £100m. for 1971 and 1972, rising to perhaps £200m. in 1973 and 1974, though with less effect thereafter. Even if, as is likely, firms use all of this reduced taxation to increase profits, rather than lower prices, the effect is small considering that company profits in 1970 fell short of the 1964 share by £2,500 million – about £1,250 million after tax.

When the Tories replaced investment grants with tax allowances they also reversed the previous bias in the investment grant system in favour of manufacturing. Further in 1974 the Regional Employment Premium, at present worth about £100m. to manufacturers, will come to an end. Both these changes are blows for manufacturing, the most vulnerable section of capital.

Manufacturers now receive lower incentives to invest in new plant and machinery than they used to. While corporation tax has fallen from 45 per cent to 40 per cent the government has cut its subsidy of investment from about $42\frac{1}{2}$ per cent under the investment grant system to $32\frac{1}{2}$ per cent under the new taxation incentive scheme.* The service sector (including the finance sector) has also benefited from the cutting of the Selective Employment Tax by around half and this is worth about £250m. p.a. Even if it were all used to increase profits most of these would probably stay in the service sector. Moreover, much of the gain would accrue in the service sector to small unincorporated businesses, cornershops, etc., and would therefore have very little effect on investment.

In his April 1971 Budget the Tory Chancellor, Anthony Barber, also announced the end of 'discrimination' against dividends. This 'discrimination' is that income tax is levied on dividends in addition to the corporation tax, while retained profits are subject only to corporation tax. This makes the retention of profits a particularly beneficial way of saving. Even when capital-gains tax is

---

* Moreover, the new system only offers a benefit to companies who are earning profits, for otherwise there is no tax bill to be reduced. *The Times* (15 July 1971) reported on a change in the Inland Revenue's rules whereby companies can go up to 3 years back to find profits against which to claim tax concessions on *current* investment.

paid on the increase in share values resulting from the reinvestment it is paid at a rate well below the standard rate of income tax, let alone of surtax. Thus, less tax is paid and it is therefore more profitable if shareholders save through company saving,* if they need cash for consumption they are better off realizing their capital gain by selling shares than by spending out of dividends on which income tax and surtax are levied.

It is unlikely that the ending of discrimination† would encourage the paying out of a higher proportion of profits as dividends, unless profits could rise sufficiently to ease the financing situation of companies. Although it might be easier for companies to raise money by selling more shares the effect is likely to be very small.

The change in the form of company taxation will not do much to advance profitability. There will be some advantage, however, for firms and industries whose lack of profitability has reduced their retentions to a particularly low level relative to dividends, since they will gain if the rate of tax on dividends falls relatively to that on retentions. There have also been official hints that stock appreciation may be exempted from tax. This and similar measures might be used as technicalities to disguise what amounts simply to a reduction of company taxes. It will become politically more difficult to make further reductions in the average burden of company taxation, though the Treasury was reported to be considering major cuts in company taxation as part of another reflationary package at the end of 1971.

There are other ways by which government aid is given to industry. Apart from expenditure of over £300m. on agriculture,

---

*Suppose a firm has £100 profit after paying corporation tax. If it pays this out the shareholder receives about £60 after income tax (less if he pays surtax). If he subscribes this £60 to a new issue he secures the returns from £40 less investment than had the company invested the £100 directly on his behalf.

†When the Labour government reintroduced the discrimination in 1965 its aim was simply to encourage retentions and thus overall investment. It is most unlikely that the 1965 change had much effect since profits have slumped so disastrously that there has been no possibility of increasing the proportion of profits retained short of drastic cuts in dividends which would have had a catastrophic effect on share prices.

the 1970/71 estimates included more than £60m. (in addition to investment grants and the regional-employment premium) for promoting local employment, £85m. for development and production of Concorde and other civil-aviation assistance, £17m. assistance for shipbuilding,* £13m. as loans to the aluminium-industry, £11m. in hotel and other tourist loans, £10m. of assistance to the Industrial Reorganization Corporation and another £50m. for miscellaneous items including industrial training and export promotion. The winding up of the Industrial Reorganization Corporation, the ending of the Regional Employment Premium and (before Rolls-Royce) some reduction in aircraft projects were announced by the Tories in 1970. Even though John Davies, the Minister for Industry, may be forced to assist more lame ducks than he would wish, a major expansion of this type of state aid might not be politically easy for the Tory party.

2. Decreasing taxation of the rich and increasing welfare charges

In three budgets between October 1970 and July 1971 the Tory Chancellor cut personal taxation by something like £900m., and he has helped the rich much more than the poor. Tax on large earned incomes was cut by £38m.† A child's investment income ceased to be assessed as part of the parents' income, which was a gift of £15 million. Capital gains tax at death was abolished – a further £15 million; and the short-term capital gains tax, applying for example to speculative gains on stocks and shares, was abolished (£1½m). These benefits, however, are obviously far too small to improve the profitability of capital. In any case *personal* incomes only have an impact on *company* financing through any effect of increased savings, so the effect on profitability is extremely remote. The projected change-over from purchase tax to value-

* Between 1967 and the end of 1971, when it was wound up, the government's Shipbuilding Industry Board distributed to the industry £19m. in grants and over £21m. in loans. (*Financial Times*, 15 December 1971.)

† The income-tax changes increased the post-tax income of a married man with two children earning £20,000 by more than 25 per cent whereas the income tax changes increased the post-tax income of a man in similar circumstances earning £1,200 a year by less than 4 per cent.

added tax, though the details of coverage are not yet announced, will also harm the poor through the wider taxation of necessities.

The working class is also hit by reductions in social services, agricultural price guarantees and housing subsidies, which will involve a saving of something like £500m. in 1974–5 on Labour programmes. These reductions include almost £50m. through charging more for school dinners and cutting down free milk, almost £100m. in higher prescription and dental charges and adjustments of the welfare milk scheme; some £150m. in reduced food subsidies (and therefore higher food prices) and £100–200m. from higher council-house rents. Those people below the official poverty line will escape some of the higher charges, provided they submit to more means tests, and those who are very badly paid will, if they come forward, benefit a bit from the Family Income Supplement which still leaves them below the poverty line. But for the working class as a whole these changes in public expenditure involve clear reductions in living standards, proportionately much greater than those suffered by higher income groups.*

The Tory government has also produced a new state pension plan which will have the effect of compelling all workers either to join a private occupational pension scheme or to contribute to a supplementary state scheme. The news of extra funds to be invested was greeted by delight at the Stock Exchange.† But the effect of all this on British capital is complex. More than 60 per

* One estimate puts the effects of all economic measures in the first year of office of the Tory government as follows:

Range of income	Gain/Loss per person per year
£1000 and under	+ £52
£1001–2000	− £15
£2001–5000	+ £76
£5001 and over	+ £1,256

(M. Meacher, *The Times*, 29 December 1971.)

† The Stock Exchange said 'it could be a tremendous fillip to the market – provided it can cope' (*The Times*, 15 September 1971). The contributions to the supplementary state scheme (perhaps £250m. p.a.), unlike contributions to the basic state scheme, will be invested in shares and bonds by an independent board of management, and of course the extra contributions to occupational schemes will increase the funds at the disposal of pension-fund managers. (*Economist*, 18 September 1971.)

cent of the contribution to the state scheme, and presumably a similar proportion in most occupational schemes, will be paid by the employers. These extra costs will reduce profits, though the funds will be available for investment in U.K. industry. However, the reduction in the profitability of industry is likely to make it more difficult for firms to raise money on the stock market, as well as leaving less profits which can be ploughed back.

It is true that the extra employee's contribution would be channelled into financing capital accumulation through the stock market. But some of the extra contributions might have been saved anyway and so would not add to private savings. Moreover, that part of the extra employee's contribution which he would *not* have saved otherwise will reduce his consumption and is therefore likely to add to wage pressure. And this effect will be magnified if employers attempt to pass on their extra contribution in the form of higher prices. In the longer run when higher pensions are paid out and pensioners consume more, the active working class must consume less or the amount of investment must be less. If the better pensions result in lower profits and a militant working class pushing harder for higher consumption the effect on British capital's position must be reckoned as adverse.

3. Nationalization, de-nationalization and lame ducks

The role of nationalization in the British economy has been widely misunderstood. On the one hand some economists have complained that the comparatively low profits in nationalized industry indicate a misallocation of capital in the economy, and that if the nationalized sector were more efficient the rate of growth of the economy would be higher.[3] On the other hand, nationalization is sometimes seen as a move in the direction of socialism. Both these views are completely mistaken. Nationalized industries are an inseparable part of the capitalist system in Britain, even though they may not obey precisely the same economic laws as private capital. Nationalized industries are formed by the purchase of assets *from* the private sector; they produce inputs *for* the private sector in the form of fuel and transport and basic industrial materials.

Compensation, therefore, can help capital. But of itself it is a subsidy to the bourgeoisie rather than to capitalist *production*; for the interest they receive on the extra national debt issued to pay for the industries taken over cannot directly help the profitability of production. The state may, however, use the nationalized industries to subsidize the private sector; low prices and profitability amount to a subsidy to production.* In practice this has always been the role of the nationalized sector in Britain.

Nationalized industries have tended to be less profitable than private industries. The figures for the share of profits in net output show this very clearly.† But the figures also show that the element of subsidy has *declined* since 1950 as successive Tory and Labour governments attempted to improve profitability and make the nationalized industries more efficient. This decline in subsidy was itself one of the pressures bearing on private capital during that time. In 1970 the profitability of the nationalized sector collapsed much more drastically than that of the private sector, though up till then it had escaped the profits squeeze altogether.‡

The recent drop in profitability in the public sector was partly the result of pressures similar to those attacking profitability in the private sector, though international competition cannot have been very important, since the majority of nationalized corporations do

* We saw in the last chapter the importance of the nationalized industries as suppliers of inputs to the private sector. Even though they sell nearly half their output direct to the consumer, private capital may still gain from the low prices charged since they help to moderate wage pressure.

† The nationalized industries are also very much more capital-intensive than the company sector, so rates of profit are much lower than the company sector's.

‡ The electricity industry made a loss of £57m. in 1970–71, as compared with a profit of £65m. in 1969–70. In the gas industry profits slipped from £14m. to £2m. British Rail's deficit was expected to be at least £22m. in 1970. The National Bus Company blamed strikes and industrial unrest for their £5m. loss. Even the profits of the travel agents Thomas Cook, which was to have been hived off to the private sector, fell noticeably. The Steel Corporation had expected to be able to raise prices by 14 per cent and had budgeted for a £30–40m. profit in 1971–72, but when the government decided to hold the price increase down to 7 per cent after intense pressure from steel users, a loss of between £50 and £100m. was being forecast. Of all the nationalized industries only the National Freight Corporation showed an improvement by cutting its losses in 1970.

not face foreign or even much domestic competition. There are exceptions like the airlines and the British Steel Corporation, which in December 1971 was forced by rising imports to lower some steel prices. For other industries there was an equivalent problem – government interference which prevented price increases in order that a stand should be taken against inflation and that some of the pressures on private profits should be reduced. Moreover, banning price increases could help strengthen the intransigence of managements in the face of wage claims. This was true both of British Rail, which faced a cash crisis in 1971, and of the Post Office, which endured a seven-week strike.

Table 8.1. Shares of Profits in Net Output of Public and Private Industry, 1950–70 (per cent)

	1950	1955	1960	1965	1969	1970
Nationalized industries	−4·3	−0·4	7·1	10·4	11·6	4·9
Company sector	23·4	24·9	23·3	20·2	14·1	12·1

Source: National Income Blue Book, 1971, tables 13, 58.

These losses or reduced profits of state industries were mildly helpful to the private sector. But there is another side to the question. The crisis in the nationalized industries has inevitably increased their need to borrow from the central government. For the financial year 1971/2 a rise in borrowings of nearly two thirds is forecast. These funds must be found by the government and so indirectly more pressure will have to be applied to taxpayers to support the position of the nationalized industries. Accordingly, the scope for reductions in the taxation in general and taxation of private capital in particular is hampered by the profit difficulties of the state sector. General increases in taxation are an alternative to price increases as a means of financing the production of nationalized industries. Their advantage over price increases is that they do not affect costs in the private sector; and since they are less obvious than price increases they may provoke less retaliation in the form of higher wage claims.

Since its arrival in office, the Tory government has talked frequently of 'hiving-off' profitable parts of nationalized industry to private buyers.*

Hiving off, even if the selling price is too low, will not have much effect on the crisis; it will only offer one or two attractive investments to private capital. Any really substantial hiving off is out of the question given the basic unprofitability of the major nationalized industries. It suits private capital very much better to have the steel industry selling to it at unprofitable prices than to have it in private hands – even supposing buyers could be found.

In any case, the Tory government has been forced by the crisis to consider further nationalization more often than hiving off. The decision of a large industrial company to go into liquidation necessarily involves the government. A large bankruptcy will cause an increase in redundancies and unemployment and probably a drop in output. It may have repercussions in other firms, which will also collapse. The bankruptcy of a large car firm, for instance, would drag down hundreds of smaller firms which supply it with parts and equipment. The Rolls-Royce collapse also led to the failure of the computer firm Systems International. With so much at stake the government is bound to intervene. The directors will naturally turn to the government for assistance as a last hope before declaring liquidation. The government then has a number of alternatives. First, it can decide to give financial assistance and prevent the collapse. Such assistance has been increasingly common in recent years.† Second, the government can decide to allow the failure to take place but to step in with assistance in forming a new private group; this is one of the things it did in the case of Upper Clyde Shipbuilders; it is also part of the solution for Harland & Wolff and the Liverpool docks. Thirdly, it

* So far, rudimentary plans for this have been announced in the case of Thomas Cook and the more specialized activities of the British Steel Corporation. There are proposals to admit private capital into the main operations of the nationalized steel industry as well as plans to sell £100m. worth of government-held shares in private industry acquired through Labour's Industrial Reorganization Corporation.

† It has gone on a large scale to Rolls-Royce, Upper Clyde Shipbuilders, Cammel Laird, Harland & Wolff (the Belfast shipyard), International Computers, and other firms, mainly those in the high technology industries.

can nationalize the enterprise; as a final alternative it can sit back and allow the failure to happen without taking action.

Part of Rolls-Royce was nationalized by the Tory government in 1971 mainly because the Ministry of Defence submitted that Britain's main aero-engine supplier could not be permitted to close down. A Labour government would be more likely, though by no means certain, to nationalize bankrupt private companies. Nationalization would protect the immediate employment prospects of the workers involved, but in the long term it is no solution. Either the nationalized corporation will continue to be run at a loss, in which case there arises the problem of financing that loss; or it will be made profitable, in which case redundancies are almost inevitable.

In principle the Tory party sets great store by the fourth alternative – permitting failures to take place without intervening: 'lame ducks' should be allowed to die so that they do not weaken the collective strength of the rest. It is a fitting philosophy for the Tory party and is, of course, perfectly logical in terms of a belief in the efficacy of competitive capitalism as well as the desire not to increase the strain on public funds. At the same time it is in a period of crisis a contradictory policy, since the failure of one firm may weaken the others.

The Tories see the psychological effect of a 'lame duck' policy as important. It is meant to threaten not only the capitalists but also the working class. A credible threat of sudden mass redundancies is a powerful weapon in wage negotiations. It can also, as at U.C.S., be used as a lever to force wage cuts before the reconstitution of the liquidated company with state help. For these reasons, therefore, the Tory strategy does not have much place for nationalization.

4. Devaluation

When the Labour government devalued the pound in November 1967, their decision was presented as an attempt to solve the balance-of-payments problem. But it also affected the distribution of income between wages and profits.

Suppose that prices of British products at home and in export markets expressed in dollars were unaffected by devaluation. If the U.K. devalued, then British firms could raise their sterling prices without losing competitiveness.[1] This would raise sterling profits, but at the same time the British working class would be faced with a general price rise (the price of imports would go up as well). If exports went up because of improved profitability, and there was no overall increase in output, there would have to be a further reduction of real wages by the taxation required to 'redirect' resources into exports. Both these effects on real wages were evident after the 1967 devaluation.

This is an extreme case: of course some firms at home do not face foreign competition at all and would have no reason to raise prices; others which do face international competition will take the opportunity of lowering their dollar prices to some extent to gain a competitive advantage. For them profits will rise a bit less but sales a bit more than if they just raised their sterling prices by the amount of the devaluation. Conversely, some foreign firms selling in the U.K. will squeeze their profits and not raise their sterling prices by the amount of the devaluation in order to prevent U.K. producers from gaining a price advantage. A number of foreign firms acted this way after the 1967 devaluation and this reduced the benefit gained by British capital; the same will again be true wherever U.K. competition is important. These factors obviously soften the impact of devaluation on the working class since the rise in prices in the U.K. is less. But the less U.K. export prices rise compared with import prices the more resources will have to be devoted to paying the import bill, leaving less for consumption and investment at home; and the government will have to squeeze hard on home demand to provide the resources required. Overall, therefore, devaluation tends to cut home consumption in order to devote more resources to exports; and to give an advantage for the capitalists in the tug-of-war between profits and wages.

In practice, however, the effects of devaluation depend on the reaction of the working class. It may press successfully for higher

[1] This is because the same price in foreign currencies would give the British exporter more pounds after the devaluation.

money wages to offset price increases. If firms try to offset this by putting up prices the competitive advantage gained by the devaluation is eroded, profit margins are maintained and there is no increase in real wages; this then stimulates further increases in money wages until eventually international competition prevents further price increases. At this stage real wages do rise and profit margins fall, and so by this time the competitive advantage of the devaluation may well have been lost. Moreover, this process gives a very important boost to inflationary expectations, which will tend to be reflected in sustained higher levels of wage pressure. This makes subsequent devaluations even harder to operate. Thus the willingness of the workers to accept the initial fall in real wages determines both the success of devaluation in improving the balance of payments, and its effects in restoring profitability. Devaluation could only help British capitalism if it was accompanied by effective wage control. This was lacking after 1967 and meant that devaluation did no more than temporarily stem the fall in the share of profits (see chapter 3).

But in any case decisions to devalue are increasingly settled by international bargaining. It is impossible to devalue while the balance of payments is in healthy (even if misleading) surplus and sterling at its strongest for years. As we argue next, entry into the Common Market may eventually make devaluation essential. But its effects on the distribution of income are unlikely to be greater than those that followed the 1967 devaluation, given increasing international competition and a growing determination of the working class to resist reductions in living standards.

5. The Common Market

Entry into the Common Market will mean a substantial reduction in real living standards in Britain. Food will be more expensive because a higher proportion of domestic resources will have to be devoted either to producing food in the U.K. or to buying expensive food from the E.E.C. Financing the British contribution to the Community's budget would involve devoting extra resources to exports in order to earn the foreign exchange to pay the contribution. The effect of these changes on the balance of payments means that entry would probably involve devaluation of the pound, and we have already seen what that involves for real wages.*

If we assume that all these costs add up to £600m. (a reasonable compromise of the estimates)[1] then private consumption, if it bears all the costs, will have to fall by about 2 per cent. But since a successful devaluation will also tend to redistribute income from labour to capital (which is more or less what restoring the U.K.'s competitiveness means) the effect on real wages would be very much greater than 2 per cent, particularly if it is combined with a coordinated drive to restore profitability by other means. It is no use arguing like Sam Brittan of the *Financial Times* that in the present situation undesirable changes in the distribution of income 'can be countered by shifts in taxes and public expenditure, which would be quite permissible within the E.E.C.'[2] These changes in distribution will have to be made if British capitalism is to survive at all.

Benefits for British industry, according to the 1971 White Paper[3] on proposed entry into the E.E.C., will arise from

opportunities opened up by the creation, at the end of the transitional period, of a permanent, *assured*, and greatly enlarged market. Manufacturers will be operating in a 'domestic market' perhaps five times as large as at present, in which tariff barriers cannot be put up against them *however well they do*.

. . . for advanced industrial countries the most favourable environment is one where markets are large and are free from barriers to trade . . . Through *increased competition* they foster the more efficient use of resources over a wide area of industry and help to check the trend to monopoly positions on the part of large scale organizations.

The abolition of tariffs and the consequent increase in intra-trade were accompanied by important changes in the performance of manufacturing industries in the Six countries. Those industries which

* Even so, the Chancellor committed himself, in a speech in the Commons reported by Peter Jay in *The Times* of 5 July 1971, not to devalue to offset the impact of joining the E.E.C. Professor Kaldor writes: 'Though the White Paper keeps silent on the subject, every economic expert in the country would agree on the present showing that if we entered the Market the pound will have to be devalued before January 1973 by something of the order of 15 per cent.' (*New Statesman*, 16 June 1971.)

competed with imports faced an *intensification of competitive pressures* as tariffs fell, *obliging them to seek ways of raising efficiency and reducing costs.* (Paras 44, 46, 50) (our emphases).

The spokesmen of the British capitalist class seem to agree with the White Paper's optimistic view, judging by their full-page advertisements in *The Times*. Most confident of all is the British motor industry, which seems unperturbed by the thought of losing sales in Britain to foreign competitors. But many other industries seem less optimistic about their ability to meet the extra competition. Publicly, the chemicals industry is in favour of entry; I.C.I.'s Chairman, for instance, said that their U.K. customers would prosper under the stimulus of membership and that this would benefit domestic sales. But it has been suggested that in private the companies are entertaining considerable doubts, and even that they have not made any plans for investment after entry.

According to recent press reports domestic appliance manufacturers already face very strong competition from E.E.C. producers and 'entry into the Common Market could be expected to exacerbate the situation'. The British Mechanical Engineering Confederation

takes the line that while it agrees Britain should enter the E.E.C., it believes membership would be painful for some sectors. There is likely to be a polarization between those companies which are in the first league (world class) for their speciality . . . which will benefit and the rest which will suffer.

Britain is likely to do well in electrical control machinery; 'dismally' in areas like machine tools and typewriters, while there is a 'vast area in between . . . where the prospects are middling to bad and where almost anything could happen'. For newsprint, entry 'could not be beneficial and indeed could be harmful'; pottery 'could suffer in the Common Market context'. The shipbuilding industry is definitely against joining because of the resulting higher wage demands, while for aircraft 'the big prize is the creation of a genuinely European aerospace industry'.

The readiness with which City worthies put their signatures to pro-E.E.C. advertisements supports the view that

. . . Whatever happens to the sterling exchange rate the City of London expects to gain from Common Market membership. Casual empiricism certainly suggests that Britain has a comparative advantage in the financial sector, and London bankers and property developers are already moving into the continental economies on a growing scale.[4]

Even excluding insurance, which may suffer from the more detailed controls in the E.E.C., the invisible earnings of the City (banking, etc.) rose from around £125m. in 1965 to £225m. in 1969 (with apparently little further increase in 1970). They expanded at a time when the importance of sterling as a reserve currency and as a trading currency was declining and when foreign borrowers were virtually unable to borrow in London because of exchange control. The growth of the need for international financing and the City's expertise in this field meant that it became the centre of borrowing and lending operations which were not conducted in sterling at all. The City was free from controls over its international business and, although the creation of a monetary union in Europe might give British banks easier access to Europe, the tighter official control of European business might be a disadvantage. There seems to be cautious sympathy for entry in the City.

What is particularly interesting is the view of the City that its prosperity no longer depends on sterling's role as an international currency. One estimate suggests that less than a quarter of the City's earnings of foreign exchange are dependent on sterling's use as an international currency. Sir Cyril Kleinwort claims:

It has not been the City that has cherished illusions – if there were illusions – about sterling's reserve currency role, or indeed about the exchange rate ... The City's interest was, and still remains only in having the maximum freedom from controls and, if possible, a stable currency and not in any particular exchange rate against other currencies or in any prestige which might be derived from sterling's use as an official reserve currency.[5]

Thus one of the historic causes of the division between financial and industrial capital, which as we saw in chapter 2 has been an important feature of British capitalism, may be evaporating.

British capital will need to be able to stand up to stiff competition if it is to survive entry into the Common Market. Certainly most members did well in the late fifties and early sixties. Their profits and investment were very buoyant as they increased their efficiency at a time of extra competition. But there is no reason for Britain to expect such benefits now. The part played by foreign competition in precipitating the present crisis makes it astonishing that British capitalists, clamouring for entry into the market, are in effect asking for more. In addition the initial adverse effects on real wages (which would involve the transfer of purchasing power from the British working class to, amongst others, European farmers) will make it all the more difficult to achieve the redistribution from wages to profits necessary to restore profitability. Only if increased competition within the Common Market can successfully be used as an argument for accepting moderation in wage demands will entry do anything to restore British capital's position.

6. Reflation and public expenditure

In April 1971 the Chancellor said of his budget measures that

... My broad aim is that these measures should after a time slow down and later stop the rise in unemployment; but of course the progress of that aim depends on the progress of de-escalation [of wage claims] ... Later, when the pay settlements have returned to more sensible levels, it should be safe to allow output to grow at a rate sufficient to reduce the level of unemployment.

... in an inflationary situation with strikes the order of the day ... the attempt to alleviate the unemployment situation would be frustrated at disproportionate cost to the balance of payments ... the extent to which a responsible government can take expansionary measures is strictly limited when it is imperative in the interests of us all that the pace of inflation should be damped down.[6]

It is quite clear from this speech that the government was using unemployment as a weapon against wage demands; that it was deliberately taking only feeble measures to stem the flood of redundancies in the hope of weakening the bargaining position of the working class.

Yet in the same speech he also implied that high unemployment arose from the 'absurdly high pay increases' through which 'workers are pricing themselves and their fellows out of a job' and that the government, therefore, had no power to alter it. In fact the redundancies have two causes. Some firms have closed plants or reduced manning because, even though they may have had orders on hand, they had become unprofitable.* In most but not all of these instances rising wages made a contribution to this unprofitability. The outcome of these redundancies is the permanent loss of jobs.† It may not be possible to offset this first kind of redundancy through expanding demand in the private sector, since profitability may be too low to justify the necessary investment in new equipment. Even so, the government can always create jobs through public-works programmes to offset those lost in the private sector.

But a second kind of redundancy has taken place in firms which, though profitable, have for the present had insufficient orders. Those laid off would be re-engaged merely if demand expanded. Thus, although it is true that wage increases contribute to unprofitability which may cause redundancy, this does not alter the fact that the government is quite able to influence the growth of unemployment, no matter which of these two kinds of redundancy has caused it. So, even though the Treasury had underestimated the depth of the slump, the failure to curb rising unemployment by reflation during the first half of 1971 was plainly deliberate.

The Budget speech also finds the government once again dragging out the balance-of-payments situation as an argument both against reflation and in favour of moderating wage demands. The argument looked rather unconvincing in view of the current account surplus of more than £660m. in 1970.

* We are ignoring the question of whether the rapid increase in real wages may, by stimulating consumption, have led to more employment than was lost through lower investment, higher imports and lower exports. The National Institute has argued that the rapid growth of real wages actually reduced unemployment in 1970 (*Economic Review*, May 1971); this is quite consistent with it also having resulted in a permanent loss of jobs in the private sector, which is the effect we are concerned with here.

† These jobs are lost when the money value of the output is less than the money cost to the firm of the output (raw materials, wages and, in the long run, interest and depreciation on capital which could be employed elsewhere). That it is capitalistically unprofitable to provide employment in a particular plant of course in no way implies that the employment would not be socially useful.

In fact, however, the balance-of-payments position was (and is) quite precarious. The surplus in the middle of 1971 was due entirely to the low level of output reflected in a high level of unemployment which kept imports down. In August 1971 the National Institute's calculations suggested that with no further erosion of competitiveness and with full employment (level unspecified) 'the level of imports might reduce the surplus to very small proportions, and possibly turn it into a deficit'.[7] Even taking account of the rather favourable trend since August it still seems likely that bearing in mind the effect on the balance of payments of entry into the Common Market there would be a deficit at full employment. Peter Jay wrote:

It is becoming increasingly clear that behind the bland exterior of Ministerial utterances the Chancellor and the Treasury must by now be chiefly worried about what would happen to the balance of payments, if they allowed the economy to move back towards full employment in the next few years.[8]

So the government may have genuinely feared the effects of reflation on the balance of payments. Not, however, the effects themselves, but because the appropriate remedy for any new balance-of-payments deficit, devaluation, would, by raising prices, only exacerbate the basic problem of wage control. The balance-of-payments argument, therefore leads us straight back again to what must have been the real fear which accounted for the government's failure to stem the rising unemployment – that wage increases would be greater if unemployment was lower and thus working-class strength increased, making the long-term task of restoring profitability even more difficult.

In contrast to this the T.U.C. was arguing that reflationary measures could substantially reduce wage claims:

The way into the situation at the present time must be for the government to take steps to reduce indirect taxes rapidly in order to provide a real breakthrough in the prices situation, so that the money level of pay settlements can be at a more modest level.[9]

But the T.U.C.'s argument is not convincing. The July 1971 reduction in purchase tax amounted to a mere $\frac{1}{2}$ per cent off the retail price index (rather less than one month's increase at the 1971 rate of inflation). In attempting to curb wage settlements this is not much for the government to hold up in front of the unions.

When obliged to introduce reflationary measures in July 1971, Barber did not rely on the T.U.C.'s pleadings but on the C.B.I.'s 'very important price initiative' which 'created a more favourable outlook for prices', leading to the possibility of 'moderating the rate of wage inflation' which 'improves the outlook for our international competitive position'. Again it is hard to take such wishful thinking seriously. In fact the government in July was responding to the political opposition to rising unemployment and to the fear that the further collapse of investment would rapidly undermine British competitiveness in several industries. And even when they came, the measures were feeble.*

This was because the government was aware that reflation, without wage control, provided no solution to the long-term question of profitability. Again, the T.U.C. thought differently:

Changes in the rates of capacity utilization in many industries have a sharper effect on profit rates than on employment and earnings ... a recovery of the economy from its present under-employed state would particularly improve unit costs in capital intensive industries and help both margins and total profits.[10]

The T.U.C.'s concern about profits is not surprising, for they believe (correctly) that a healthy capitalism requires high profits. But they are wrong in suggesting that profit margins could be restored painlessly for the workers by an expansion of output.

Our estimate is that only about one sixth of the fall in the profit share since 1964 was the result of stagnation. Getting back to full employment, particularly over an extended period of time, could not do much more than stabilize the profit share, unless there were a drastic reduction of international competition or improvement in Britain's competitiveness. But merely maintaining the present profit share, even with higher output, is not sufficient. Given the state of international competition and the determination of British workers to maintain and improve living standards, this means that British capitalists will have no remedy but to attack

---

* If the rate of growth expected by the Treasury were achieved it would take about six years to get back to $1\frac{1}{2}$ per cent unemployment.

the working class – by attacking wages, probably in combination with devaluation.

Until the T.U.C. realizes that faster growth by itself is not enough, it will remain quite unprepared for the coming intensification of the attack on working-class living standards.

But would an increased part of the national income devoted to public expenditure offer a solution to the problem of reduced profitability? The first point is that for it to have any relevance at all to the problems of private capital, the expenditure must constitute an increase in demand for the output produced by private capital. This will be true of some civil expenditure (construction of schools, payment of unemployment benefits which increase private consumption) and some military expenditure (armaments). But both categories of expenditure contain other elements which absorb resources directly in the state sector (for example, the employment of teachers and soldiers). This latter type of expenditure leaves less resources at the disposal of private capital and so can do nothing to improve its condition.*

Still, even supposing government expenditure does keep up the level of demand for the output of private capital, it will only avert the pressure on profitability if it can neutralize its causes – wage increases and international competition (see chapter 3). If the government provides private capital with a market for its products with profitability guaranteed by cost-plus contracts, then in effect a section of private capital is removed from the competitive struggle which prevents wage increases being passed on in the form of higher prices. In this respect, arms expenditure may be more effective than civil expenditure if it employs more capital which is thereby removed from the area of competition. Also it may be politically easier to reserve defence expenditure for domestic producers than for civil expenditure. For, to improve profitability, it is absolutely necessary that the expenditure *should* be reserved for domestic producers. It would do U.K. capital no good at all if profitable contracts for armaments were allocated to the lowest cost producers if these were not from the U.K. On the other hand civil expenditure may tend to be concentrated in construction

---

*Though even these will have indirect effects, for teachers spend their pay on the output of private capital.

which, by its nature, is an industry better protected from international competition than most. Government transfers such as unemployment benefit do nothing to solve the *profitability* problem as they do not provide guaranteed profitable markets, though by increasing overall purchasing power they may help to maintain full employment.

This suggests that from the point of view of maintaining profitability government expenditure is merely a convenient way of protecting certain industries from the full blast of international competition. It is a relatively respectable form of protectionism. This means that it can only be important for a very limited number of industries – armaments obviously being the best example – and cannot be an answer to the general problem of declining profitability. It could only have some effect on the profitability of industry as a whole if the expenditure somehow moderated the pressure for higher wages. This can hardly be true of military expenditure, except during a war in which patriotic motives are exploited. But it might possibly be the case that an increase in civil expenditure, for example on health and housing, might help to moderate wage claims generally. If this happened the share of profits could perhaps rise, but it would have to do so at the expense of real wages, thus in the end renewing the wage pressure.

If higher government expenditure is to raise the proportion of national income which capitalists can invest, both these increases must be offset by lower wage earners' consumption; it therefore cannot leave the wage earner better off even if his standard of living is reckoned to include the public expenditure. Resources cannot be conjured out of the air and devoted to welfare expenditure without fewer being devoted to something else. Public expenditure does not provide a magic formula for increasing the living standard of the working class without reducing what is available for profits and investment.

7. The creation of unemployment

We have already argued in section 6 that the recent rise in unemployment was deliberate government policy. Between 1954 and

1964 unemployment was low – between 1 and 2 per cent of the labour force. Only once (in 1963) did the average number of unemployed reach half a million, and this was partially due to the exceptionally bad winter. Since 1966, however, unemployment has never been below half a million, and by January 1972 had risen to over 1 million* – higher than at any time since the 1930s, when unemployment never fell below one million and sometimes reached three million. The January 1972 figure meant that unemployment was running at nearly 4 per cent, or nearly 5 per cent for male workers only.† This was the result of the combination of very slow economic growth and the profits squeeze.

As one would expect, vacancies have moved in the opposite direction. The number of vacancies began to fall early in 1966 at the same time as the number of unemployed began to rise fast. Since then, with the exception of 1968, when they came together very slightly, they have continually diverged. For no significant

---

*The average length of unemployment has also grown. The percentage of unemployed who at any given time had been unemployed for 2 weeks or less averaged 23·2 per cent in 1963, and 14·5 per cent in June 1971. The number who had been unemployed for a year or more rose from 58,800 in April 1967 to 111,800 in April 1971. There are variations as between regions and industries. In January 1972 male unemployment was under 5 per cent in the South and some of the Midlands, but was over 9 per cent in the Northern region and in Scotland, and well over 10 per cent in Northern Ireland. Even the South East, with 3·4 per cent, faced mass unemployment. About 9 per cent of male construction workers were unemployed in June 1971, more than 5 per cent of coal miners, and almost 5 per cent of male textile workers were also out of work, while in chemicals and the engineering industries less than 3 per cent of male workers were unemployed.

Between the end of 1969 and the early months of 1971 the number of people working overtime fell by about one quarter to about 1¾ million and the average number of overtime hours worked fell from 8½ to less than 8 hours. Up to the end of 1970 short-time working had not risen very markedly and was still lower than in the 1962–3 slump; but from December 1970 it rose quickly and was more than twice as high on average in the first half of 1971 as in the first half of 1970.

†A recent analysis suggests that when all forms of under-recording are taken into account there were more than 1¼ million people out of work in Britain in September 1971 (5·5 per cent) as compared with registered unemployment of about 900,000 (Guy Standing, *New Society*, 14 October 1971). Thus registered unemployment is a considerable underestimate of those out of work.

period since the mid-fifties have there been more vacancies than unemployed.

The growth of unemployment has a purpose – to turn the advantage against the working class in bargaining for wages. Unions are expected to exert less pressure for higher wages in a climate of high unemployment and therefore of insecurity for workers, who know that if they lose a job it will be hard to find another. In the

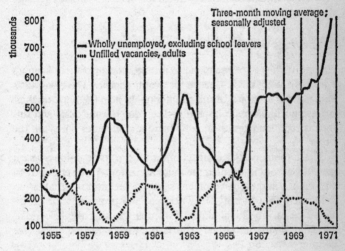

Figure 13. Unemployed and vacancies 1955–71
Source: Department of Employment Gazette, October 1971

middle of the 1960s it was generally accepted by economists that the rate of unemployment and the rate of growth of wages moved in a simple, almost mechanical, inverse relationship to each other.

Although unemployment is bound to have some effect on the workers' bargaining strength, enough has changed to make such a simple view untenable now. In fact in the last five years unemployment and the rate of growth of money wages have increased together. It has been argued that workers and trade unions are less worried than in the past about restraining wage demands during periods of high unemployment for a number of reasons: they may expect that unemployment will not rise very much; redundancy and unemployment payments and supplementary benefit may give potentially unemployed workers a greater feeling of security. This may help to explain why rising unemployment is not having its expected effect. But the increased militancy of wage demands cannot be so explained. The slow growth in living standards in the late sixties and the increasing realization of bargaining strength are the real causes.

8. Incomes policy

Capitalists have not been able to put up their prices and keep up with their wage costs – hence the profits squeeze. Devaluation as explained in section 4 of this chapter might help them put up their prices; but their main hope is to keep down wage costs and this means redundancies on the one hand and incomes policy on the other.

The Labour party's connections with the trade unions were a great asset to it in running the incomes policy. At the end of 1964 the T.U.C. and the government signed a declaration of intent on incomes with a 'norm' of $3\frac{1}{2}$ per cent and provisions for exceptional cases. The main effect of all this was that the Prices and Incomes Board published reports on which no one acted (see chapter 9, section 1).

In July 1966 the Labour government faced its second balance-of-payments crisis. It responded with a wage and price freeze, which was to be followed by six months of severe restraint in which the norm for wage increases would be zero. The zero norm in fact lasted until early 1968, when it was replaced by a $3\frac{1}{2}$-per-cent norm. The statutory freeze undoubtedly held back wages while it was in operation. Our analysis suggests that it may have held down prices even more, but that the lost profits were regained next year. Incomes policy may have had the perverse effect of encouraging high claims (if not settlements) later on. It forced the unions to offer justifications for claims, whereas such justifications had not been required in the period of a theoretically free labour market. This made it a powerful instrument of education for the labour movement at all levels. And when there was a positive norm it was undoubtedly regarded as a floor; every worker expected at least the norm and there were, under the policy, a number of legitimate loopholes through which it could be exceeded (low pay, especial growth of productivity, need to attract labour, etc.).

It was the impossibility of combining high levels of employment with moderation in wage claims and settlements which attracted so many people to incomes policy in the late fifties. But after 1967 it could no longer be seen as an alternative to unemployment and devaluation, for both had already happened. Incomes policy obviously came to be thought of as the cause of the miserable increases in living standards from 1966 on, even though these were really the result of the devaluation and deflation. The opposition became so great that by mid-1969 the Labour government was completely disarmed in the battle against wage increases. Its last year in office saw a wages free-for-all. In June 1970, when the Tories came in, there was nothing they could immediately do to stem the tide. They professed ideological hostility even to the idea of an incomes policy, though it was originally a Tory invention. But they felt in any case that the unions were unlikely to cooperate in an incomes policy while the government was putting the Industrial Relations Bill through the Commons.

An incomes policy like that of 1964 no longer provides a way out for capital. For the 1964 policy was based on freezing the distribution of income; money wages were supposed to rise in line with average productivity so that average costs would stay constant. Firms could then maintain constant profit margins by keeping prices stable (on average), and the distribution of income would be fixed as real wages grew in line with productivity.* But capital now requires that the growth in real wages should be kept well *below* the growth in productivity.† This is a deal which Vic Feather

---

* Labour's first White Paper on incomes policy was actually rather soft on prices, allowing that firms should raise prices relative to costs (so as to increase their profit margin) if 'unable to secure the capital required to meet home and overseas demand'. On the other hand it was hoped, perhaps even believed, that other firms would be able to 'reduce the return sought on investment' and cut prices which rested on excessive market power (thus reducing their profit margins).

† '... if there was to be a freeze on incomes and prices at the current

could hardly be expected to accept, even though he did move from implacably opposing the Industrial Relations Bill in March 1971 to attempting to secure agreement on a T.U.C.-operated voluntary incomes policy at the meeting of the National Economic Development Council in the next month.

Naturally, therefore, aside from the C.B.I.'s insignificant price initiative, all the attention has been concentrated on devising unilateral schemes for keeping down wage increases rather than on any agreed plan for prices and incomes. These schemes include one from a Tory M.P. and a Professor of Economics to subsidize firms incurring loss of profit from strikes which result from their resistance to wage claims; and the obverse from the *Economist* to tax firms which succumb to excessive claims. In September 1971 the government was widely reported to be considering the second plan. No doubt it is also considering taxing unions which put in excessive claims or taxing away 100 per cent of all increases in working-class incomes.* One way or another they must find a way of keeping wage increases down while allowing prices to rise.

9. The Industrial Relations Act

The failure of incomes policy and mass unemployment to protect capital from wage pressure has shifted the emphasis of governments to legal control of workers' bargaining strength. In the face of a great storm of protest from the labour movement, the Labour government was forced to abandon its Industrial Relations Bill in June 1969 in exchange for a promise by the T.U.C. to implement

* When we wrote this we meant it ironically. On 30 September 1971, however, the *Financial Times* reported on a lecture by Professor James Meade which suggested that workers who put in claims above a 'norm' set by the government should lose rights to redundancy payments and supplementary benefits. In addition the unions concerned should be liable to a tax on strike benefits paid out. Professor Meade denied that he was an advocate of union bashing and described his viewpoint as 'liberal socialist'!

level of industrial profits, this freeze would have a disastrous effect on investment . . .' (a speech by David Montagu, chairman of a merchant bank, in March 1971, quoted by Charles Levinson, *Capital, Inflation and the Multinationals*, Allen and Unwin, London, 1971).

certain reforms (later contained in the T.U.C. pamphlet *A Programme of Action*).* This defeat for the Labour government (later presented by Wilson as a triumph in which he forced the union leadership to see sense) meant that, after the crumbling of the incomes policy, there was nothing the government could do to control the wage explosion of 1970.

The Tories' Industrial Relations Act of 1971† creates a legal framework for industrial relations. All agreements between unions and employers about wages or anything else are to be legally enforceable, unless this is specifically excluded in the agreement. In the first instance administration of the Act will be in the hands of informal industrial tribunals and also of the powerful National Industrial Relations Court (N.I.R.C.). The Commission on Industrial Relations will provide a sort of probation service for the Court, and the Chief Registrar of Trade Unions and Employers' Associations will oversee the unions' constitutions. In most cases breaches of the provisions of the Act are 'unfair industrial practices' and can be prosecuted in the courts.

The attack begins with membership. Full protection of the law is now given to anyone who is unwilling to join a trade union. In other words, with minor exceptions, the closed shop[1] is outlawed.‡ In some industries this will severely weaken the workers' bargaining strength. On the other hand, some employers use closed shops as an instrument of labour discipline. A threat from the union leadership to expel a man from the union carries with it a threat of the loss of his job, without the management needing to say any-

[1] In a *closed shop* all workers must be union members.

* There were mass unofficial strikes against the Bill in February and May. Even union leaders who secretly welcomed its attempt to strengthen the union leadership relative to the rank and file were unable to support it. The pursuit of the Bill would have irrevocably split the Labour party.

† Its origins go back to a pamphlet called *A Giant's Strength*, published by the Inns of Court Conservative and Unionist Association in 1958, and *Fair Deal at Work*, published by the Tory Party in 1968. But it also revived some of the proposals of Labour's white paper, *In Place of Strife*, especially concerning a number of 'reforms' of collective bargaining.

‡ The importance of this is indicated by the fact that very nearly 4 million workers in Britain work under pre- or post-entry closed shop conditions – that is about 40 per cent of all trade-union members and about one fifth of all workers (*Donovan Report*).

thing. This is most important in those industries like the railways with very centralized management and only a few unions, where bargaining is centralized, and where local wage bargaining is not a problem.

The Act aims to control the workers' bargaining power, especially that of the shop stewards and leading rank-and-file members, through an ingenious combination of anti-strike provisions, financial penalties on the trade unions, and provisions for registration and control of union rules. The first step is to make all trade unions register with the Registrar. This is done by making non-registration very burdensome.*

The registration of a union will only be confirmed when its rules are approved by the registrar. These must include full details of the circumstances in which officials of the union (full-time or shop stewards) may call a strike. All powers and duties of shop stewards must be detailed; and this is something which many unions do not do at present. Since many of these rules have been unwritten, the need to spell them out will undoubtedly tend to reduce the nominal power of shop stewards. As one observer has pointed out, the requirements of registration could lead in practice to considerable reductions of shop steward activities:

* Workers do not have a statutory right to join a non-registered union; a non-registered union can neither become a 'sole bargaining agent' in a 'bargaining unit' nor use the machinery of the Act to obtain an agency shop – the Act's 'alternative' to a closed shop under which workers need not join the union but they can opt instead either to pay dues to the union (without being members) or to pay the same amount to charity. It cannot use the Act to impose a procedure about disputes or bargaining on the employer. 'It cannot compel an employer to disclose information about his undertaking for the purpose of collective bargaining ... and it will have a much less favourable position with regard to strike action.' (A. D. Hughes in S. Chomet, *Industrial Relations Bill*.) Officials of an unregistered union have no immunity from prosecutions for inducing breach of contract in furtherance of a trade dispute. For a registered union the limit to the fine which can be imposed for an 'unfair industrial practice' is £5,000 for a union with membership of under 5,000 and £100,000 for a union with over 100,000 members; for an unregistered union there is no limit. And the private property of its members and officials is not protected. Moreover, unregistered unions may lose tax exemption on their provident funds (worth £12m. in 1968/9 according to *The Times*, 5 July 1971). Thus the unions face difficulties if they do not register.

(a) a union may hesitate to give its stewards authority to make agreements which could become legally enforceable, if only by mistake;

(b) a union is unlikely to delegate to shop stewards the power to call a strike because of the financial risk in terms of strike pay and of possible claims on union funds resulting from unfair industrial practices;

(c) a shop steward acting outside the scope of his authority could be liable as an individual for an unfair industrial practice and be faced with a demand for compensation. He may therefore err very much on the side of caution in implementing the rules which define his authority. [11]

It is just as likely that the leadership of unregistered unions will, to avoid conflict with the government, attempt to police their members more rigorously.

In fact the Act enjoins a union to take all 'reasonably practicable' steps to prevent its members from committing an unfair industrial practice; otherwise it is itself guilty of an unfair industrial practice. In other words a union may be acting illegally if it does not try to break unofficial strikes. In these ways the union leadership would become the main defence of the employers and government against shop floor militancy. This is more subtle than an attempt at more direct control of unofficial strikes and local bargaining. The Tories obviously calculate that the Act will make workers fight their union leaders instead of their bosses.

Unofficial strikes will only be legal when notice has been given; the length of notice is the same as that required in the contract of employment. Only in this case will unofficial strike leaders have any legal protection against damages. This would probably make about 90 per cent of strikes in recent years illegal. In reacting against day-to-day management decisions about dismissals, work methods, rates of pay and many other things, the working class at shop-floor level would be shackled if the provisions of the Act were really enforced. The Act is not meant to stop all strikes, but rather the sudden unpredictable strikes against which the employer is most powerless. A Tory Minister at the Department of Employment and Productivity (Paul Bryan) said that, 'Put in one sentence *our objective is to make strikes in Britain a last resort rather than the first resort they so often are today.*' [12] Strikes are better in the Tories' view if they are national, official, taken after long notice and after the workers' demands have failed at a number of levels first. The employers, and behind them the system of industrial courts and the government, can then prepare their counter-attack.

But the Act will also reduce the likelihood of *official* strikes. At the request of the Secretary of State, the N.I.R.C. can either call for a ballot of union members, or impose a two-month deferment of the strike if it 'is likely to endanger the national economy, national security, public health or public order'; and almost any national strike could be put in this category. The industrial correspondent of the *Sunday Telegraph* concludes that

Once we become familiar with the list of unfair practices and take into account the reluctance of unions to disburse their funds in lavish compensation to employers, it becomes clear that the freedom to strike has been curtailed by the Act, if not by specific injunction, then by the possible financial deterrent.[13]

Sympathy strikes and political strikes, like those which took place against the Bill and to show solidarity with the U.C.S. workers, are specifically outlawed. So are strikes resulting from disputes between trade unions. But employers often present what are really disputes between themselves and sections of workers as inter-union disputes – this occurred, for instance, in the case of the lock-out of the National Graphical Association by Newspaper proprietors in September 1971. The Act also removes the right to picket outside people's homes; and this is an attack on collective action against scabs and blacklegs.

Edward Heath has claimed that the Act is 'a measure which gives fresh rights and fresh opportunities to the individual trade unionist'.[14] The emphasis is, of course, on 'individual' and the 'fresh rights' are mostly illusory. For example, there are provisions about unfair dismissal and the compensation which can be claimed in the N.I.R.C. Yet the employer who is found guilty of wrongful dismissal is not obliged to reinstate the workers concerned. The compensation may strike some employers as a cheap way to get rid of a militant. Similarly, the Act forbids the dismissal of individual workers for union or strike activities. It does not, however, outlaw the victimization of a whole group of workers involved in an act of indiscipline. Group victimization, like that at Pilkingtons in St Helens in 1970, remains perfectly legal.

The Act also obliges companies to release to the workers' representatives financial and other information about the Company necessary for collective bargaining purposes. But of course it is the company which decides what is necessary; and it need not reveal any information which would be 'seriously prejudicial' to it for other reasons than bargaining. In any case failure to provide information necessary for bargaining is not an 'unfair industrial practice'. Some of this information is already available for shareholders, though there is of course a contradiction for firms between the image of wealth which they aim to present to shareholders and the image of poverty which they wish to present to workers.*

Sir John Partridge, the head of the C.B.I., was speaking for most employers when he said that the C.B.I. 'strongly supports the principles embodied in the government's Industrial Relations Bill'.[15] But the *Guardian* noted that 'some employers are also deceiving themselves. They hope that when the Bill is law the judges will do their job for them.'[16] This clearly was not going to happen. In the face of the unions' opposition more than 100 of the largest companies had agreed by July 1971 that wage deals should not be made legally binding; they included Esso, Ford, British Leyland, Courtauld, British Oxygen and Hoover.[17] It was clear that, beginning with registration, there was to be a struggle over the implementation of many of the Act's provisions, not to mention the cases which might be brought under it. But the Government had certainly calculated that even if the provisions of the Act could not be implemented at once they would gain from the consternation and disunity it would cause within the trade-union movement (see chapter 9).

The success of all these government policies in redistributing income back to capital depends entirely on the reaction of the

* When the T.U.C. submitted its list of desired information to the C.I.R., the labour editor of the *Financial Times* commented (24 May 1971):

'. . . other demands such as production, distribution, sales and other costs, performance indicators, up-to-date valuations of fixed assets and stocks, and plans for expansions, close-downs, mergers and takeovers would obviously be resisted either by companies themselves or by the City for a variety of reasons.'

working class to the attack on their living standards. This is why hopes are pinned on the third group of policies which we described – those aimed at undermining the strength of the working class. Policies which redistribute income in a mechanical way (taxation or devaluation for example) are always liable to be offset by successful wage demands. The evolution of the crisis, therefore, depends increasingly on the response of the workers.

Chapter 9
Workers in the
Capitalist Crisis

1. The wages struggle

Wages in money terms have risen faster in the last two decades than in any previous twenty-year period of British history. Up to 1964 real wages also rose fast; since then, however, rising prices and higher taxation have eaten up more and more of the money increases (as shown in chapter 5). Gains have also been made not only in wages but also in hours and holidays.*

In the fifties and early sixties a gradual change was taking place in the structure of the wage-bargaining system and of the labour movement. National bargains had been very important during the war, but afterwards the focus slowly shifted to local, 'domestic' or factory agreements. This meant that rises in actual earnings tended increasingly to exceed rises in nationally agreed rates. One historian of industrial relations claims that they 'have moved almost continuously apart' since 1939.[1] Between 1955 and 1968 hourly earnings for manual workers rose on average one per cent a year faster than hourly wage rates. This difference, which is known as wages or earnings 'drift', is significant in itself, but it is not the most important aspect of the growth of domestic or shop-floor bargaining.

The strength of the shop stewards has grown steadily. There are at least 175,000 shop stewards in Britain, 2,000 of them full-time, compared with about 3,000 full-time union officers.[2] A well-known study of the car industry, for instance, decided that 'the shop steward organization has become the real union'.[3] This local organization not only helped in the negotiation of plant-level

*The proportion of workers getting more than two weeks' holiday a year rose from 6 per cent in 1963 to 60 per cent in 1970, and the proportion getting three weeks rose from 2 per cent to 54 per cent. Between 1950 and 1969 average hours worked fell slightly from 47·3 hours a week to 46·5; but the standard week fell from 43·8 hours to 40·4, so a higher proportion of work was done at overtime rates.

wage agreements but also strengthened the workers' ability to resist disadvantageous changes in work methods, and encroachments on customary rights. As one academic expert remarked, there has been 'a progressive loss of managerial control over pay and work, and therefore over labour costs, at plant level'.[4]

Falling profitability has led to disputes of increasing bitterness and frequency over wages. The weakness of the capitalists has been that in many industries they cannot endure a long strike for fear of competitors encroaching on their markets. In the sixties this led both capitalists and government into experiments with incomes policy (see chapter 8). Large sections of the trade-union leadership were willing to support this policy which they believed to be in the national interest, but they kept running into opposition from their rank and file and from the shop stewards' movement. In its first period up to 1966, incomes policy 'never impinged on company or plant level bargaining'.[5] And though the policy was strengthened, the overall growth of wages, in fact, was *higher* during the whole period of incomes policy than before. At the same time the government and the employers attempted to introduce into wage bargaining the new techniques like productivity deals which got closer to the root of the problem of rising wage costs (discussed in chapter 7, section 3). These too met growing workers' resistance, especially when inflation accelerated. Many of them were abandoned.

By 1969 the Labour government had lost faith both in such innovations in drawing up wage agreements and in a national incomes policy negotiated with the leaders of trade unions. They looked instead to a 'reform of industrial relations'; in other words, they decided to attack those sections of the working class which had been foremost in the resistance to earlier attacks on wages – in particular the shop stewards' movement. The defeat of this policy in June 1969 (see chapter 8) left the Labour government with no wage strategy and led directly to the wage explosion of 1970.

Enormous claims, owing a lot to the discontent aroused by a tiny increase in real disposable income (see chapter 5), were for more than a year remarkably successful. The change of government in June 1970 had no immediate effect and the scale of wage settlements continued to climb. The Tory government inherited no effective wage-control measures. It even lacked the tactical weapon of a bad balance-of-payments situation, a 'national' problem which had been used frequently as a propaganda device to conceal what was really at stake in wage bargaining. With a strong balance of payments from 1969 onwards, the government was forced to reveal more clearly that what was at stake was not 'national' interest but profitability.* Government incomes policy, according to a Tory statement in September 1970, was 'to require industries in the public sector to resist wage claims which could have an adverse effect on the economy of the country'. There was no short-term policy for the private sector, though some form of penalty for awarding wage increases was being prepared (see chapter 8). Hopes were now focused on the Industrial Relations Act.

Between the end of 1970 and the end of 1971 prices rose by about $9\frac{1}{2}$ per cent. The average worker would find that income tax would take a higher proportion of any increase he received than of his present income. As a result it was necessary during that period for workers to be obtaining annual wage increases of well over 9 per cent before they could even begin to feel confident that their real disposable income was going to be maintained. To get a mere one-per-cent increase in their real living standard under those conditions might require rises in money earnings of 12–15 per cent.† Anything less than this would have to be counted as an economic defeat, since it would involve a reduction in real living standards. A large proportion of workers, especially in industries which did worse than average, who obtained increases during this period were, therefore, accepting drops in their living standards;

*The Treasury in its submission to the Court of Inquiry on Electricity Pay in 1970 (Wilberforce Inquiry) argued that the 'sharp narrowing of profit margins is having adverse effects on investment plans ... This has serious implications for future growth and the balance of payments, particularly in view of the already low level of industrial investment in this country compared with that of most of our main competitors.' Cmnd 4579, p. 6.

†This tax effect would have been reduced by the cut in the standard rate of income tax which increased the disposable income of an average manual worker with 3 children by about 3 per cent. But this cut in income tax was in turn just about offset by increases in national insurance contributions, health and welfare changes and rent increases for local-authority housing (Michael Meacher, *The Times*, 3 April 1971).

for very low-paid workers the drop might have been substantial (see chapter 5). Hourly wage rates and average earnings in fact each grew about 10 per cent in this period. These are averages; some workers, like provincial company busmen, airport manual workers, nurses, manual gas workers, co-op workers, wool textile workers, postal workers and electrical workers, did worse than average; car workers, electrical contracting workers and policemen did better.

After a victory for the council workers late in 1970, the Tories' resistance to public-sector claims began to have some success, not least because the union leaders seemed surprised by the seriousness and determination of the new strategy. The power workers' work-to-rule in December 1970 was a defeat in that industrial action was abandoned in an ignominious way in the face of the government attack. In the end the result was to some extent ambiguous since the court of inquiry under Wilberforce made an award which both government and union counted as a victory. The real implications of the government's attitude were unfolded in the course of the Post Office workers' strike. After a remarkable seven-week fight the leaders suddenly and unexpectedly called off the strike and agreed to a Committee of Inquiry which awarded a settlement scarcely higher than the Post Office's offer (9 per cent instead of 8 per cent). This then was a major economic and political defeat for the workers. It was a political defeat for all workers, as well as being an economic setback for the postal workers themselves. In December 1971 the leaders of 1 million council workers recommended acceptance of wage increases of around 8 per cent, compared with settlements of between 14 per cent and 18 per cent the previous year.

For most employers in the present critical situation the need to keep wage increases as low as possible is urgent. There may even be efforts to obtain decreases in money wages, especially when these can be backed with credible threats of redundancy or even liquidation unless the workers accept them. In recent agreements the question of decreases, usually as part of a change in the salary structure, have been features of negotiations in the electricity industry (for engineers, where a reduction in the highest rates was accepted by the union), in the Midland Bank, where a proposal to cut the salaries of the top paid clerks was rejected by the union, and at a Plessey factory in Liverpool, where an attempt was made in July 1971 to impose a productivity deal which would have reduced the pay of a number of engineers who were already badly paid by local standards.[6] It is well to remember that the last period of wage cutting in recent history was that of the inter-war crisis (see chapter 2).

In early October 1971 the wage struggle, having been dormant for a while, showed signs of erupting again. In the previous six months the number of strikes and days lost had been greatly reduced and the proportion of wage settlements involving reductions in living standards seemed to be growing. But it was the calm before a storm. To undo a significant part of the last few years' damage to profitability, capital needed a respite like this to last for several years. Meanwhile, the workers in the industries where wage increases of less than 12–15 per cent had been accepted were smarting under what to them was an all-too-clear defeat. The Union of Post Office Workers and the main railway unions (N.U.R. and A.S.L.E.F.) had lodged new claims immediately, or very shortly after, the previous ones had been settled to their disadvantage. The leaders of some of the other unions who had yet to lodge claims spent some time assessing the consequences of making claims of the size which their rank-and-file members were increasingly demanding. It seemed inevitable that large claims would land the unions in difficult, painful, political struggles like those earlier in the year. These were signs of a 'hot autumn'.

The national engineering deal was to expire at the end of 1971. The engineers' leaders, as well as cancelling the 50-year-old procedure agreement, made a wage claim of 35–40 per cent together with a demand for equal pay for women, a reduction in hours to 35 and an increase in holidays to four weeks, all without loss of pay. This was at a time when output was not expected to expand for at least a year. The Engineering Employers' Federation described it as 'phenomenal'[7] and had not replied two months after it was submitted. The Shipbuilders' National Association received a similar claim with 'dismay', saying it would bankrupt the industry. Of the other large unions the miners' claim for 35–40 per cent on basic rates seemed destined to cause a major dispute. The Coal

Board in October made a 7-per-cent offer. The miners were contemplating their first national strike since 1926. Among other groups of workers who had in late 1971 lodged still unsettled claims for more than 20 per cent were the bakery workers (43–59 per cent), building workers (50 per cent and a 35-hour-week), council workers (22 per cent), farmworkers (40 per cent), London dockers (30 per cent) and railwaymen (22 per cent and better holidays).[8]

Claims of this size were explicable entirely as an effort to defend the living standards of all union members and improve those of some. Their effect in some cases, however, is to subject capital to a pressure which actually threatens its survival. This pressure is not what the union leaders intend; and they are often not even aware that it exists. As a result they were unprepared for the inevitable response. Since the wage explosion of 1970, the employers had had time to build up some political defences. This time they had the backing of the government, which was urging settlements of 6–7 per cent. They also had the Industrial Relations Act, though how that would affect immediate events was still very uncertain. (See chapter 8.)

2. The strike weapon

Since the war strikes in Britain have been frequent, mostly short and unofficial. But very recently they have tended to become not only more frequent, but also longer. The number of stoppages in 1970 (nearly 4,000) was the highest since the war. The number of working days lost through strikes grew even more. In 1969 this was more than 6 million; in 1970 it surpassed 10 million; and it had already passed this figure by the fourth month of 1971. The number of workers taking strike action in recent years is comparable to that in the seven years after the First World War, and larger still than in the pre-war years, though the strikes have been shorter.

The official figures underestimate the amount of industrial strife. They do not, for example, take account of go-slows, overtime bans and working to rule, all of which have become more common since the war (though the overtime ban is a decreasingly useful weapon in a time of crisis when anyway the amount of over-time falls). The figures also fail to pick up many of the shortest stoppages. In the motor industry (one of the most strike-prone) it was estimated in 1967 that '60 per cent of all stoppages lasted for less than four hours'.[9] Even the official figures show that roughly a quarter of all stoppages last for less than a day. As well as being short, strikes are nearly all unofficial,* which is one indication of how strong the shop stewards' movement has become.

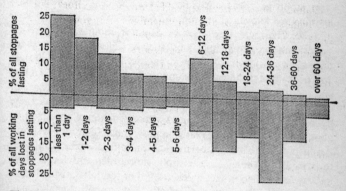

Figure 14. Proportion of all working days lost in strikes of different lengths, 1970
Source: Department of Employment Gazette May 1971, Table 5.

Although in 1970 about three quarters of strikes lasted less than a week, the average number of days lost for each striker has been rising – from 2·1 days in 1968 to 8·5 in 1971. This is the result of a growing number of very long, exceptionally bitter official disputes over wages, such as the council workers' strike of 1970, the Ford dispute and the postal workers' strike of 1971. Early in 1971 similar situations which might have emerged in the steel industry and in the railways were averted by the readiness of the union

*In the period from 1964 to 1966 the Donovan Report found that out of an annual average of 2,272 stoppages of work only 74 were official, 2 partly official, and 2,171 unofficial; the remaining 25 were lock-outs or strikes by unorganized workers. Out of the 757,800 workers involved, 653,400 were participants in the unofficial disputes, which accounted for 1,697,000 of the 2,452,000 working days lost. (*Donovan Report*, p. 97.)

leaderships involved to accept the defeat of their claim without calling strikes.

From 1940 to 1960 the proportion of strikes over 'working arrangements, rules and discipline' rose very greatly. In the view of one observer this reflects 'an implicit pressure for more democracy and individual rights in industry'.[10] That pressure has not subsided but as a cause of disputes wages have become increasingly prominent. The number of wage disputes as a proportion of total work stoppages rose from 48 per cent (52 per cent of working days lost) in 1964 to over 63 per cent (85 per cent of working days lost) in 1970. The increasing share of disputes about wage *increases* rather than other wage questions (such as differentials or rates for particular jobs) is much more dramatic, however. In 1960 only 16·6 per cent of disputes were about wage increases; by 1964 it was still only 21·4 per cent. By 1970 it had risen to 55·4 per cent. Of course, the categories in which the government presents these figures can be a bit misleading. A strike which may appear to be about a wage increase can really be about much broader questions. An example of this was the remarkable unofficial strike at Pilkingtons in 1971 where an ostensibly simple demand for a wage increase contained in fact a declaration of total dissatisfaction of the rank-and-file workers with both their union leadership and their employers.[11] Nevertheless, wages are becoming a much more important strike issue than they used to be, and this is a measure of the real economic position of workers and capital. It shows both the rising militancy of workers over wages which culminated in the wage explosion of 1970 and the increasing resistance of employers to these claims.

In the early 1920s, a period of crisis in some ways similar to the present, much of the loss of working days was due to lock-outs. Considering the present crisis, therefore, the rarity of lock-outs may seem surprising. Part of the reason is that employers have not wanted to stop production for fear of losing markets; it also reflects the employers' weaker bargaining position. In any case, it is very difficult to draw the line between strikes and lock-outs. What is thought of technically as a strike may in fact have been invited by the employers. The Ford strike of early 1971 was an example of this since the employers summarily rejected a wage claim in the sure knowledge that it would force the workers into a strike. In December 1970 the airlines (B.O.A.C. and B.U.A.) threatened a lock-out. In September 1971 the newspaper proprietors locked out the National Graphical Association over a wage demand. In this case the lock-out appeared to reflect the desperate financial position of the newspapers; other employers can be expected to follow suit. In October 1971 Coventry engineering employers, in reply to one-day-a-week strikes against their cancellation of the toolroom agreement, locked out toolroom workers for one day each week.

Another important recent development is the increase in political strikes, which are not included in official statistics. These came into prominence during the struggle about the passage of the Industrial Relations Bill in 1970 to 1971. A one-day strike on 12 December, 1970 had the support, according to the Department of Employment, of 350,000 workers. Two further one-day stoppages were called on 1 March and 18 March, 1971, this time with the support of the A.E.F. and the T.G.W.U. Strike action against the Bill ceased after the narrow defeat of this strategy at the special T.U.C. Congress on the matter on 18 March. Later in the year the government's plans for large-scale redundancies after the liquidation of Upper Clyde Shipbuilders provoked strikes and a huge demonstration on Clydeside. And strikes against unemployment were planned in the autumn.

But in a way strikes about wages are becoming equally political. Given that the Tory government's wages policy is part of a programme to rescue British capitalism, a strike against that wages policy is a strike against capitalism, and hence is really political. A wage claim is increasingly likely to result in a confrontation with the government. In nationalized industries this, of course, is important from the outset – as in the electricity work-to-rule of late 1970 and the postal workers' strike of early 1971. The government treated both these disputes as political struggles. The tactics against the electricity workers included scarcely-veiled incitements to public violence against the workers by cabinet ministers on radio and television. The only people who failed to accept the nature of these disputes were the trade-union leaders. Everyone else, including the government, the press and most of the workers, had little doubt that they were political.

In both public and private industry the political relevance of strikes in the immediate future will be partly decided by the way in which the anti-strike provisions of the Industrial Relations Act are implemented. The imposition of fines on unofficial strikers, or the frequent use of the forced strike ballot or the 60-day cooling-off period could very quickly escalate the political significance of wage demands and strikes. The exact effects depend on the position adopted towards the government and the rank-and-file workers by the union leadership, whom the Act attempts to use as an anti-strike police force.

3. The strategy of the unions

Membership of unions grew from 10·3 to 11 million in 1970, a bigger rise than the total increase over the previous nine years. But at a time when the British working class is more than ever organized into trade unions, its official leadership is economically and politically blind. While British capitalism has entered a crisis which it may not survive, the trade-union leaders behave as though capitalism will muddle on for ever.

The most obvious weakness of the trade-union movement is its disunity. This was clearly a main cause of some of the defeats over wages which occurred in the first half of 1971. The Tory government was determined to resist wage increases of more than 8 per cent in the public sector. One by one the unions in public-sector industries – the Post Office, the electricity industry, the steel-workers, the railways – submitted their claims; one by one they confronted the government, and one by one they suffered defeat in varying degrees. There were even crucial disagreements between unions in the same industry. The railway unions, for instance, could not agree about industrial action; and the Union of Post Office Workers received scarcely any assistance from the Post Office Engineers. An attempt by Tom Jackson, the postal workers' leader, to establish a joint pay strategy in the public-sector unions over the months after his strike's ignominious defeat, achieved almost nothing. In August 1971 the unions concerned and the T.U.C. could agree to do no more than exchange information.

Table 9.1. Facts about Strikes, 1960–71

	No. of stoppages	Wage disputes as % total No. of stoppages	Wage increase disputes as % of total stoppages	Total No. Working days lost '000	% Working Days lost in wage disputes	No. of Workers involved '000	Average No. days lost per worker
1960	2,849	48·9	16·6	3,024	43·5	819	3·7
1961	2,701	48·6	17·1	3,046	65·6	779	3·9
1962	2,465	45·9	15·5	5,798	75·3	4,423	1·3
1963	2,081	46·2	18·5	1,755	69·1	593	3·0
1964	2,535	47·9	21·4	2,277	51·9	883	2·6
1965	2,365	50·1	27·5	2,925	56·1	876	3·3
1966	1,951	45·6	22·3	2,398	68·6	544	4·4
1967	2,133	46·6	30·2	2,787	57·7	734	3·8
1968	2,390	51·7	38·9	4,690	75·9	2,258	2·1
1969	3,146	57·2	49·5	6,846	57·0	1,665	4·1
1970	3,943	63·1	55·4	10,980	84·7	1,801	6·1
1971	2,223	52·0	39·9	13,558	n.a.	1,173	11·5

Source: Department of Employment, *Gazette.*

Disunity was partly the result of inability or unwillingness to recognize the attack on the working class for what it was. The General Secretary of the T.U.C., Vic Feather, realized that 'unemployment is being used as an economic policy',[12] but our analysis shows that this ought to be understood in a wider context. For whatever the level of overall demand and employment in the economy, British capital will either have to restore some of its lost profitability at the expense of the working class, or die. Unemployment is part of the capitalists' strategy for survival because it is likely to weaken the bargaining position of the workers and their ability to resist reductions in their real wages. Unemployment is now exposing, as it did in the 1930s, the weakness which results from disunity. Although the T.U.C. has protested about the level of unemployment, unions often do not keep their former members when they become unemployed. Their voice is therefore excluded from the organized labour movement and their position weakens the bargaining strength of those who remain at work. A direct fight against unemployment would throw the unions into a more direct conflict with the government; and this may be why so many union leaders shirk it. The T.U.C.'s day of action in November 1971 against unemployment contained no call for strike action.

The almost universal trade-union demand for rapid reflation in these circumstances is being firmly resisted because it will cause little direct improvement in profitability and may worsen it through intensifying wage pressure. (See chapter 8.) The unions' faith in reflation is misplaced. There is no economic solution to the crisis in which the interests of capital and labour can be satisfied at once.

When the boilermakers' leader, Dan McGarvey, asserted that 'The employers will complain about the effect on their profits, but they should come along with us',[13] he only succeeded in showing that he did not understand that the essence of the situation was a clash between labour and capital. The same applied to the A.U.E.W. General Secretary, Jim Conway, when he claimed not to understand 'why we look on profit as a dirty word. It is in our own interests, and we have got a vested interest in the profitability of a company.'[14] In October 1971 Vic Feather repeatedly argued that 'management and unions must work more closely together to stop the slide to economic disaster, since the government's policy is to stand aloof.' [15]

The mistaken ideas of the union leaders that reflation could solve everything and that the economic interests of capital and labour coincide are linked to a misunderstanding of the wage struggle. (See chapter 8, section 6.) We have argued that the growth of wages in the 1950s and 1960s contributed to the present crisis. This does not mean that the unions were wrong to press their demands, however: quite the opposite. To begin with, the unions are right to argue against the Tory wage strategy by saying that 'the workers in one industry cannot be expected to accept a moderation of their wage claims merely on general arguments about inflation . . . or . . . unless the workers concerned were satisfied that there would be some compensating policies elsewhere'.[16] But there is a more fundamental point. The unions exist to advance and protect the workers' wages and conditions; but when the wage struggle really does threaten the survival of the capitalist system, as it does now in Britain, it is time for workers not to moderate their wage demands but to destroy the system which exploits them and for whose difficulties they will otherwise have to suffer. They must see through the argument that they should reduce their wage claims in the national interest; the interest which moderation serves is really that of the capitalists.

The official trade-union leaders are at present far from acknowledging this consequence of the wage struggle. They are right to argue, as Jack Jones, leader of the T.G.W.U., did recently, that 'only the unions, by putting purchasing power in the hands of our members, have kept unemployment at the level it is. Without our action in stimulating consumption, unemployment could have been ½m. higher.'[17] But the union leaders go wrong when they attempt to cover up the fact that increasing wages are one of the causes of falling profit margins, which provoke the failures, redundancies and low investment with which the capitalists have responded.

In another way the trade-union leaders conceal the real strength of the labour movement by belittling the importance of strikes. The T.U.C. report to the Special Congress on the Industrial Relations Bill spoke of 'the fiction that the British economy is

being threatened by industrial disputes'. The Mineworkers'
General Secretary, Laurence Daly, said at the Congress that it was
'essential to expose the fallacy about the impact on the British
economy of strikes both official and unofficial'.[18] Of course, as
many people point out, sickness and injuries lose many more
working days every year than strikes; but they are wrong to conclude that sickness should give capitalism more concern than
strikes. Sickness seldom stops a production line and 'sick people
do not raise wages'.[19] Strikes, because they obtain real gains for
the workers, are a more powerful threat to the capitalist system
than most union leaders are prepared to admit.

The British trade-union leaders do not deny the existence of
conflicts between capital and labour. Too often, though, they act
on the assumption that some mutually satisfactory compromise is
possible. The movement does not realize that the distribution of
income between capital and labour *can* be altered; and it denies
that there is any fundamental contradiction between capital and
labour or that capitalist crises occur because of this contradiction.
Such an attitude was a feature of the contributions from both left
and right of the trade-union leadership in the Special Congress of
the T.U.C. against the Industrial Relations Bill in March 1971.
(See chapter 8.) There was underlying acceptance of the need for
'improving industrial relations'. Jack Jones said that 'other, more
peaceful measures than the Industrial Relations Bill could have
been adopted to reduce industrial disputes'. Frank Chapple of the
Electricians said that 'the whole exercise, which divides the nation
from top to bottom, is to a large extent self-defeating'. Hugh
Scanlon of the A.U.E.W. spoke of unifying the trade-union movement 'around industrial action in order to bring some common
sense to the government who are determined to destroy the trade-
union movement'. But our economic argument shows that the
government did not lack common sense; its attempt to crush the
unions was, in its own terms, completely rational. Its reasons for
introducing the Bill can only be understood as an attempt to help
capitalism weather its crisis. (See chapter 8.)

The T.U.C. attitude to incomes policy is another example of
lack of political and economic understanding. In 1971 the leaders
of the T.U.C., in spite of their verbal opposition to so many of the

Tory government's policies and especially to the Industrial Relations Act, were still prepared, even anxious, to be given a chance to participate in the planning of the economy along with the government and the C.B.I.; they were even arguing for the renewal of incomes policy in order to combat inflation. Yet the only incomes policy acceptable to the C.B.I. and the Tory government at present is one which will guarantee a major reduction in the growth of wage levels in order to restore lost profitability (see chapter 8). The government, unlike the T.U.C., does not see higher unemployment and an incomes policy as alternative policies.

There are likely to be more and more liquidations, closures and redundancies as capitalists try every available method for reducing their costs (see chapter 7). This means that the labour movement will face tactical challenges for which its experience over the last 25 years has given it absolutely no preparation.

In a number of recent strikes, especially in the shipbuilding industry, the employers have made the threat that, unless the strike ends, the firm will be forced into liquidation. This threat was made specifically in the strike of 70 boilermakers at Cammell Laird in April 1971; and it had some effect in ending the strike, though not until the supposed deadline had passed. Later in the year a strike of general shipyard workers in the Swan Hunter yards was met by a statement by the head of the group, Sir John Hunter, to the effect that a continuation of the strikes and leapfrogging wage demands in the yard would make liquidation inevitable; but he did not fix a date. This threat may be used more by the employers; the Engineering Employers' Federation (E.E.F.) made a similar threat in August 1971. The growth of liquidations is giving it some credibility (see chapter 6, section 3). But employers can hardly wonder at its general ineffectiveness after years of total concealment of all company information from the workers, after the well-known window-dressing of accounts and after capitalists' chronic lamentations about lack of profits. Besides, a threat of liquidation is a two-edged weapon, since a firm which advertises difficulties is not going to find it easy to raise loans.

In 1971 one thousand workers were laid off every day. Most of these redundancies have not been seriously resisted by the trade unions. It is often in the political interests of the leaders to lose members as long as they can get benefits for those who remain at work. In this way ambitious trade-union leaders can be obstacles to working-class unity. But there are increasingly numerous examples of walk-outs and strikes in opposition to redundancy. In September 1971 such strikes occurred in British Aircraft Corporation factories, where production of the Concorde was halted, in the Perkins Diesel engine company in Peterborough, and by A.S.T.M.S. members at G.E.C.-E.E. plants when the company refused to negotiate a redundancy agreement. These tactics had some success. British Leyland had to withdraw 750 redundancy notices at its Birmingham van-body plant in October 1971 in response to a week's strike by the whole workforce and a threat to occupy the factory. Dartmouth Auto Testings were forced to withdraw 110 redundancy notices for foundry workers in Smethwick after a protest march through the town by 1,000 workers. But a proposed strike against 3,000 redundancies at B.S.A. in November 1971 collapsed in the face of threats by the company to go into liquidation. And at the Perkins factory at Peterborough the draughtsmen were reported to have offered to cut their working week and take a cut in pay to save seven workers from redundancy.[20] This shows a real sense of solidarity, but it is no way to fight redundancy. It is completely defensive and, through work-sharing, simply serves to spread the burden of exploitation more evenly over the working class.

A clearer expression of the workers' militancy is the growth of factory occupations or threats of them. In September the Plessey electronics factory in Alexandria, Dumbartonshire, was occupied when the company attempted to close the factory; a similar occupation was being threatened at the Waltham factory of G.E.C. Semiconductors. But up to October 1971 the most important case was the occupation since June of the four yards of Upper Clyde Shipbuilders after government plans to close down two of them had been announced following the company's bankruptcy. The government never wavered from this plan, though it attempted to weaken the workers by periodic hints that it would consider changes, and even encouraged a remarkable alliance between the shop stewards leading the occupation and a Scottish millionaire, Archibald Kelly, who seemed ready to buy all four yards in the unlikely event that the government would give him the financial aid they had refused to U.C.S. It was an impractical plan but it gained time for the government. The government used the several weeks' respite to implement some redundancies although many of the redundant workers continued to work, paid by a levy on their mates. The government also expected that the period of false hopes would allow some of the workers' funds and determination to be exhausted. In September the government gave its support to Govan shipbuilders, a new company headed by Hugh Stenhouse, Treasurer of the Scottish Conservative Association, which planned to keep open two of the yards as the Tories had intended all along.

The U.C.S. workers organized themselves against this campaign, in particular refusing to have the four yards considered separately. They got massive spontaneous support throughout the country, but little of this got transferred into an effective strategy in the labour movement. While Anthony Wedgwood Benn, on a visit to the Clyde for the Labour party, expressed great enthusiasm for the workers' action in occupying the yard, the labour leaders did little to back this up. The Scottish T.U.C. concentrated on pressuring the government to improve the employment position in Scotland in general, and the T.U.C. advocated a development authority for Clydeside. Dan McGarvey, the leader of the union to which most of the U.C.S. workers belonged, after standing aloof for some time, intervened at the end of September to negotiate with the management of the new company. He agreed with them that the four yards of U.C.S. should be broken up; and in exchange they decided to 'consider' whether they might take on three rather than two yards. Thus the stand of the U.C.S. workers was sabotaged.

An open clash between the U.C.S. workers and the liquidator or the government was avoided up to the end of 1971 for two reasons. First, the government and liquidator shrewdly kept holding out new hopes that many of the jobs could be saved, while for the time being they did not need to break the occupation which had not by then interfered directly with their own intentions and policies. Second, the leaders of the occupation and the others who claimed to speak for the workers had been proposing solutions (more subsidy and less redundancy) which, while they did not fit in with the government's economic policy, still amounted to demands that the government should do something to help out by subsidizing some private company to run all the yards, or else that the workers should run them as cooperative ventures inside a capitalist economy. But it was the working of the capitalist system which had brought U.C.S. to a position of bankruptcy and which made it essential that some of its capital had to be scrapped and some of its workers lose their jobs; in addition both the government and potential new managements insisted that profitable operation of the remaining yards would depend on the 'right' wage agreements being made with the workers. Under capitalism, therefore, the problem of the U.C.S. failure could not be solved without substantial cuts in the living standards of the workers; the only question was which workers should suffer most.

In January 1972 workers occupying the Fisher-Bendix plant of the Thorn electrical group obtained a settlement which gave at least partial, temporary guarantee of work for most of the 600 threatened with redundancy by the plant's closure. The Plessey workers got a similar settlement at the same time. But these relatively small occupations, unlike U.C.S., had not directly involved the government.

The workers of U.C.S. (or of the many other firms which are likely to face similar problems) cannot win a fight against the government without the support of the working class in the country as a whole. That unity is very unlikely to develop around detailed demands about how many yards or plants, how many redundancies or how much subsidy there should be in individual firms. It could, however, develop around genuinely socialist demands – for the nationalization of the enterprise without compensation and under workers' control, for its continued operation regardless of profitability in capitalist terms until alternative work can be found, that is, for the right to a job. Maybe such demands would not have changed what the government or potential buyers of U.C.S. would have done in 1971; it is something which would have much more immediate impact when an occupation occurs not in a bankrupt factory, which the capitalists do not want, but in one which is profitable.

Situations, such as that which arose at U.C.S. in 1971, along with many other effects of the crisis which we have mentioned, are making clear to growing numbers of workers, if not to the union leaders, the irrationality and injustice of the capitalist system. And they are focusing attention on the political steps which are necessary for the building of a more rational and juster socialist alternative.

Chapter 10
Politics

Trade unions work well as centres of resistance against the en-croachments of capital. They fail partially from an injudicious use of their power. They fail generally from limiting themselves to a guerrilla war against the effects of the existing system, instead of simultaneously trying to change it, instead of using their organized forces as a lever for the final emancipation of the working class, that is to say the ulti-mate abolition of the wages system. (Karl Marx – *Wages, Price and Profit*, p. 55.)

World capitalism is now experiencing critical economic changes which are helping to undermine 25 years of relative political stabi-lity both between and within the capitalist centres. Political events and prospects in Britain should be seen first against this political background.

At the end of the Second World War the major capitalist coun-tries, except for the United States, were economically weak, and some of them physically devastated. Initially under United States patronage, and later more independently, most capitalist countries reconstructed their economies with astonishing speed. 'Economic miracles' were performed in Western Europe and Japan. In the United States and Britain, however, there was nothing miraculous. The secret of rapid economic growth, of expanding trade, and of increasing accumulation of capital, eluded them.

Underdeveloped countries suffered too. Their share of world output fell, even though their share of the world's population was rising. The gap in average incomes between underdeveloped and advanced countries has widened very greatly. It seems likely that this new prosperity of capitalism has been accompanied by a deterioration in the standards of living of most people in under-developed countries. In most underdeveloped countries small groups have of course benefited from capitalist expansion; and these have usually held political power too, often with the economic or even military help of the large capitalist nations. On those occasions when governments pledged to reform have taken over political power, they have hardly ever succeeded. The combined power of groups at home and abroad which showed a vested interest in maintaining the *status quo* has usually been too much for them.

Published figures suggest that a colossal amount of capital – in the form of official loans and grants and also of private investment – has moved from the developed, capitalist countries to underdeveloped countries since the war. But much of this money flows straight back to the developed capitalist economies. Countries may receive aid only in return for a promise to buy certain products from the donor country, which may be sold at high prices; interest will be paid from the developing country, and profits will be 'repatriated'. And, of course, there is massive scope for corruption. A few underdeveloped countries appear to have had enormous success in expanding their exports to the developed, capitalist countries. But, in doing so, they have made themselves completely dependent on markets whose continued existence they cannot rely on. As a result of the present crisis these markets may disappear, either through a collapse of demand or through an increase in protectionism. At the height of their prosperity the developed capitalist economies have done little or nothing to help the underdeveloped countries; and now that they are beset with economic problems themselves, the underdeveloped countries are liable to be forced to suffer too.

Post-war prosperity improved the material living standard of many though by no means all of the people in advanced capitalist countries. At least the mass unemployment and terrible uncertainty, which had formerly been the normal experience of the working class, were significantly reduced. From the early 1960s, however, all the major capitalist economies ran into problems which threatened to make continued expansion and prosperity impossible. The growth of international trade and investment which had sustained the prosperity of the fifties became a source of increasingly threatening competitive pressure.

At the same time economic expansion had changed the expectations of the workers. To varying degrees in different countries, they came to expect steadily growing wages against a background of secure employment; and, when they were thwarted, they were correspondingly more militant. Everywhere these expectations of the working class came into increasingly open conflict with the capitalists' need for profitability and competitiveness.

The effects of these pressures have typically been felt in three areas. First, private capital has suffered a setback in profitability. Second, capital accumulation and economic growth have been jeopardized. And third, the working class has become more aware of and more angry about the way their lives are dominated by decisions over which they have no control. These effects are common to the individual capitalist countries.

At the same time, the great expansion of world trade and investment has meant that the economies of different capitalist countries have increasingly become interlocking pieces of capitalism as an international system. This has increased each country's vulnerability to foreign competition; and that has been decisive in threatening profitability. Capitalist governments, though they have a common interest in combining against the working class, have in practice been more divided by international competition. And the system of fixed exchange rates established after the war to provide a stable basis for world trade has become more and more of a battlefield.

The level at which each country's exchange rate was fixed determined how competitive its exporters could be, given the wages they had to pay. Countries whose capitalists were doing well (and which had balance-of-payments surpluses as a result) were unwilling to revalue their currencies and undermine the competitive power of their capitalists. Nor did they want to control wages, which they would have had to do if they were to maintain profits after revaluation. But the enormous increase in the amount of money which large corporations can move around internationally makes it very hard to resist the pressure to revalue, since governments fear that the inflow of 'hot' money may increase inflation.

The dollar crisis of 1971 took the conflict over exchange rates to a new level with the United States imposing a tax on imports which would be removed only when Japan and other countries had been forced to revalue. It presented the prospect of a trade war between the major capitalist countries, and this would inevitably have led to a widespread slump. The deteriorating economic conditions in the major capitalist countries have made world currency crises both more severe and more dangerous; and currency problems themselves aggravate the problems which give rise to them.

For instance, the currency crisis of late 1971 threatened simultaneously to damage the booming capitalism of Japan, to intensify competition in Europe if Japanese producers lost part of their American market, and because of Nixon's wage freeze to worsen the relations of capital and organized labour in the United States. The effects of a shock in one part of the system can be felt in many places.

These economic conditions in the world capitalist system are causing increasing political turbulence both internationally between countries and at the national level between classes. But politics affects the economic situation too. For instance, the French government had to devalue after the political events of May–June 1968 and the problems of Italian capitalism have an important political basis. And it is not only through their economic effects that political events in one country influence the international economic situation. They can also act, as they often have in the past, as an inspiration to political action in other countries. In these ways the influence of economic and political events in other capitalist countries will be transmitted to Britain.

We have tried to show in this book how the economic crisis of capitalism is especially severe in Britain. What is now likely to develop out of this situation? There seem to be several possibilities. First, the present crisis could drag on for some time to come with neither capitalists nor workers making any decisive move. This would mean economic stagnation, more company liquidations and redundancies, high and possibly rising unemployment, and also the continuation of high wage claims and settlements partly wiped out by rising prices. But this situation is not at all stable. One side or the other is almost certain to get the advantage. And the working class can only do this if armed with a realistic political strategy. As long as the fight is conducted according to the capitalist rules then the capitalists have the most effective weapons: the threat of bankruptcy, redundancies and higher unemployment, and the ability to manipulate taxation and the exchange rate.

If the capitalists are victorious the real wages of the workers will be reduced, or at the very least their growth will be drastically held back for several years. There is a chance that the capitalists may be able to achieve this, as they have in the past, without much of a struggle; they may get the cooperation of a trade-union leadership prepared to hold down working-class living standards for fear of worse economic consequences. Without this cooperation capital will attempt to weaken workers' organizations through growing political attack.

The only way working-class living standards can now be protected is through a successful revolutionary struggle. And this would also open the way to eliminating all the poverty, inequality and oppression of the capitalist system.

We have shown that the fall in the profitability of capital, in an internationally competitive atmosphere, has been greatly accelerated by working-class wage pressure. This may make it sound as though we are arguing on the side of capital against the workers. After all, capitalists always say they cannot afford to pay higher wages. But our findings ought to strengthen and not weaken the working class if they are interpreted in the right way. We have shown that capitalism will be unable to continue accepting the rate of wage increase which has prevailed in the recent past without jeopardizing its own existence. This means that the working-class leaders must adopt a new attitude to wage demands: they must realize that wage claims are becoming political weapons in a battle in which the existence of capitalism is at stake.

And although the last two decades of working-class pressure on wages has been unusually successful, we have shown that there is no longer any plausibility in the reformist idea that wage claims are the only issue that workers' leaders need to bother about. The very success of struggles based on the narrow reformist perspective which never challenges the system has made reformism outdated and irrelevant. The struggle for living standards has become a political struggle.

We are not saying that present trends will somehow lead capitalism to fall automatically. On the contrary, the capitalist class in Britain is preparing an economic and political counter-offensive. The Conservative government was formed in June 1970, at a moment when the economic condition of capital was worsening fast after the Labour government, for nearly a year, had provided no effective support for capital against the wage attack. This represented a very sharp turn to the right in British government policy. There was no sign of the so-called liberalism of the Tory administrations of the 1950s and early 1960s. There was a clear understanding within the Tory government of the necessity of resisting any further encroachment on profits.

The sophisticated incomes-policy strategy was replaced by a cruder plan in which the working population was attacked by unemployment, the Industrial Relations Act, cuts in public social expenditure, and fierce resistance to wage claims in the public sector. There seemed no basis for compromise in relations between a Tory government with these intentions and the organizations of the working class.

By the end of 1971, although the attempt to implement the Industrial Relations Act had only just begun, there was no sign that the Tories' other policies in support of capital were beginning to work, since the fall in the share of profits had not been significantly reversed. It is predictable, therefore, that the Tory government will be forced towards more ferocious policies.

Between 1964 and 1970 the Labour government tried to serve two masters. It would not challenge capitalism, so it tried to support it; but it could not make its policy acceptable to the trade unions on whom it depended. Such contradictions are bound to beset a working class party in power, if it does not oppose capitalism but tries instead to make it run more efficiently and more humanely.

In 1971, in opposition, the Labour party naturally took, in words at least, a move to the left, though its credibility in doing this was still sadly compromised by its recent actions when in power. But some left-wingers were brought into the shadow cabinet, the Industrial Relations Act was opposed (though quite ineffectively and on the grounds that it would provoke militancy) and new measures of public ownership were incorporated into party policy. At the annual party conference resolutions were passed for the nationalization of banks and insurance companies, though against the advice of the leadership.

None of these moves, however, involve any basic change in the Labour party leaders' attitude towards the capitalist system. They persist in asserting that the economic crisis is simply a question of inadequate demand and would be solved by a policy of government spending. Our analysis, however, has shown that such reformist policies are based on illusions about the present condition of British capitalism. The British working class must not be taken in by them.

But the proposals of most trade-union leaders stick closely to Labour party policy. During the last years of the Labour government the leaderships of the unions and the party drifted apart for a time, on the question of incomes policy and Industrial Relations legislation. But when the Tories attacked, the trade-union leaders forgot their differences with the Labour party. This was in spite of the fact that the party was still led by Harold Wilson and Barbara Castle, who had tried so hard in office to implement anti-union policies and did not seem penitent out of office.

There is a grave danger that now, as on many occasions in the history of capitalism in Britain, the leaders of the working class will fail to face the contradiction between the workers' demands and the ability of the system to meet them; that they will fail to carry the fight to a higher political level; and that they will obstruct the development of a revolutionary strategy.

This is the lesson of Black Friday, 1921. That day marked, as one historian wrote recently, 'the end of the romantic notion that the Labour movement, through its own solidarity, could challenge economic facts *without* challenging the government and society of which these economic facts were a part'. [1] The terrible condition of the working class during the long inter-war crisis was due to the failure to make that challenge.

Yet in 1968 George Woodcock, then General Secretary of the T.U.C., said:

We have to oppose governments' policies but in the end I do not want to get into a fight with the Government. There is no future in getting into fights with governments in the kind of world in which we live today.[2]

If British workers follow this defeatist line their future will be bleak. They will find better advice about the choices which face the labour movement at a time of economic crisis in this statement by Trotsky:

... the trade unions in the present epoch cannot simply be the organs of democracy as they were in the epoch of free capitalism and they cannot any longer remain politically neutral, that is limit themselves to serving the daily needs of the working class. They cannot any longer be anarchistic, i.e. ignore the decisive influence of the state on the life of people and classes. They can no longer be reformist, because the objective conditions give no room for any serious and lasting reforms. The trade unions of our time can either serve as secondary instruments of imperialist capitalism for the subordination and disciplining of workers and for obstructing the revolution, or, on the contrary, the trade unions can become the instruments of the revolutionary movement of the proletariat.[3]

The capitalist crisis is converting the fight for the rights, wages and conditions of the workers into a simultaneous fight for a revolutionary political strategy inside the labour movement. This is clear to a growing number of workers in Britain. But the desperate underlying economic situation of capitalism, which makes these tasks so urgent now, is not realized widely enough. There is still a need for information and the correct analysis of it. It is this aspect of the political struggle for socialism to which we hope this book will make a contribution.

The way that capitalism deals with economic problems is anarchic, inhumane and irrational. So the economic crisis makes the success of a revolutionary movement and the building of a better system more urgent.

Socialism resulting from revolutions in the advanced countries will have little in common with what has passed for socialism in countries with Social Democratic or Labour governments or in the U.S.S.R. and Eastern Europe. By abolishing the private ownership of capital and redistributing income a socialist system could almost immediately provide a decent standard of life for everyone. By planning what is produced and how much is invested socialism could ensure that living standards improve and that production reflects social need and not the quest for private profit. Changes

215

could be made in an orderly way without workers needing to suffer periods of hardship and unemployment. Working methods could be democratically controlled by the workers themselves. A real contribution could be made to economic development in poorer countries. It is the pursuit of profit which prevents these things from happening now.

However obvious its failures or however deep its economic crisis, the capitalist system is not going to just collapse. Its supporters will continue to attempt to implement policies which will preserve it. It needs therefore to be dislodged by conscious and organized political action.

Postscript

1. Profits and growth

Economic trends in late 1971 and early 1972 have showed a large drop in inflation to about 6 per cent a year, stagnant industrial production and the continued climb of the unemployment figures well beyond the million mark. In 1971 the share of profits in the national income rose somewhat – from 10 per cent in the first half of the year to 11·1 per cent in the second.* (For earlier figures see appendix Table C.1.)

For several reasons this cannot be taken as any indication of a permanent reversal of the profits squeeze. First, although by January 1972 the annual rate of wage increase was down to $8\frac{3}{4}$ per cent, the preceding months had been a period of 'phoney war' in the wage struggle as negotiations proceeded on the large claims lodged in the summer of 1971 (see pp. 193–4). The success of the miners gave another sharp upward push to the wages index, and other claims were being militantly pursued. Second, a good deal of the gains in profitability came not from the home market, where price increases were slowing down, but from the export market where there was an exceptionally high rise in British prices; this meant temporarily higher profits but long-term loss of markets. Moreover international competition threatened to become more severe in the wake of the international money crisis. Third, part of the gain in profitability came from a large increase in productivity (6 per cent in 1971) which was a result of the continued surge of redundancies.

Productivity may continue to increase fast if the Treasury's prediction (and the T.U.C.'s aim) of 5 per cent annual growth of

*The second figure is adjusted down by 0·2 per cent to remove the strictly once-for-all effect of reducing the Selective Employment Tax.

production up to 1973 is achieved. There is good reason, however, to doubt the feasibility of this, especially of the prediction that exports would grow by 6 per cent. This seemed highly optimistic in view of a recent decline in export volume, an estimated 5 per cent loss of competitiveness of British products in 1971, and the prospect of at best only a small acceleration in the growth of world trade in 1972. The forecast 12 per cent rise in private industrial investment in 1972 also seems unlikely. For there was a 10 per cent fall in manufacturing investment in the last quarter of 1971 and profit prospects and confidence received a severe setback from the miners' strike. In any case even the achievement of the growth target would not fundamentally alter the deep problems facing British capitalism. It would at most reduce the unemployment rate by $\frac{1}{2}$ per cent a year. And a year or two of expansion could not restore profit margins to anywhere near their early 1960s level without a successful attack on real wages (see pp. 61–4, 133–5).

2. The budget and the coming devaluation

The budget of April 1972 implicitly recognized the seriousness of the profitability situation by a £365m. p.a. increase in the value of investment incentives, now worth 35 per cent of the cost of investment (compare appendix Table F.1). These, together with the £35m. assistance to U.C.S., £50m. to the shipping industry, £10m. of special government orders for the machine-tool industry and the creation of the Industrial Development Board to consider specific cases for financial assistance, mark a total reversal of the lame duck policy (see pp. 165–6). Also, contrary to their avowed aim of increasing investment at home, the government relaxed restrictions on overseas investment (see pp. 147–50).

The budget also contained a long list of new tax concessions to the rich (see also p. 160). Death duties were cut by about one third (£150m.); there was favourable treatment for executives buying shares in their own firm; tax relief was granted on interest payments exceeding £35, that is on large loans only.* Meanwhile

*This means that the effective rate of interest to a surtax payer can be

workers getting less than £19 a week will not benefit from the increase in tax allowances. And old-age pensions rose by a pathetically small 75p.

In the budget speech the Chancellor hinted strongly that future balance-of-payments problems would be met with devaluation. The government has apparently learned the lesson that devaluation is a necessary weapon in capital's struggle to improve profits. But the weapon is not as strong as it looks. First, a further devaluation, by reducing the growth of real wages and consumption below that of output (see pp. 105–7, 166–8), would again prove an instant stimulus to wage pressure.* Second, as the monetary crisis of 1971 showed, it may be very difficult for one government to devalue when and by how much it wants.

3. The international monetary settlement

The realignment of exchange rates agreed in Washington in December 1971 resulted in an effective devaluation of the dollar by about $7\frac{1}{4}$ per cent against the average of other currencies. Italy devalued slightly while other countries revalued upwards – Japan by 13 per cent, Germany by $6\frac{1}{2}$ per cent, the U.K. by 2 per cent and France by 1 per cent. The dollar devaluation was less than the U.S. government wanted but it has created a serious situation for the exporting industries in Germany and Japan. Japanese exports are expected to fall by around 10 per cent and home sales to suffer from a 10 per cent increase in imports; German exports

*Recently a prominent Labour economist has argued that the failure to devalue in 1966 was 'largely responsible for the deterioration on the home front – notably with respect to rising prices, worse industrial relations and higher unemployment – in the last two years of the Labour Government'. (W. Beckerman, *The Labour Government's Economic Record 1964–70*, Duckworth, London, 1972, p. 63). But the only certain thing about an earlier devaluation is that the wage explosion it provoked would also have come sooner. And as events in 1969 and 1970 proved, the government's only policy for dealing with that was maintaining unemployment.

down to about 1 per cent, compared with over 20 per cent commonly paid on hire purchase loans.

are expected to fall by 8 per cent. And as exporters struggle to keep their markets they will be forced to accept slimmer profit margins. Exchange-rate adjustments can redistribute profits between countries; but the intensification of competition will tend to reduce profits overall so limiting further expansion (see pp. 98–102). Protectionist sentiment grew: the Chairman of I.C.I., explaining why its profits had virtually halved between the beginning of 1971 and 1972, urged the limitation of cheap imports. On the other hand the U.S. is pressing for the extension of the trade liberalization concessions already gained by Nixon's measures (see pp. 88–9). The U.S. is increasingly concerned that the enlarged E.E.C. will turn into an inward-looking defensive block, a view supported by E.E.C. insistence that trade agreements with Japan should contain a safeguard clause permitting a ban on imports in the event of 'market distortions' (i.e. too much competition).

There was little or nothing in the Washington agreement to make future crises less likely, and speculation against the dollar continued into 1972. The ritual increase in the gold price means nothing: the $30 billion which central banks accumulated in 1971 cannot be exchanged. For the American government refuses to sell gold at least until the multinational companies, which reputedly made $3 billion from the realignments, decide to return their funds to the U.S. There remains no general agreement about how the role of gold and the dollar in the international monetary system should be reduced. While the mystique of exchange-rate changes may have been diminished by the multilateral bargaining, it has showed the reality of the conflicting interests which are at stake. Even so, a prominent economist could still complain that 'decisions about prices, including the prices of foreign currencies, ought to be taken out of politics' (F. Machlup in *The Banker*, March 1972).

4. The miners' strike and its aftermath

In 1926 a million miners struck for nine months and lost dismally. In their next national strike in 1972 280,000 miners struck for 7 weeks and won. Nearly 11 million working days were directly lost in the strike (compare p. 199) and many millions more through lay-offs during the power crisis. It was the biggest and most significant industrial dispute in Britain since 1926 and it dealt a very damaging blow to the Tory government's economic and political strategy.

The government probably realized that the social solidarity of miners' communities ruled out a propaganda assault on them similar to that on the power workers a year earlier (see p. 197). Instead it hoped that the mere 55 per cent majority in the strike ballot and the political differences of the N.U.C. leaders would eventually cause support for the strike to collapse.

But, though the T.U.C. did nothing, the government had not reckoned on the active support which the miners received from other workers – in particular the refusal of most drivers to cross the miners' picket lines at ports and power stations. Most dramatic was the sympathy strike of Midlands engineering workers, whose support helped to close the Saltley coke depot.

The success of the pickets precipitated a massive fuel crisis, in which the government was forced to reduce electricity supplies by half. They could only have given further resistance to the wage claim by using troops to move coal. The government capitulated by setting up the Wilberforce Court of Inquiry. Its offer of £4·50 to £6 a week far exceeded the Coal Board's December offer of £2. Moreover in a late night Downing Street meeting the N.U.M. secured further important concessions, including longer holidays, and these increased the cost of the settlement by a third.

The laboriously constructed policy of imposing a pay norm on the public sector (see pp. 180–82) collapsed as the miners' success stimulated wage pressure. In March 1972 engineering workers in the Manchester area started factory occupations to support their national wage claim. In the public sector the railway unions rejected British Rail's second offer. Thus the miners' victory threatens to affect profitability throughout the economy, and it worsens the financing problems of the nationalized industries (see pp. 162–4).

Many Tories were hoping that the Industrial Relations Act, which came into operation at the end of February 1972, would redress the balance (see pp. 182–8); and by the end of March a fine of £5,000 had been imposed on the Transport and General Workers' Union. But it would be a desperate gamble for the government to use the Act in the face of such a determined challenge as the miners' strike.

The miners' victory was not only a setback in capital's struggle to restore profitability. It was also a demonstration of the power of militant and united trade unions. Finally, it showed how quickly the industrial power of the working class could be transformed into political strength.

April 1972

Appendices

In these appendices we present some further material which is relevant to the argument of this book but which we thought it better to omit from the text. Appendix A is concerned with the treatment of the distribution of national income in conventional economic analysis and, we hope, should be comprehensible to people with no formal training in economics. This is also true of appendix B, where we relate our analysis of the crisis in Britain to Marx's views on capitalist development. Appendices C–G are rather more specialized, being concerned with various problems of measurement, and also with testing some of the hypotheses we have put forward in this book. Non-economists may find the discussion of the undervaluation of assets in appendix E useful and may also like to browse round the data for different firms and industries in appendix E, and for different countries in appendix G. Otherwise the later appendices are rather heavy going and appendix D in particular will only make any sense to people with some knowledge of econometrics.

Appendix A (for chapters 2, 3, 4)
The share of labour according to bourgeois economics

The question of how income is divided between labour and capital is, implicitly by admission, the weakest section of orthodox economic theory. If you look for a discussion of this crucial economic question in the two most famous general economics textbooks in current use (by Samuelson and by Lipsey) you will find almost nothing. Of course in many places you will find a simple statement that the share of labour in the national income has remained constant for more than a century. This is simply false, as all of the experts on the subject now agree (see p. 43). But the myth has had a deep effect on the construction of theory. For instance Nicolas Kaldor, one of the most prominent modern theorists of income distribution, has said:

No hypothesis as regards the forces determining distributive shares could be intellectually satisfying unless it succeeds in accounting for the relative stability of these shares in the advanced economies over the last 100 years or so, despite the phenomenal changes in the techniques of production, in the accumulation of capital and in real income per head.[1]

The American economist R. Solow has also claimed that 'the division of the national income between labour and property incomes is among the slower changing characteristics of our economy, or any Western economy . . .'[2]

Economists are now becoming more aware of changes in the distribution of the national income.[3] But there is still extreme

[1] N. Kaldor, 'Alternative Theories of Distribution', in *Essays on Value and Distribution*, Duckworth, London, 1960, p. 210.

[2] R. Solow, in T. Schultz and R. Aliber, *Guidelines,* Informal Controls and the Market Place, Chicago U.P., 1966, pp. 18–19.

[3] See for example the well-known textbook, Lloyd G. Reynolds, *Labor Economics and Labor Relations*, 5th ed., Prentice-Hall, Englewood Cliffs, N.J., 1970, pp. 215–16.

caution among them about admitting that the organizational strength of the trade unions can have anything to do with these trends. To admit this would be to admit the efficacy of class struggle and to destroy the myth of potential harmony and equilibrium which underlies orthodox bourgeois economics. The denial of the relevance of class struggle sometimes goes to quite absurd extremes. One economist concludes that 'only during 1930–39 is there any evidence of a positive correlation between the level or growth of union activity and a relatively high or rising share of labour in national income. If one ignores the *basic upward trend in both union membership and labour's share* over the past sixty years, there is no observable stable relationship between the two series.'[1]

Much of bourgeois economic theory (especially what is called neo-classical theory) is based on the assumption that there is 'perfect competition' – that is, large numbers of firms trading at prices set in the 'market', bidding freely for workers who are not organized. Full employment is ensured by money wages and prices being flexible, or, in more sophisticated versions, by government management of monetary and fiscal policy. There is a limit to the possible real wage at full employment which is the amount of output produced by employing the last man, for if the real wage was greater than this 'marginal product of labour' it would not be worth while for a firm to employ him. If there is competition between firms they will be prepared to bid up the real wage until it is equal to the marginal product of labour; and competition between individual workers will prevent any agreement amongst them to insist on a higher wage. Output will then be at its maximum possible given the productive capital stock which exists.

After the workers are paid, the remainder of the product goes to capital; and the rate of profit is said (by analogy to the case of labour) to be the 'marginal product of capital' and to be a measure of the contribution of capital to the process of production. This rate of profit is supposed to represent the reward required for savers if they are going to continue saving in the form of productive capital. It is a reward for postponing their consumption (i.e. for saving) and a reward for the riskiness of saving in the form of

[1] B. M. Fleischer, *Labor Economics*: Theory and Evidence, Prentice Hall, Englewood Cliffs, N.J., 1970, pp. 185–6 (our emphasis).

accumulating productive capital rather than simply buying government bonds.

Before seeing what happens to the theory without the assumption of competition, it is worth looking at it in terms of its own assumptions (perfect competition), even though they are totally irrelevant to modern capitalism. The theory provides an explanation of the determination of the wage level on the assumption that full employment is maintained. If output and the wage level are known, the rest must go to capital; and so (with a given method of production) the rate of profit is determined. Where the theory is so misleading is that it apparently provides a justification for exploitation rather than just an explanation.

Because workers do not own the capital they work with, they have to sell their labour power (their ability to work) in the labour market, and therefore can be exploited in the sense of receiving less than the full value of what they produce. But the statement that the 'marginal product of capital' is equal to the rate of profit seems to imply that capitalists are getting a profit which measures their contribution to the productive process.

However, while capital certainly increases the productivity of labour, as Joan Robinson says, '*owning* capital is not a productive activity. The academic economists, by treating capital as productive, used to insinuate the suggestion that capitalists deserve well by society and are fully justified in drawing income from society'.[1] Even if it was necessary in a capitalist society to pay a rate of interest in order to get people to save (and the evidence is that it is not)*, it is circular to say that interest or profit is *justified* by being required for saving and therefore capital accumulation. It is *explained* in a capitalist society by a shortage of capital; it can only be justified if the capitalist society

---

[1] *An Essay on Marxian Economics*, Macmillan, London, 1966, p. 18.

*In his standard textbook on *Macroeconomic Theory* (Macmillan, New York, 1961), G. Ackley writes 'Although we have seen that an a priori case can be made that rational consumers will save more at high than at low rates of interest, almost no one today believes this factor to be significant.' There is no empirical evidence which clearly supports this classical idea. One recent study found that saving was *reduced* by high interest rates (W. E. Weber, 'The Effect of Interest Rates on Aggregate Consumption', *American Economic Review* 1970, pp. 591–600).

itself, with the means of production owned by a few, can be justified.

If perfect competition amongst workers and amongst producers is not assumed, we move closer to the real world where relatively few firms dominate an industry and workers are organized into unions. Then the 'neoclassical theory' has virtually nothing to say about income distribution because while it is based on competition among workers and among capitalists it ignores the fundamental contradiction *between* capital and labour. Everybody recognizes that there is in fact bargaining between firms and unions but such conflict is alien to the theory. The general view is that, although trade unions can force up money wages, these can usually be passed on by firms in the form of higher prices, so that, regardless of how the distribution of income was originally determined, it is likely to remain more or less constant. So, according to Joan Robinson, 'we know that [strong trade unions] can sometimes squeeze profits a little bit for a little time, but in the main, rises in money wage rates are offset by rising prices (percentage gross margins vary much less than the level of money wage rates)'.[1] This view, we believe, takes too little account of one of Marx's pair of antagonisms which determine the outcome of capitalist development – namely competition between capitals, which in the present situation predominantly takes the form of competition between different capitalist countries.

The 'neoclassical theory' is the foundation of the view that any success of unions in pushing up wages above the (quite unmeasurable) competitive level is an unjustified use of economic power; and that, although 'monopoly profits' (any profits over and above those which would be earned under perfect competition) are 'bad', other profits are justified. But any justification of profits based on their role in capitalist society is logically trivial: it says no more than that profits are imperative for the health of capitalism.

[1] 'The Relevance of Economic Theory', *Monthly Review*, January 1971.

Appendix B (for Chapters 2, 3, 9)
Marx's view of exploitation and capitalist crisis

The central importance which we attach to Marx's analysis of capitalism makes it necessary for us to give a brief outline of how we believe the recent fall in profitability and its consequences relate to Marx's famous theories of the falling rate of profit and capitalist crisis.

Marx's starting point was the labour theory of value. This says that commodities have value according to the amount of labour which has to be used to produce them. Commodities are produced by a combination of raw materials, capital equipment and labour. Part of a commodity's value is imparted to it by the labour which has been used to produce the raw materials and keep the capital equipment from deteriorating (this part of value is called constant capital). Further value is added to this by the labour directly used in the production of the commodity concerned. But the labour force, in return for producing the net product of society, only receives a portion of that product in the form of wages; it is as if the workers spend only part of their working-time working for themselves while the rest is spent working for the capitalists. Thus, of the total value added by labour a part becomes surplus value pocketed by the capitalists. The basic feature of capitalism which leads to this situation is that the means of production (raw materials and capital equipment), without which the workers cannot produce, are in the hands of the capitalists. The ratio between what the capitalists keep (surplus value) and what they are obliged to pay the workers to keep them at work (wages or variable capital) is called by Marx the rate of surplus value or sometimes rate of exploitation.

This notion of exploitation is central to Marx's writing on capitalism. Though there is a moral side to it, it is essentially a scientific concept which he uses as a tool of analysis. Exploitation is not a piece of the wickedness of employers; it is an inseparable part of the capitalist system. Unless the workers produce more value than they receive in wages then there are no profits to be earned. And without profits capitalism could no longer exist. Its purpose is to make profits, and its continuation depends on profits to finance the continued accumulation of capital. Without profits the incentive to produce and the means of producing both disappear. No one capitalist can opt out of exploitation and pay the workers the full value of their output, or even a significant amount more than the going rate, because he would be eliminated in the competitive struggle by those with higher profits and access to capital.

It is not hard to see that the rate of profit which capitalists earn on their capital is very closely linked with the rate of exploitation of their labour force. The rate of profit will fall if surplus value falls relative to constant plus variable capital. If we imagine (as Marx does in the famous section of *Capital* Vol. III, in which he discusses the law of the falling rate of profit) that the rate of exploitation remains constant, then the rate of profit will fall only if constant capital rises relative to surplus value, and so to variable capital at the same time. Marx attached special importance to the ratio between constant and variable capital which he called the organic composition of capital.* He believed it likely that the organic composition of capital, the amount of raw materials and capital equipment used in relation to the amount of labour in production, would rise over time. This would come about as a result of a constant search by capitalists for new methods of production which saved labour; and these were likely to use more capital relative to labour (or rather constant relative to variable capital) than before. Hence, if the rate of exploitation remained constant the rate of profit would fall. This is the essence of Marx's famous law of the falling rate of profit.

*In symbols c = constant capital, v = variable capital and s = surplus value. If the rate of exploitation $\dfrac{s}{v}$ is constant then the rate of profit $\dfrac{s}{c+v}$ will fall if the organic composition of capital $\dfrac{c}{v}$ rises. Compare this formulation with the other one, using non-Marxist terminology in the footnote on p. 54.

If the rate of exploitation is reduced then the rate of profit can still fall, even if the organic composition of capital does not rise. The dramatically falling rate of profit in Britain does not seem to have been caused to any significant extent by the increasing organic composition of capital but rather by an increase in labour's share of the product (very roughly the equivalent of a decrease in the rate of exploitation). Logically this possibility is allowed for in Marx's analysis; just how it relates to his expectations of what would happen in practice is harder to say.

It is clear what Marx thought about the course of wages relative to profits in an economy with a competitive labour market, without strong trade unions and where capital accumulation only took the form of increasing the amount of capital without changing its technical composition.[1] If labour became scarce relative to capital accumulation, wages would rise. This

increase only means at best a quantitative diminution of the unpaid labour that the worker has to supply. This diminution can never reach a point at which it would threaten the system itself . . . [because] . . . a rise in the price of labour resulting from accumulation of capital implies the following alternative:

Either the price of labour keeps on rising, because its price does not interfere with the process of accumulation . . . *Or*, on the other hand, accumulation slackens in consequence of the rise in the price of labour, because the stimulus of gain is blunted.[2]

And so demand for labour would fall and so would wages.

Elsewhere Marx considers the accumulation of capital with increasing organic composition which by raising the amount of capital equipment per man would increase the productivity of labour. He emphasizes the tendency of capital accumulation of this type to swell the reserve army of labour and thus to keep down wages and increase pauperism. But at this point in his argument he does not say explicitly what may happen to the rate of exploitation or to the distribution of income.[3] But earlier he had argued, again ignoring trade unions, that 'hand-in-hand with the increasing productivity of labour, goes, as we have seen, the

[1] *Capital*, vol. I (Lawrence and Wishart, London, 1970), chapter XXV, section 1, pp. 612–21.

[2] *Capital*, I, p. 619.

[3] *Capital*, I, chapter XXV, sections 2–4.

cheapening of the labourer, therefore a higher rate of surplus value, even when the real wages are rising. The latter never rise proportionally to the productive power of labour.'[1]

It would seem from this passage as though he envisaged a long-term rise in the rate of exploitation (even though the paragraph from which it comes begins with a speculation about what would happen when productivity rises and the rate of exploitation falls).

Marx on many occasions envisaged that a reduction in the rate of exploitation in the short run would play an important part in causing crises. He objected to an idea, common in his time and still, especially among trade unionists, that the source of capitalist crisis was always to be found in under-consumption – that is, in the fact that workers were not paid enough to purchase all they produced. In fact, he argued:

... crises are always prepared by precisely a period in which wages rise generally and the working-class actually gets a larger share of that part of the annual product which is intended for consumption. ... It appears, then, that capitalist production comprises conditions independent of good or bad will, conditions which permit the working-class to enjoy that relative prosperity only momentarily, and at that only as the harbinger of a coming crisis.[2]

Throughout his work Marx consistently sees capital as subject to pressures from two sides; it is these pressures which have combined to produce the present crisis in capitalism. One comes from the exploited proletariat demanding improvements in its conditions, the other from the competition of other capitals, which not only produces constant accumulation and a rising organic composition of capital, but also restricts capitalists' ability to raise their prices and so tends to restrict their profit margins.

Much of this competition in the British economy in recent times has been international; Marx says little about international competition, since he was mainly analysing the capitalist system

---

[1] *Capital,* I, chapter XXIV, section 4, p. 604. Also see J. Steindl, *Maturity and Stagnation in American Capitalism*, Blackwell, Oxford, 1952, chapter XIV.

[2] *Capital*, II, chapter XX, section 4, pp. 410–11. Also see P. M. Sweezy, *The Theory of Capitalist Development*, Monthly Review Press, New York, 1956, chapter IX.

as a whole, rather than in one country. Competition of any kind, however, conditions the attitude of capital towards the workers' fight for wages:

> If it were in the power of the capitalist producers to raise the prices of their commodities at will, they could and would do so without a rise in wages. Wages would never rise if commodity prices fell. The capitalist class would never resist the trade unions, if it could always and under all circumstances do what it is now doing by way of exception, under definite, special, so to say local, circumstances, to wit, avail itself of every rise in wages in order to raise prices of commodities much higher yet and thus pocket greater profits.[1]

On an earlier occasion Marx had devoted an important lecture to attacking the argument that the amount and proportion of total production available to be paid out as wages were fixed:

> ... the bowl from which the workmen eat is filled with the whole produce of the national labour, and what prevents them fetching more out of it is neither the narrowness of the bowl nor the scantiness of its contents, but only the smallness of their spoons.[2]

The class struggle, and the institutions which represented the working class (the spoons) were therefore crucial in determining what happened to relative and absolute wages. But at the level of trade unions the class struggle could achieve only so much. If the profitability was really reduced, then the inevitable result was a crisis in which capital accumulation would fall and unemployment rise.

Crises for Marx also possessed a political significance which escapes most bourgeois economists. In the *Communist Manifesto* he writes of 'the commercial crises that by their periodical return put the existence of the entire bourgeois society on trial, each time more threateningly'. On the purely economic side crises were regarded as the natural reaction of capital when it was hard-pressed to restore the conditions for capital accumulation and to defeat the strength of the working class. For a crisis really to threaten bourgeois society, therefore, it was necessary for the working class to conduct 'general political action'.

[1] *Capital*, II, chapter XVII, section 1, p. 340.
[2] *Wages, Price and Profit*, Progress Publishers, Moscow, 1970, pp. 8–9.

Appendix C (for Chapter 3)
Measuring the share of profits

In the appendix we discuss further the problems in measuring the profit share and give a table of yearly figures.

The Importance of the Company Sector

The profit shares shown in the text are shares of company profits in the net output of the company sector (the sum of profits, wages and salaries, and rent generated in the company sector).*

Net output by sectors as a percentage of total domestic product (Net of stock appreciation and capital consumption)

	1950	1955	1960	1964	1970
Companies	55·9	58·9	59·8	59·6	56·5
Personal sector	22·4	19·0	17·6	17·4	18·0
Government	21·7	22·1	22·6	23·0	25·5

Source: National Income Blue Book 1971, tables 13 and 58.

Between 1950 and 1960 there was a substantial shift in the production of output from the personal† to the company sector, reflecting the incorporation of small businesses, and from 1964 to 1969 a shift from the company sector to the government sector,‡ reflecting nationalization of steel and the fact that part of the higher

* Rent is a very stable proportion (about 1 per cent) of net output, and we have ignored it.
† Mainly incomes generated in the unincorporated enterprise sector (self-employed).
‡ Output of nationalized industries, local authorities (e.g. teachers' pay) and the central government (e.g. pay of the armed forces).

government expenditure consisted of output produced by the government. Thus, as can be seen from Table C.1, between 1964 and 1970 the proportionate fall in the share of company profits in total domestic product was greater than the fall as a share of net output, but overstates the fall in the share of profits in the output of the capitalist sector.

Stock Appreciation

The figures in Table C.1 (columns 1 and 2) show clearly that the deduction of stock appreciation (S.A.) makes a considerable difference to profit shares. Between 1964 and 1970 the fall in the share before deducting S.A. was 6 points (about $22\frac{1}{2}$ per cent), whereas after deducting S.A. the fall was 7·5 points (about 29 per cent). If stock appreciation is expressed as a proportion of the initial level of stocks a *rate of stock appreciation* is derived which shows the percentage nominal gain on holding stocks as a result of price increases during the year. If the rate of stock appreciation in the company sector is compared with the increase in the price of final output (G.D.P. at factor cost) during the same year, the correspondence is not very great, but over the period as a whole the average rate of stock appreciation was 4 per cent p.a., whereas the average price rise of G.D.P. was about 4·1 per cent p.a. It appears, therefore, that there were virtually no *real* capital gains as a result of S.A. as it more or less just offset the rise in the average price level.

Capital Consumption

Deducting capital consumption (C.C.) makes a considerable difference to the estimate of the fall in the profit share as a comparison of columns 2 and 3 in Table C.1 show: the share fell by 43 per cent between 1964 and 1970 when C.C. is subtracted, as compared with 29 per cent if it is not. We want to sort out whether this increased burden of capital consumption is solely due to the fall in the utilization of capacity; in other words, whether a fixed amount of depreciation is subtracted from a smaller volume of gross profits.* One estimate gives a fall in capacity utilization between 1964 and 1970 of 5·7 per cent, admitted to be perhaps on the high side. We can then calculate that if output had been say 6 per cent higher,† and if the share of profits after S.A. stayed at its actual 1970 level, then the share after S.A. and C.C. would have been 12·5 per cent rather than 12·1 per cent (assuming an unchanged *level* of C.C.). Thus even with constant capacity utilization the fall would have been 41 per cent after C.C. is subtracted as compared with 29 per cent when it is not. Clearly the burden of capital consumption as a proportion of value added has been rising independently of the cycle, and this implies that if the share of profits after C.C. is to be held constant the share before deducting C.C. must rise.

There appear to have been two factors at work. First there has been some upward trend in the fixed capital intensity of production: the ratio of company value added to fixed capital at current prices fell from 0·69 to 0·63 between 1958 and 1970, years of comparable utilization of capacity.‡ This could have occurred as a result of a slow rise in the price of company sector output as compared with the rise in the price of capital goods, an increase in the 'real' fixed capital intensity of output (more machines per unit of output) or a shift within the company sector towards industries with greater capital-intensity. There are not the data available to say which of these has been operating.

The second factor is that the capital consumption estimates by the Central Statistical Office appear to show an increase in the rate of depreciation (ratio of C.C. to net capital stock) – between 1964 and 1970 it increased from 0·33 to 0·38. These capital consumption

* As calculated by the national-income statisticians capital consumption is independent of utilization of capacity. This follows companies' accounting practice and is almost certainly the best estimate to make since most depreciation is from obsolescence rather than physical wearing out.

† Allowing something for company output increasing more than G.D.P. as a whole. The estimate is from F. W. Paish, *The Rise and Fall of Incomes Policy*, Institute for Economic Affairs, London, 1971.

‡ The ratio fell from 0·70 in 1964 to 0·63 in 1970; this could only be accounted for by the fall in utilization of capacity if utilization was 11 per cent less in 1970, which seems completely implausible. This is *fixed* capital intensity. If stocks are added to get closer to total capital intensity the rise has been very much less.

estimates are made on the basis of fixed assumptions as to the lives of the assets, so that there seems to have been a change in the asset composition of the company capital stock which would account for this rise, that is, a higher proportion of plant and machinery which has a shorter life and which is depreciated faster.* It may actually be that the C.S.O. has underestimated the true rise in capital consumption; as a proportion of the profits of non-financial companies C.C. rises from 14·6 per cent in 1950–52 to 24·8 per cent 1967–9. But for quoted companies in the same sector depreciation as published in their accounts rose from 13·5 per cent to 28·7 per cent. Now the figures for quoted companies are at historic, not replacement, cost (making no allowance for the fact that prices have risen since the assets were bought), so that they would be expected to be well below the C.S.O.'s replacement-cost estimates. The fact that by the end of the period the company account figures were higher suggests that the C.S.O. uses assumptions of longer asset lives than do the companies themselves and one would expect the assumptions used by the companies themselves to reflect more nearly the competitive situation of obsolescence. The C.S.O.'s estimates may be too low, therefore, and if the rate of obsolescence has speeded up recently,† which is quite possible, the increase in capital consumption and thus the fall in the profit share would also be underestimated.

Financial Companies

The treatment of financial companies in the national accounts is, at first sight at least, peculiar. Their profits are taken as being the 'difference between bank charges, commissions etc. on the one hand and management expenses on the other'. This figure is negative and growing (from £61m. in 1950 to £508m. in 1970). Financial companies make most of their income by the interest

* This is not apparent in the net capital stock estimates but it is the capital stock gross of depreciation on which the capital consumption figures are based.

† 'In view of the world chemical industry's problems I.C.I. is now anticipating shorter lives for some of its plants and has increased the depreciation charge accordingly' (*The Times*, 26 November 1971).

Table C.1. Profit Shares 1950–1970

	Share of Company Profits in Company Product (per cent)				Share of company profits in gross domestic product net of SA, gross of CC
	Gross of SA and CC	Net of SA gross of CC	Net of SA and CC	Net of SA, gross of CC excluding financial comps.	
1950	32·3	27·4	23·4	29·8	14·8
1951	33·8	29·3	25·4	31·7	16·0
1952	29·6	29·8	25·7	32·1	16·0
1953	29·4	29·8	25·8	32·1	16·1
1954	29·9	29·5	25·5	31·9	16·2
1955	29·8	28·9	24·9	31·3	16·5
1956	28·1	27·0	22·6	29·5	15·4
1957	27·9	27·0	22·4	29·7	15·4
1958	26·4	26·5	21·8	29·1	15·2
1959	27·4	27·0	22·5	29·7	15·5
1960	28·1	27·6	23·3	30·4	16·0
1961	25·8	25·2	20·5	27·7	14·6
1962	24·6	24·1	19·0	26·6	13·9
1963	26·3	25·6	20·9	28·1	14·7
1964	26·9	25·9	21·2	28·6	15·0
1965	26·1	25·0	20·2	27·9	14·4

Share of Company Profits in Company Product (per cent)

	Gross of SA and CC	Net of SA gross of CC	Net of SA and CC	Net of SA, gross of CC excluding financial comps.	Share of company profits in gross domestic product net of SA, gross of CC
1966	23·5	22·4	17·6	25·3	12·8
1967	23·7	23·1	17·7	26·2	13·1
1968	24·1	22·1	16·6	25·2	12·3
1969	22·5	20·1	14·1	23·4	11·0
1970	20·9	18·4	12·1	21·6	10·2
Quarterly 1970(1)					10·0
1970(2)					10·4
1970(3)					10·2
1970(4)					10·2
1971(1)					10·1
1971(2)					9·8

Source: National Income Blue Book 1971, tables 1, 13, 17, 27, 58.

they receive on their investments (net of what they pay) and this more than covers the deficit of expenses (wages, etc.) over commissions. It might be thought that this net interest should be counted in as net output (value added) by the financial sector, thus making their profits positive and increasing the share of total profits in company value added. But a substantial part of the total interest these companies receive is paid *by* industrial and commercial companies (about one third of total income including income from overseas). To show this contributing to the profits of financial companies would be double counting, as the gross profits of industrial and commercial companies are shown *before* payment of interest. The rest of domestic interest comes from the government (national debt) and from the personal sector (consumer credit, bank overdrafts, etc.). These items are treated in the national income accounts as 'transfer payments', that is, they do not represent a payment for factor services which contribute to the G.D.P., and accordingly are not shown in with the profits of financial companies in reckoning company value added. This corresponds to the treatment of financial companies we argued for in the text. But there is a case for leaving out the expenses incurred by financial companies in their dealings with the government and consumers. We cannot do this but we can go to the other extreme and leave out financial companies altogether. This has been done in column (4) of Table C.1 by making an estimate of the financial companies' contribution to company net product.* This is subtracted from total company net product, at the same time subtracting the (negative) profits of financial companies from total profits. The resulting series for the share of profits in net product of industrial and commercial companies shows a similar trend to the corresponding series for the company sector as a whole. The fall between 1964 and 1970 is slightly less steep (24 per cent instead of 29 per cent).

*Estimated as the sum of their profits (negative) and income from employment generated in the banking, insurance and finance sector.

Appendix D (for Chapter 3)
The statistical results

Table D.1, which follows, presents a selection of the statistical results we obtained trying to explain the fluctuations in the share of profits over the period 1950–69.

The general significance of the rate of change of wages, the rate of change of productivity and the rate of change in export prices can be easily seen in the table. The following notes amplify statements in the text.

(a) *The increasing effect of money wage changes* even in the period up to 1964 can be seen by comparing equations (3) and (7). In equation (3) the wage variable is an index number form and is substantially more significant than in equation (7) where the percentage change is used. The index number specification builds in an accelerating effect over time since a given percentage change in money wages represents a bigger change in the index in later years when the index is larger. The same result shows up very well in equation (9) where the increasing effect of money wages is built in by means of a time trend which is multiplied by the wage change variable. Comparison of the multiple correlation coefficient in equation (9) and equation (10) shows that it *is* the effect of wage changes which is increasing and not just a time trend towards bigger falls in the profit share which is being captured in equation (9). Equation (9) is used to estimate the effect of wage changes at the beginning and end of the period as reported in the text.

(b) The argument that the important thing is the *rate of change* of money wages and not the *acceleration* of money wage changes is illustrated in equation (6), where the lagged rate of change of money wages is included. If it was only the acceleration which affected the profit share, the coefficient of the lagged rate of change would be equal (and opposite in sign) to the coefficient of the current rate of change (i.e. no effect of wages on the profit share if this year's wage increase is the same as last year's). Though the coefficient of the lagged rate of change is of the opposite sign it is completely insignificant, and much smaller than the coefficient of the current rate of change.

(c) Comparison of equations (1) and (2) shows that the export price variable is very much more significant when calculated in dollars, i.e., abstracting from devaluation, which should have pushed up the profit share by allowing sterling prices to rise. We used equation (8) calculated on the data for 1950–64 to make 'predictions' for 1965–70 – using the actual changes in the explanatory variables. This is because the index number form in equation (3) gives ridiculous results when extrapolated. Overall the fall in the profit share was predicted very well by this equation, provided the effect of devaluation on world export prices was ignored. On the basis of equation (8) there 'should' have been a rise in the profit share of 2 points, whereas in 1968 after devaluation it actually fell by one point. It is also interesting that the fall in the profit share in 1966 (the year of the freeze) was about 1 point more than 'forecast', but this was made up the next year.

(d) We attempted to test the Kalecki* hypothesis that a rise in import prices would tend to increase the share of profits since firms calculate their mark-up in total costs so that when import prices rise so do profits. The import price variable was quite insignificant in equation (4). The importance of money wage increases for increasing labour's share is not the rather mechanical effect suggested by Kalecki of profits rising in proportion to *total* costs, i.e. slower than wages. Rather it is due to the *inability* of firms to raise their prices.

(e) We attempted to increase our information about international competition by seeing if a particularly big rise in the ratio of imports of U.K. manufacturers to output of manufactures, which we would take to be a sign of increasing foreign competition in the U.K. market, was associated with a fall in the share of profits. If anything, the reverse appeared to be true, though the variable was not significant in equation (5). An explanation would

* M. Kalecki, *The Theory of Capitalist Dynamics*, Allen and Unwin, London, 1964, chapters 1–3.

be that relatively large increases in imports occur when U.K. firms do put up their prices to protect their margins.

(f) The model was also tested on data for individual industries, though a major problem was the absence of a long run of stock–appreciation data by industry group. We hoped to find that in industries which seemed *a priori* to be relatively protected from international competition (bricks, etc., construction and distribution) wage pressure would be relatively unimportant, whereas in chemicals, engineering and vehicles it would be particularly important due to intense international competition. No such pattern could be distinguished; wage changes generally seem to have had a significant effect, but with no obvious tendency for this to be greater where international competition was stronger. This may suggest that internal competitive pressures are also important in restraining price increases in oligopolistic industries when costs go up. But there *is* one additional piece of evidence which suggests very strongly that external competition has an important effect on the rate at which wage increases can be passed on. This is the result that when, for the company sector as a whole, the export price variable was omitted the coefficient of the wage variable was both smaller and less significant. This implies that at least to some extent it is the rate of wage increase *relative* to export price increase that affects the profit share. This further suggests that the reason why we failed to find the expected pattern of wage effects when we examined individual industries may have been that we were forced to use the export price index for manufacturers as a whole rather than separate export price indices for each industry.

Table D.1. Equations Explaining Fluctuations in the Share of Company Profits in the U.K.

S_s	Change in share of gross trading profits in company value added after deduction of stock appreciation.
P	Change in index of GDP per person employed.
W	Change in index of income from employment per head.
X	Change in world export prices of manufactures in dollars.
XX	As X except in £ terms so that devaluation shows up in increase in world export prices.
M	Change in index of import prices into the U.K.

V   Change in index of volume of imports of manufactures relative to domestic production.

W_{-1} Change in income from employment per head in previous year.

t   Time trend (1 in 1950, 20 in 1969).

1950–69 $\bar{R}^2$

(1) $S_s = 1.16 + 0.30P + 0.12XX - 0.29W$ 0.43
$ (2.2) \quad\;\; (2.0) \quad\quad (3.9)$

(2) $S_s = 0.43 + 0.47P + 0.23X \;\; - 0.26W$ 0.61
$ (3.8) \quad\;\; (3.5) \quad\quad (4.8)$

1950–64

(3) $S_s = 0.44 + 0.40P + 0.23X \;\; - 0.25W$ 0.48
$ (2.9) \quad\;\; (3.2) \quad\quad (2.2)$

1950–69

(4) $S_s = 0.58 + 0.44P + 0.19X \;\; - 0.27W + 0.02M$ 0.58
$ (2.9) \quad\;\; (1.5) \quad\quad (4.7) \quad\;\; (0.4)$

(5) $S_s = 0.41 + 0.44P + 0.24X \;\; + 0.29W + 0.04V$ 0.64
$ (3.7) \quad\;\; (3.8) \quad\quad (5.4) \quad\;\; (1.6)$

(6) $S_s = 0.22 + 0.52P + 0.27X \;\; - 0.35W + 0.09W_{-1}$ 0.59
$ (3.6) \quad\;\; (3.2) \quad\quad (4.7) \quad\;\; (0.7)$

Bracketed figures are 't' values. When greater than 2, the relevant coefficient is statistically significant at the 5-per cent level. $\bar{R}^2$ is the multiple correlation coefficient. Data from table C.1 and National Institute Economic Review, November 1971, Tables 2, 6, 8, 15, 19.

Percentage models (explanatory variables in form of percentage changes)

1950–64 $\bar{R}^2$

(7) $S_s = 0.67 + 0.31P + 0.23X \;\; - 0.30W$ 0.37
$ (1.8) \quad\;\; (2.8) \quad\quad (1.5)$

(8) $S_s = 0.65 + 0.37P + 0.19X \;\; - 0.21W - 0.01tW$ 0.38
$ (2.1) \quad\;\; (2.2) \quad\quad (1.0) \quad\;\; (1.1)$

1950–69

(9) $S_s = 0.80 + 0.35P + 0.10X \;\; - 0.12W - 0.02tW$ 0.41
$ (2.0) \quad\;\; (1.5) \quad\quad (0.6) \quad\;\; (3.5)$

(10) $S_s = 2.1 \;\; + 0.29P + 0.11X \;\; - 0.31W - 0.13t$ 0.26
$ (1.5) \quad\;\; (1.5) \quad\quad (1.4) \quad\;\; (2.6)$

Appendix E (for Chapter 3)
The rate of profit

In this appendix we explain our calculations for the rate of profit and in particular deal with the problem of valuing assets.

Pre-tax Rate of Profit. This is income from trading and other activities less depreciation, divided by end-year book value of net assets (equal to book value of shareholders' capital, ordinary and preference, plus book value of long term loans).

Post-tax Rate of Profit. As above, except that taxation, including an estimate of income tax on debt interest and dividends, is subtracted from pre-tax net profits. The resulting post-tax profits are equal to ordinary and preference dividends and long-term debt interest (net of tax) plus the amount retained in reserves (retained profits). The retained profits figure includes investment grants received in the year; this is in order to make the post-1966 figures comparable to the earlier years when investment incentives were all in the form of reduced tax charge.

Rate of Return on Ordinary Shareholders' Assets. This is identical to the rate of profit on net assets except that interest on long-term debt and preference capital is subtracted from the profit figure, and the book value of these items of capital is subtracted from the asset figure.

Because the return on long-term debt and preference stock does not fall when profits fall, the fall in the rate of return on shareholders' assets (Table E.1, column 5) is slightly greater than the fall on net assets (column 4). Although interest rates rose, they remained (after-tax) less than the return on net assets, so the return to shareholders' capital still gained from the increased 'gearing' (see p. 123).

Stock Appreciation. There are no published figures for stock appreciation in quoted companies in particular industries and we calculated this from national income estimates of stock appreciation in rather broad industry groupings by assuming* that within a grouping (e.g. engineering) all the component industries (e.g. vehicles, electrical engineering, etc.) had the same ratio of stock appreciation to stocks. The ratio of the stocks of U.K. quoted companies (including their stocks overseas) to total stocks held by the engineering industry in the U.K. (including those of foreign subsidiaries, unquoted companies, etc.) was very low (less than 50 per cent) and this meant we arrived at a low figure for stock appreciation in quoted engineering industries. Since engineering industries are important, and stock appreciation in them very heavy in the last few years, this meant that we arrived at a considerably smaller figure for stock appreciation in the quoted company sector as a whole than an earlier estimate based on total profits in the manufacturing sector.† Although our new estimate may well be on the low side – the ratio of trading profits in the quoted sector to total U.K. profits in engineering was more than 60 per cent – we think it better to use this 'conservative' estimate.

Undervaluation of Assets. In these estimates of the rate of profit based on company accounts, capital is shown in the companies' books at what it originally cost (historic cost). In a time of inflation this will give an underestimate of the current value of capital employed. Similarly depreciation is reckoned at the historic cost of the assets wearing out, so that depreciation in the accounts is an underestimate of what must be set aside from profits to replace these assets. The underestimate of capital employed, and the overestimate of profits net of depreciation, combine to give 'too high' an estimate of the rate of profit. It definitely *is* too high. Suppose £100 is invested and gives £10 profit per year – the rate of profit is 10 per cent. If the price level doubles (and profits with it) the rate of profit calculated on the book value (historic cost) of the

*This assumption makes our estimates of rates of profit after S.A. in individual industry groups subject to a wide range of error.

†In our paper in *New Left Review 66* we used this higher estimate of stock appreciation, which meant that the rate of return in 1969 was more than 1 per cent lower than our new estimates.

investment rises to 20 per cent. But the £20 profit is worth no more in *real* terms than the original £10 – the *real rate of return* is unchanged. If the investment was repeated it would cost £200 (as the price of investment goods has doubled), it would yield £20 and have a real rate of return of 10 per cent; the original investment will be shown as earning its real rate of return of 10 per cent only if the capital is revalued at current replacement cost (£200). The older on average are the assets employed (i.e. the less new investment there is), and the faster prices have risen since they were bought, the more they will be undervalued in the books, and the more will measured rates of return exaggerate the real rate of profit.

Undervaluation of assets was probably at its peak around 1952, when the capital stock was old and there had been rapid price increases; it may have declined thereafter due to the high level of investment reducing the average age of the capital stock and also to more modest price increases.

From 1956 on it is possible to calculate a real rate of profit for the company sector as a whole using estimates in the *National Income Blue Book* of the value at replacement cost of the company sector capital stock and the value of stocks.* The rate of profit measured in this way (Table E.1, column 6) and from the company accounts shows a very similar trend up to 1964, suggesting little change in undervaluation. But since 1964 the *Blue Book* series shows a very much sharper fall, part of which is probably due to the fact that the acceleration of inflation has *increased* the undervaluation of capital in company accounts. The increase in undervaluation will have been biggest in 1970 since prices of capital goods rose by $7\frac{1}{2}$ per cent in 1970 as compared with about $3\frac{1}{2}$ per cent during 1964–9 and not much more than 2 per cent in 1954–64.

Industry and firm rates of profit – post-tax

Individual industry post-tax rates of profits are calculated in the same way, and from the same basic source, as the rate of profit for

*This will still overestimate the true rate of profit in that no financial assets are included in capital employed.

Table E.1. Rates of Profit 1950–70

Rates of profit on net assets of quoted companies in manufacturing, construction, communications and distribution per cent

	Before Tax incl. SA (1)	excl. SA (2)	After Tax incl. SA (3)	excl. SA (4)	Selected years. as (4) except on shareholders' assets only (5)	Ratio of profits before tax, but after SA and CC Co. Capital Stock (6)
1950	18·2	15·6	8·4	5·7	6·7	n.a.
1951	19·5	17·0	8·4	5·9		n.a.
1952	16·0	16·9	6·4	7·3		n.a.
1953	16·4	16·6	6·8	7·0		n.a.
1954	17·0	16·6	8·0	7·5		n.a.
1955	16·8	16·0	8·2	7·4	8·6	n.a.
1956	15·7	14·8	7·5	6·6		12·0
1957	14·9	14·1	7·1	6·3		11·6
1958	14·0	14·0	7·2	7·2		11·0
1959	14·8	14·5	8·1	7·7		11·6
1960	15·3	14·9	8·5	8·1	9·1	12·5
1961	13·4	13·0	7·4	6·9		10·8
1962	12·3	12·0	6·7	6·4		9·8
1963	13·1	12·5	7·2	6·6		10·7
1964	14·4	13·7	7·8	7·1	7·9	11·0
1965	13·6	12·8	8·6	7·8		10·2
1966	12·1	11·3	5·7	4·9		8·3
1967	12·1	11·7	6·5	6·1	7·0	8·8
1968	13·3	11·6	6·8	5·2	5·9	8·1
1969	12·9	11·1	6·5	4·7	5·0	6·8
1970	12·0	9·7	6·3	4·1	4·5	5·8

Source: Columns 1–5. 1950–59 *Economic Trends*, April 1962, Tables 1A, 1B, 1C. 1960–70 *Business Monitor M3*, 1971, Tables 4 and 5.
Column 6. *National Income Blue Book*, 1971, Tables 13, 58, 61, 67 and earlier years.

the industrial and commercial sector as a whole. For the years before 1967 this industry data was published in successive issues of *Statistics on Incomes, Prices, Employment and Production*. Industry stock appreciation estimates are those used to build up the figure for the sector as a whole. From 1967 onwards the figures are from *Business Monitor* M3. These figures are built up from the accounts of British companies quoted on U.K. Stock Exchanges, so that foreign subsidiaries are excluded.

The firms' rates of profit are calculated to be as far as possible comparable to the industry profit rates. They were calculated from company accounts* by adding (a) distributions (ordinary and preference dividends, debenture and other loan interest) after deducting income tax; (b) returns to 'minority interests' (profits payable to other companies which have joint subsidiaries); (c) the difference between cash flow and depreciation (an estimate of retained profits including investment grants). The sum of these items gives post-tax profits which are then divided by capital employed (net assets) to give a rate of return. For example, for Courtauld in 1969:

Ordinary and Preference dividends	£18·75m.
Debenture and Loan Interest	£10·93
	29·68
less income tax @ 41·25%	12·24
= Net distributions	17·44
Cash flow	37·00
less depreciation	28·21
= Retained Earnings	8·79

Net distributions + Retained earnings + Minority interest (2·80m.) = £29·03m.
Net assets (including goodwill) at end year = £459·3m.

$$\text{Rate of profit} = \frac{29·03}{459·3} = 6·32\%$$

The firms which were chosen were the largest three or four firms in each industry for which data were readily available. To get an idea of importance in an industry net assets for individual

* Using the analysis of company accounts issued by Moodies Services.

firms and for industries at the end of 1969 are also shown. Where acquisitions make comparisons of a firm's rate of return from year to year particularly hazardous, the break is indicated by the sign //. Where a post-tax rate of return could not be calculated and a pre-tax rate was available from *The Times* list of 1,000 largest companies (e.g. for the motor firms) we used the pre-tax rate indicated by ( ).

All the rate of profit figures will be biased upwards due to valuation of assets and depreciation at historic cost, and for firms the fall in the rate of profit will also be underestimated since no attempt was made to estimate stock appreciation for individual firms.

Table E.2. Rates of Profit in Different Industries and Firms

	1950	1955	1960	1964	1967	1968	1969	1970
Food Net Assets £995m.	11·6	9·1	8·0	7·2	7·6	8·0	6·0	5·8
excl. S.A.			8·0	7·2	7·3	5·7	4·5	2·8
Tate and Lyle £145m.				(13·4)	(8·6)		(5·9)	(9·8)
Reckitt and Colman £110m.				8·2	4·7		6·7	6·9
Cadbury Schweppes £165m.				8·2	7·8	//	4·5	5·0
Associated British Foods £141m.				11·6	9·0		11·4	12·9
Drink Net Assets £2,089m.	7·8	7·6	7·8	7·2	5·3	5·7	5·4	5·3
excl. S.A.			7·8	7·2	5·1	3·9	4·1	4·1
Allied Breweries £331m.				5·4	4·7		5·0	5·4
Bass Charrington £324m.						5·5	4·0	4·9
Distillers £317m.				10·0	5·9		7·1	7·6
Whitbread £205m.				4·3	3·7		3·8	4·5
Tobacco Net Assets £637m.	8·5	6·5	7·7	8·5	6·2	6·5	6·7	6·9
excl. S.A.			7·7	8·5	5·7	3·4	4·0	3·9
Imperial Tobacco £488m.				8·1	5·8		6·1	7·2
Gallaher £121m.				9·5	5·8		7·0	7·6
Carreras £49m.				8·8	5·4		8·0	7·4

Table E.2 – *contd.*

	1950	1955	1960	1964	1967	1968	1969	1970
Chemicals Net Assets £3086m.	7·7	7·5	8·0	6·9	6·5	7·8	7·3	6·5
excl. S.A.			8·0	6·9	5·6	7·4	7·1	5·0
I.C.I. £1559m.				7·1	6·7		8·6	7·1
Unilever £548m.				9·2	9·5		9·0	9·2
British Oxygen £159m.				6·5	6·1		6·8	8·0
Boots £110m.				8·9	8·5		7·2	9·7
Metal Manufacture Net Assets £660m.	11·5	12·6	8·9	5·9	5·4*	6·1	7·3	7·1
excl. S.A.			8·9	4·2	4·5	5·3	1·1	6·0
Tube Investments £235m.				5·3	4·0		4·9	8·1
Delta Metals £86m.				11·4	6·0		8·2	8·5
Thomas Firth & J. Brown £36m.				7·1	4·3		2·5	5·9
Glynwed £39m.				17·3	17·7		12·9	7·9
Electrical Engineering Net Assets £1991m.	13·8	11·6	6·4	7·6	6·7	8·2	7·6	7·2
excl. S.A.			5·5	6·0	5·9	5·9	4·1	4·9
General Electric £691m.				8·2	2·7	//	4·7	5·0
British Insulated Callendar's Cables £211m.				6·4	7·5		5·1	5·9
Joseph Lucas £111m.				6·4	8·7		7·9	6·2
Thorn Electrical £150m.				9·1	17·6	//	21·7	27·8

*From 1967 excludes nationalized steel companies

	1950	1955	1960	1964	1967	1968	1969	1970
Non-Electrical Engineering Net Assets £1380m.	11·8*	10·6*	7·4	6·3	6·3	6·2	6·2	6·4
excl. S.A.			6·6	4·8	5·5	5·3	2·3	2·5
International Computers £124m.				n.a.	n.a.	4·4	3·9	5·5
Vickers £117m.				2·8	3·2		4·5	3·1
Associated Engineering £54m.				6·0	5·4		7·4	6·2
Babcock and Wilcox £45m.				3·5	4·7		1·6	3·2
Alfred Herbert £33m.				9·1	4·5		1·3	2·2
Vehicles Net Assets £1060m.	9·5	12·3	9·1	8·8	4·0	7·1	6·0	1·4
excl. S.A.			8·0	6·8	2·9	3·7	0·9	−3·3
Hawker Siddeley £189m.				6·7	4·8		5·5	5·2
Rolls-Royce £221m.				4·9	6·2		4·3	
British Aircraft Corporation £69m.				(5·6)	(13·2)		(13·1)	
B.S.A. £26m.				3·4	6·8		2·0	1·8
Ford Motor £240m.				(5·9)	(3·2)	(22·1)	(18·0)	(11·3)
Vauxhall £125m.				(22·6)	(7·7)		(1·4)	(−4·2)
Chryslers (Rootes) £73m.				(−0·5)	(−14·6)		(1·4)	(−13·7)
British Motor Holdings				(19·7)	(0·2)			
Leylands £408m.				(21·8)	(14·9)	(15·8)	(16·0)	(6·3)

*Includes shipbuilding

Table E.2 – contd.

	1950	1955	1960	1964	1967	1968	1969	1970
Shipbuilding Net assets £130m.			5·6	1·9	1·4	7·7	0·4	-5·2
excl. S.A.			5·0	0·8	1·3	6·3	-2·7	-5·2
Cammell-Laird £34m.				5·4	7·6	6·2		
Swan Hunter Group £27m.				2·6	2·5		-4·4	-10·0
Harland and Wolf £9m.				-4·9	-19·2		-31·8	-39·9
Doxford and Sunderland £17m.				4·0	3·2		4·2	
Metal Goods (n.e.s.) Net assets £791m.	8·2	11·4	9·6	8·4	7·9	7·7	7·3	9·0
excl. S.A.			8·5	7·2	7·9	5·2	4·6	6·5
Guest, Keen & Nettlefolds £296m.				6·3	3·2		3·0	3·6
Metal Box £123m.				8·2	9·5		8·2	10·2
Johnson, Matthey £46m.				9·6	13·4		8·4	8·3
British Ropes £37m.				6·6	5·7		5·4	5·0
Textiles Net assets £1299m.	14·5	8·3	7·0	7·3	6·1	8·3	7·2	6·4
excl. S.A.			6·7	8·1	7·2	5·1	6·5	4·8
Courtaulds £459m.				7·8	5·4		6·3	5·0
Coats Patons £174m.				7·2	5·8		5·9	4·8
Turner and Newall £107m.				7·5	5·1		5·4	6·2
English Calico £85m.				6·4	n.a.		4·5	3·8

	1950	1955	1960	1964	1967	1968	1969	1970
Clothing and Footwear Net assets £381m.	14·7	9·8	9·7	6·7	6·0	6·1	5·9	5·3
excl. S.A.			9·2	7·4	6·8	3·6	5·4	3·8
Leather, Leather Goods £28m.			4·7	7·4	3·2	9·2	9·3	10·0
Sears Holdings £186m.				5·5	6·5		6·6	8·0
Burton Group £72m.				2·9	3·5		5·5	4·4
Barrow, Hepburn & Gale (leather) £7m.				5·5	3·3		5·5	7·4
Bricks, Pottery, Glass, Cement, etc. Net assets £823m.	9·5	9·6	9·1	9·4	7·7	7·7	6·9	8·1
excl. S.A.			8·3	8·8	7·7	6·6	5·8	6·3
Associated Portland Cement £210m.				8·7	8·0		3·4	3·4
Thomas Tilling £92m.				9·6	9·3		7·0	8·7
William Baird £32m.				(12·6)	(8·7)		(8·2)	(6·4)
Pilkington Bros. £140m.				n.a.	n.a.		5·0	5·3
Timber and Furniture Net assets £109m.			8·0	7·7	5·5	7·5	5·0	5·1
excl. S.A.			6·8	5·9	5·5	4·7	2·3	0·8
Duport £23m.				5·3	4·2		6·8	5·6
Boulton and Paul £11m.				5·4	6·8		5·1	

Table E.2 – contd.

	1950	1955	1960	1964	1967	1968	1969	1970
Paper, Printing & Publishing Net assets £1287m.	10·8	10·4	8·0	6·8	9·0	5·9	6·5	5·9
excl. S.A.			7·4	6·1	9·0	4·8	5·3	4·2
Bowater Paper £282m.				3·9	3·8		3·3	3·1
Reed Group £281m.				5·6	3·5		5·3	3·7
International Publishing £128m.				7·2	5·8		3·7	
Wiggins Teape £94m.				3·6	3·5		5·5	
Other Manufacturing Net assets £549m.			6·6	7·4	10·1	8·0	6·6	6·0
excl. S.A.			5·3	6·0	10·1	6·0	4·3	2·3
Dunlop Holdings Ltd. £269m.				7·4	6·0		5·6	4·4
Goodyear Tyre and Rubber £43m.				n.a.	n.a.	8·2	4·7	5·7
British Match £52m.				7·4	6·4		6·0	4·9
Nairn & Williamson £13m.				3·9	-1·0		1·6	5·9
Lines Bros. £21m.				6·1	10·2		2·3	n.a.
Construction Net assets £348m.	9·1	10·7	7·5	9·7	11·9	8·1	8·5	10·2
George Wimpey £40m.				15·5	12·2		9·6	6·1
John Laing £22m.				11·2	4·2		6·2	4·6
Richard Costain £20m.				5·2	6·0		6·7	12·4

Wholesale Distribution Net assets £683m.

	1950	1955	1960	1964	1967	1968	1969	1970
excl S.A.	9·0	7·2	7·4	7·3	8·1	6·8	6·5	7·5
Brooke Bond Liebig £100m.			6·6	5·4	6·7	5·1	3·7	2·3
Booker McConnell £48m.				7·7	7·5		6·2	6·5
Powell Duffryn £39m.				6·0	7·0		5·0	2·6
				6·5	4·9		5·8	7·2
Fitch Lovell £27m.				5·6	5·7		6·2	6·3

Retail Distribution Net assets £1233m.

	1950	1955	1960	1964	1967	1968	1969	1970
excl. S.A.	6·4	9·1	9·2	8·5	6·6	7·4	6·9	8·2
Great Universal Stores £223m.			9·0	7·6	6·5	6·0	5·5	6·1
Marks & Spencer £170m.				10·5	10·7		9·8	10·0
F. W. Woolworth £166m.				10·0	8·7		11·4	13·6
Unigate £111m.				11·4	8·0		7·4	6·7
				6·1	6·3		4·9	5·5

Transport and Communication (excl. ships) Net assets £372m.

	1950	1955	1960	1964	1967	1968	1969	1970
			7·5	7·1	8·6	6·6	6·9	3·4
British Electric Traction £154m.				9·4	5·0		5·6	5·2
Transport Development Group £49m.				7·6	5·4		6·6	7·6
William Cory £26m.				5·6	3·5		4·2	5·6

Table E.2 – contd.

	1950	1955	1960	1964	1967	1968	1969	1970
Miscellaneous Services Net assets £859m.			9·2	9·0	6·1	6·3	6·7	7·1
E.M.I. £136m.				8·7	6·7	//	6·0	6·0
Rank Organisation £186m.				9·3	10·0		15·6	4·0
J. Lyons £106m.				6·1	4·3		3·8	3·6
Redifusion £61m.				8·8	9·4		7·0	
Oils (not included in the Industrial and Commercial sector)								
Shell Transport & Trading £1991m.				7·2	6·5		7·7	6·5
British Petroleum £1955m.				8·0	6·1		5·9	5·9
Burmah Oil £761m.				9·5	8·9		3·9	5·6

Appendix F (for Chapters 3 and 8)
Company taxation

In this appendix we discuss changes in the burden of company taxation. The proportion of company income taken in taxation in a particular year depends on the tax rate and the amount of tax allowances generated by the current and previous years' investment. Suppose the tax rate is 50 per cent and there is a 100 per cent tax allowance on new investment (free depreciation). If the company did no investment it would pay half its income in taxation, giving an apparent tax rate of 50 per cent. If, however, the company does an amount of investment just equal to its profits then the tax allowances will exactly offset the profits and no tax will be paid – an apparent tax rate of 0 per cent. Now the *real* situation of the company's profitability is the same in both these cases, but it will apparently be much more profitable in the second case, when it is undertaking investment. A calculation of true profitability should include tax concessions received on *replacement* investment but *not* those received on *net* investment. The inclusion of the latter in post-tax profits overestimates profitability.* Actual taxation incentive systems are complicated, but table F.1 is of some help in unravelling the various factors behind the divergent behaviour of pre-tax and post-tax profits.

The fall in the apparent tax burden (line d) between 1950–54 and 1955–9 resulted from a sharp fall in the average tax rate (line a) and a substantial increase in the investment level (line c). These more than offset a slight fall in the value of investment incentives (line b). The fall is even greater if it is calculated on true company income (line e), with stock appreciation excluded, for the

---

*This is clear, since replacement investment keeps the capital stock intact and thus tax concessions for doing this should be included in an assessment of profitability just as taxes levied on the profits from the existing capital stock should be taken into account.

Table F.1. Taxation and Investment Incentives

	1950–54	1955–59	1960–64	1967–9	1970
a. Average tax rate*	51·0	44·1	47·5	48·6	48·6
b. Proportion of cost of investment paid by government in tax concessions or grants†	35·7	35·2	46·5	43·0	42·6(32·5)
c. Ratio of fixed-capital formation to company income	19·9	28·8	34·0	36·3	40·8
d. Actual taxes as per cent of company income	44·0	35·9	33·4	34·1	33·0
e. As (d) but after deducting SA from company income	46·5	36·5	34·2	36·1	35·9

Source: National Income Blue Book, 1971, Tables 13, 27, and p. 113.

*Total taxes (including foreign taxes on profits earned abroad for company sector as a whole from *Blue Book* and an estimate of the tax remission as a result of tax allowances on new and existing capital stock) as a proportion of company profits, non-trading income, and income earned abroad.

†Calculated from rates of annual, initial and investment allowances, investment grant rates and tax rates using a discount rate of 10 per cent. Refers to plant and machinery, for 1967–70 for manufacturing only and does not include additional regional incentives. The figure in parentheses for 1970 refers to value of investment incentives under the Tories' scheme of October 1970 and the same figure applies after 1971 changes, which reduced taxation as well as increasing incentives.

high level of S.A. in the early fifties had caused more taxation to be paid. Between 1955–9 and 1960–64 a rise in the average tax rate was offset by a massive increase in the value of incentives and a further big increase in the amount of investment on which they could be claimed. Between 1960–64 and 1967–9 (1965 and 1966 are excluded because the change in the tax and incentive system makes it difficult to calculate sensible figures) the apparent tax burden rose slightly, with a rise in the tax rate and fall in incentive rate being nearly offset by a higher investment level; but when S.A. is excluded from company income the increase in the apparent burden is a good deal greater (line e).* In 1970 there was a further rise in investment relative to income; but this was offset by higher stock appreciation, so that taxation did not fall as a proportion of income.

So the relative stability of post-tax profitability in the early sixties was mainly attributable to higher rates of investment incentives received on greater net investment, rather than any substantial reduction in taxation on existing capital. By contrast the rise in the apparent tax burden in the late sixties does reflect a greater weight of taxation on profits currently earned, reversing the trend of the fifties. Thus recent faster fall in our measure of post-tax profitability is not distorted by changes in investment incentives.

As far as the incentive for new investment is concerned it is the difference between the tax rate and the proportion of the cost of investment which is offset by investment incentives which counts. When lines (a) and (b) are equal this means that profits taxation is being exactly offset by incentives, so pre-tax and post-tax profitability are equal. Between 1955–9 and 1960–64 the gap narrowed from almost 11 per cent to 1 per cent. Some widening occurred with the switch to corporation tax and investment grants in 1966, and the gap was further increased by the Tories' changes, for the fall in corporation tax from 45 per cent to 40 per cent is less than the fall in the value of incentives.

* We had to make these calculations for the company sector as a whole (including financial companies and U.K. companies operating mainly overseas). Industrial and commercial companies in the U.K. were affected a good deal more.

Appendix G (for Chapter 4)
Profitability and demand in international capitalism

Apart from the U.S. and the U.K. it is impossible to get direct information about how the share of profits fluctuates in the capitalist sector. In most cases we do know how the national income is distributed between wages, self-employed incomes and profits, but these figures do not help much in making inferences about profitability in the capitalist or company sector. This is partly because some wages are earned in government employment, where there are no profits. However, the main problem lies in interpreting the figures for self-employed incomes, which are a very important, though diminishing proportion of total incomes in all the European capitalist countries and in Japan.

The economists' usual method of dealing with these is simply to rather arbitrarily allocate part to labour and part to capital and treating them as wages and profits. But this method is useless here, since much self-employment, especially in the less advanced countries, lies outside the modern organized capitalist sector altogether. So splitting their incomes between profits and wages will not tell us much about the fate of capital. In a few countries the problem is even harder because in the only available statistical evidence some self-employed incomes are lumped together with profits.

There are two sets of figures which are particularly relevant to the profits crisis. The first is the ratio of employed people – wage and salary earners – to the total working population (that is, employed plus self-employed); we have called this the 'employee ratio'. The second is the proportion of the national income (wages and salaries, self-employed incomes and profits) going to these employed people as wages and salaries – the 'wage ratio'. Since there is a tendency for self-employed people to become wage and salary earners, the employee ratio is rising all the time. For this reason, as long as the productivity of the workers does not change much when they leave self-employment to become employees, the wage ratio will tend to rise at more or less the same pace as the employee ratio.* If the wage ratio rises *faster* than this the likelihood is that it is rising not only because more people are moving as employees into the capitalist sector, but also because the workers are on average getting a rising share of the product in that sector. On the other hand, if the wage ratio rises more *slowly* than the employee ratio this suggests that the share of profits in the capitalist sector is rising more than enough to offset the rise in the wage ratio which results from the move out of self-employment.

So far we have assumed that the productivity of the workers who move from self-employment into wage or salary employment does not change. But what if the productivity of the workers employed in the capitalist sector is on average higher than the productivity of self-employed workers because they are equipped with better machines, and so on? In that case the total national income rises; and it is possible, therefore, that even when the wage ratio rises somewhat slower than the employee ratio, the share of profits in the income of the capitalist sector is falling.†

---

*A numerical example may help. Suppose half the working population is self-employed and the other half employed, and that national income of 100 is split up as follows: 25 wages, 25 profits, 50 self-employment incomes. The employee ratio is therefore 50 per cent and the wage ratio is 25 per cent. Suppose a further quarter of the population transfers from self-employment, that the share of wages in the output of the capitalist sector remains at 50 per cent, and that total income is unchanged. The national income will then be $37\frac{1}{2}$ wages, $37\frac{1}{2}$ profits, 25 self-employment incomes, and the wage ratio will have risen from 25 per cent to $37\frac{1}{2}$ per cent – a rise of one half. Furthermore, the employee ratio will have risen from 50 per cent to 75 per cent – also a rise of one half. O.E.C.D., in *Inflation: The Present Problem* (1970), analyses the distribution of income using these two ratios.

† If output does rise as a result of the transfer of labour, then the wage ratio may rise much slower than the employee ratio (perhaps one third to one half as fast) even though the distribution of income within the capitalist sector remains constant. Although wages and salaries would rise in proportion to the increase in the employee ratio, the *ratio* of wages and salaries to national income would rise less fast because national income would be going up. To go back to the numerical example in the last footnote: suppose, after the transfer of labour, national income goes up 10 per cent because self-employment incomes are reduced less than incomes in the capitalist sector rise. In that case national income will be 110 and will be

Table G.1. Wage Ratio in Capitalist Countries (per cent)

Country	Sector	1950–54	1955–9	1960–64	1964	1965	1966	1967	1968	1969	1970
U.K.	Corporate	68·5	70·2	71·7	71·4	72·1	74·7	73·8	74·8	76·9	78·4
	Manufacturing	64·9	67·6	69·2	69·1	70·1	72·7	70·8	72·2	75·2	76·6
U.S.	Corporate	71·0	71·7	71·4	70·2	69·1	69·4	70·4	70·5	71·7	73·3
	Manufacturing	69·2	70·7	71·5	70·2	68·8	69·3	70·8	70·8	72·2	
France	G.D.P.	49·5	52·5	53·2	54·7	54·9	54·5	54·4	55·0	54·8	
Germany	G.D.P.	52·0	53·8	56·2	56·9	57·4	57·9	57·8	57·5	57·5	59·1
	Manufacturing	59·6	60·3	61·5	62·1	62·1	63·7	63·6	60·7	61·9	
Italy	G.D.P.	43·5[1]	45·4	49·5	52·8	52·0	51·3	51·6	51·9	51·8	53·7
	Manufacturing	53·6[1]	57·8	61·7	65·3	62·8	60·9	63·4	62·7	63·7	
Japan	G.D.P.	44·5[2]	45·9	45·6	46·0	48·4	48·2	47·2	46·4	46·7	
	Manufacturing (large companies)				39·6	41·8	41·0	40·3	41·3	40·9	41·3
Netherlands	G.D.P.	49·2	50·9	54·7	57·2	58·1	60·1	59·4	59·8	60·3	62·0
	Manufacturing	54·6	56·6	60·2	62·5	62·8	64·5	63·6	63·4	64·2	
Sweden	Manufacturing	66·5[2]	67·1	70·1	69·4	69·3	70·9	71·0	69·9	69·0	
Canada	G.D.P.	55·4	57·5	58·6	58·2	59·2	60·0	61·8	61·9	62·8	64·0
Belgium	G.D.P.	48·4[3]	50·3	52·9	54·4	55·2	56·6	56·7	56·8	57·0	

(1) 1951–4   (2) 1952–4   (3) 1953–4

Note: Output is gross of depreciation in every case, and it is domestic output, i.e. excluding income from abroad. In the case of U.K. and U.S. it is net of stock appreciation; for other countries there is no mention of stock appreciation and it is assumed that output is defined net of stock appreciation.

The wage ratio is wages and salaries and employers' contributions to social security as a proportion of output. For U.S. and U.K. the corporate sector excludes financial companies. U.K. data from Table C.1 column (5).

Sources: Series of shares in G.D.P. are all from O.E.C.D. *National Accounts 1950–68* supplemented by O.E.C.D. country surveys. Other data:

U.K.: *National Income Blue Books* (1970, Tables 13, 17, 64, 65)

U.S.: *Surveys of Current Business* (Tables 1.12, 1.13, etc.)

Germany: *Statisches Jahrbuch*, Table XXIII/4

Italy: *Annuario Statistico Italiano 1970*, Table 396 and National Accounts 1951–68

Japan: Analysis by Bank of Japan of 75 per cent of large firms

Netherlands: *Statistical Yearbook* Tables P5 and P7

Sweden: Kindly supplied by O.E.C.D. National Accounts Division

Interpretation: Except for U.K., U.S. and Japanese manufacturing, self-employment complicates comparisons over time and between countries (see text pp. 262–6), and they should be judged in conjunction with facts on employee ratios (see Table G.2), but the dramatic increase in the wage ratio in most countries in 1970 appears quite clearly.

To avoid these difficulties we have tried in chapter 4 to use information about income of the manufacturing sector rather than about the national income as a whole, partly because self-employment is less important in this sector and partly because the problems of government-employed labour do not usually arise there. The case of Italy, where the two sets of data give rather different results, suggests that inferences based on national income alone (France, Belgium and Canada) should be treated with especial caution.

Our figures for the rates of growth of the two ratios (presented in Table 2) suggest that in the Netherlands, Italy and Belgium there has been a marked downward trend in the profit share between 1950–69 (because the wage ratio has been growing faster than the employee ratio). In Canada, France and Germany the differential is not very large, although the wage ratio has risen more slowly than the employee ratio, so it seems safest to conclude that there has been no strong trend either way. In Japan, however, the wage ratio has risen so much slower than the employee ratio that a strong upward trend in the share of profits is indicated.

------

split up into 37½ wages, 37½ profits and 35 self-employment incomes. The wage ratio will have risen from 25 per cent to 34·1 per cent, which is a smaller proportional increase than that of the employee ratio.

Table G.2. Trend Rates of Growth of Wage Ratio and the Employee Ratio

		Proportional rate of growth of wage ratio % p.a. 1950–69	Proportional rate of growth of employee ratio % p.a. 1950–69	Employee 1950 %	Ratio 1969 %
France	G.D.P.	0·52	0·88	60·4	76·7
Germany	G.D.P.	0·47	0·77	66·6	81·4
	Manu-facturing[1]	0·14	0·22	88·0	93·4
Italy	G.D.P.[2]	1·03	1·27	51·2	65·6
	Manu-facturing[2]	1·01	0·40	76·3	82·1
Japan	G.D.P.[3]	0·26	2·68	43·8	63·5
Nether-lands	G.D.P.	0·79	0·54	71·9	82·7
	Manu-facturing	0·64	0·25	87·5	93·1
Canada	G.D.P.	0·47	0·68	70·8	86·4
Belgium	G.D.P.[3]	1·15	0·51	72·7	78·6

(1) 1950–68   (2) 1951–69   (3) 1953–69

Notes: Proportional rates of growth are estimated by least squares.

The *employee ratio* is the number of employees as a proportion of employees plus self-employed.

Sources: Wage Ratio: See Table G.1.

Employee ratio: O.E.C.D. *Manpower Statistics 1950–62*, Paris 1963. O.E.C.D. *Manpower Statistics 1959–69*, Paris 1971.

For Italian manufacturing industry: *I Conti Economica Nazionali e Territorali* September 1969.

Interpretation: When the trend rate of growth of the wage ratio is greater than the rate of growth of the employee ratio the implication is that the share in the capitalist sector has been growing. In the reverse case interpretation is less clear cut (see text, p. 263). In the Italian case there appears to be a possible inconsistency between the results for G.D.P. and for the manufacturing sector. Because the problem of self-employment is less severe there we rely on the manufacturing sector data.

Table G.3. Determinants of Annual Changes in the Wage Ratio

This table presents the results of testing an econometric model to explain changes in the wage ratio. The dependent variable is the wage ratio as calculated in Table G.1.

w " " " compensation per head.
w_{-1} " " " " " lagged one year.
p " " " output per head.
x " " " world export prices of manufactures.
e coefficient of change in employee ratio.

Country	Sector	const.	e	w	w_{-1}	p	x	$\bar{R}^2$	$(w+w_{-1})$
U.K.	Corporate	0·016		0·29*		−0·30*	−0·12*	0·43	0·29
U.S.	Corporate	−0·005		0·19*	0·18*	−0·47*	−0·11	0·67	0·37
	Manufacturing	−0·011		0·28*	0·25*	−0·40	−0·08	0·88	0·53
France	G.D.P.	−0·017	1·72*	0·11*	−0·05	0·02	−0·11	0·35	0·06
Germany	G.D.P.	−0·002	0·36	0·16*		−0·16*	−0·09*	0·15	0·16
	Manufacturing	0·009	1·12*	0·27*		−0·44*	−0·26*	0·64	0·27
Italy	G.D.P.	−0·008	0·74*	0·15*		−0·38*	−0·06	0·91	0·15
	Manufacturing	−0·007	1·57*	0·27*		−0·21*	−0·00	0·62	0·27
Japan	G.D.P.	0·003	0·55*	0·13*	0·12*	−0·40*	−0·12	0·86	0·25

Netherlands	G.D.P.	0.001	0.51	0.19*		-0.31*	-0.14*	0.51	0.19
	Manufacturing	0.011	-1.20	0.28*		-0.48*	-0.11	1.20	0.28
Sweden	Manufacturing	-0.016		0.48*		-0.35*	-0.16	0.59	0.48
Canada	G.D.P.	-0.002	0.31	0.28*		-0.38*	-0.06	0.75	0.28
Belgium	G.D.P.	0.007	0.74*	0.21*	-0.09	-0.36*	-0.11	0.74	0.12

*Significant coefficient at the 5 per cent level.

Notes: Period 1950–69 except as indicated in Table G.2.
For Sweden absence of employment figures means that wage and output changes were totals and not per head.

Sources: As for tables G.1 and G.2, together with output data from national accounts and export price data from National Institute Economic Review November 1971, table 19.

Interpretation: The equation was re-estimated leaving out lagged wage change when that variable was nowhere near significant. Some of the values for e are implausibly high but re-estimating the equation leaving out the employee ratio made virtually no difference to the coefficients. We present our conclusions on pp. 74–5.

Table G.4. Public and Private Demand (per cent of G.N.P. at current market prices)

	1950–54	1957–61	1964–8
U.K.			
Govt. Expenditure on goods and services	21·9	20·0	22·0
of which Defence	8·2	6·3	5·8
Private consumption	67·9	65·5	63·4
'Private' investment	9·7	13·4	14·2
Budget surplus	−1·1	−0·1	−0·7
U.S.			
Govt. Expenditure on goods and services	20·1	21·2	22·5
of which Defence	10·8	7·5	8·5
Private consumption	63·3	63·6	61·7
'Private' investment	15·9	14·4	14·9
Budget surplus	0·7	−0·1	−0·1
France			
Govt. Expenditure on goods and services	16·2	15·9	16·0
of which Defence	6·5	5·7	3·9
Private consumption	67·4	63·2	60·6
'Private' investment	16·4	20·0	23·0
Budget surplus	−1·3	1·2	0·7
Germany			
Govt. Expenditure on goods and services	16·7	16·5	19·9
of which Defence	4·6	3·0	3·7
Private consumption	61·2	58·2	56·8
'Private' investment	20·0	22·0	21·5
Budget surplus	4·2	4·0	0·3
Italy			
Govt. Expenditure on goods and services	14·8	14·9	16·1
of which Defence	3·1	2·5	2·3
Private consumption	70·2	64·6	63·9
'Private' investment	16·8	19·9	17·8
Budget surplus	−3·1	−0·9	−2·0

	1950–54	1957–61	1964–8
Japan			
Govt. Expenditure on goods and services	17·1	17·3	18·1
of which current	10·9	9·1	8·9
Private consumption	64·7	57·4	54·4
'Private' investment	18·3	25·1	26·9
Budget surplus	0·0	0·0	−1·4

Note: Government expenditure plus private consumption and private investment does not add up to 100 per cent of Gross National Product because net exports may not be zero (if net exports are positive the country is doing some net foreign investment).

Sources: The basic source for this table is O.E.C.D., *National Accounts 1950–68*, Paris 1970.

Definitions follow standard national accounting principles except for:

Budget surplus: The excess of taxation (including social security contributions) plus government property income (rent, interest and incomes of some public enterprises) *over* government expenditure on goods and services (current and capital), current grants to persons, capital transfers and debt interest.

Private investment: Total gross domestic fixed capital formation plus stockbuilding, less that undertaken by the General Government, i.e. nationalized industries' investment is included.

Figures for total government investment for Japan were taken from O.E.C.D. Annual Survey Japan 1970, Table D. This appears to remain a constant proportion of total G.D.F.C.F. and stockbuilding over the available period 1960–68, and the figures for 1950–54 and 1957–61 were computed by assuming the same held true over the period as a whole.

Sources and References

Chapter 2

To avoid cluttering up the text with reference numbers the sources of individual facts and figures have not been marked separately. Instead the most important books used are listed below and the general areas for which we have used these books are indicated in a key. We hope that, as well as enabling people to check up on a particular piece of information, this will be helpful to those who want to read more about labour and economic history. The particular numbered references from the text (mostly the source of quotations) are listed after the key and bibliography.

Key to areas covered:

A: Growth of national income, industrial output, productivity and investment.

B: Inflation and prices.

C: Foreign trade, the balance of payments, the exchange rate, international competition and foreign investment.

D: Rate of profit and the distribution of national income.

E: Wages and salaries, size of the labour force, unemployment.

F: Trade unions, strikes, the labour movement.

G: The structure of industry, monopoly, nationalization.

List of books used:

Aldcroft, D. H., *The Inter-War Economy:* Britain 1919–1939, Batsford, London, 1970 (A, D, E).

Armitage, S. M. H., *The Politics of Decontrol of Industry:* Britain and the United States, Weidenfeld & Nicolson, London, 1969 (D, F).

Arndt, H. W., *The Economic Lessons of the 1930s*, Frank Cass, London, 1963 (A, E).

Branson, N., and Heinemann, M., *Britain in the Nineteen Thirties*, Weidenfeld and Nicolson, London, 1971 (E, F).

Brown, A. J., *The Great Inflation 1939–1951*, Oxford U.P., 1955 (B).

SOURCES AND REFERENCES

Brown, K. D., *Labour and Unemployment 1900–1914*, David & Charles, Newton Abbot, 1971 (E).

Deane, P. and Cole, W. A., *British Economic Growth 1688–1959*, 2nd edition, Cambridge U.P., 1969 (A, B, C, D).

Emmanuel, A. 'White Settler Colonialism and the Myth of Investment Imperialism', mimeographed paper from international symposium on imperialism, Elsinore, 1971 (to be published) (C).

Employment, Department of, *British Labour Statistics:* Historical Abstract 1886–1968, London, 1971 (E, F).

Feinstein, C. H., 'Changes in the Distribution of the National Income in the United Kingdom since 1860', in J. Marchal and B. Ducros (eds.), *The Distribution of National Income*, Macmillan, London, 1968 (D).

Harman, C., 'The General Strike', *International Socialism*, 48 (F).

Hart, P. E., *Studies in Profit, Business Saving and Investment in the United Kingdom 1920–1962*, Allen & Unwin, London, 1965 (D).

Hobsbawm, E. J., *Industry and Empire*, Penguin, Harmondsworth, 1970 (G).

Hobsbawm, E. J., *Labouring Men*, Weidenfeld & Nicolson, London, 1964 (F).

Hutchinson, K., *The Decline and Fall of British Capitalism*, Charles Scribner's, New York, 1950 (A).

Kendall, W., *The Revolutionary Movement in Britain 1900–1921*, Weidenfeld & Nicolson, London, 1969 (F).

Lewis, W. A., *Economic Survey 1919–1939*, Allen & Unwin, London, 1949 (G).

Martin, R., *Communism and the British Trade Unions 1924–1933*, Oxford U.P., 1969 (F).

Mitchell, B. R. and Deane, P., *Abstract of British Historical Statistics*, Cambridge U.P., 1962 (C, F).

Mitchell, B. R. and Jones, H. G., *Second Abstract of British Historical Statistics*, Cambridge U.P., 1971 (C, F).

Pelling, H., *A History of British Trade Unionism*, Penguin, Harmondsworth, 1969 (F).

Phelps Brown, E. H., and Browne, M., *A Century of Pay*, Macmillan, London, 1968 (A, C, E, F).

Pollard, S., *The Development of the British Economy 1914–1967*, 2nd edition, Arnold, London, 1969 (A, B, C, E).

Richardson, H. W., *Economic Recovery in Britain 1932–39*, Weidenfeld & Nicolson, London, 1967 (A, D, E).

Roberts, B. C., *National Wages Policy in War and Peace*, Allen & Unwin, London, 1958 (E).

Rogow, A. A., *The Labour Government and British Industry 1945–51*, Blackwell, Oxford, 1955 (B, G).

Royal Institute of International Affairs, *The Problem of International Investment*, Oxford U.P., 1937 (C).

Smith, C., 'The Years of Revolt', *International Socialism*, 38 (F).

Strange, S., *Sterling and British Policy*, Oxford U.P., 1971 (C, G).

The Times, *The British Economy, Key Statistics 1900–1970*, London, 1971 (A–G).

Worswick, G. D. N. and Tipping, D. G., *Profits in the British Economy 1909–1938*, Blackwell, Oxford, 1967 (D).

References:

1. quoted in Phelps Brown and Browne, p. 136.
2. Phelps Brown and Browne, pp. 130–40.
3. Phelps Brown and Browne, p. 163.
4. Phelps Brown and Browne, pp. 188–95.
5. Pollard, p. 78.
6. Pollard, pp. 79–80.
7. Pollard, p. 82.
8. Arthur Henderson and G. D. H. Cole, quoted in Hutchinson, p. 174.
9. Armitage, pp. 79–124.
10. Harman, p. 24.
11. Lewis, p. 42.
12. Hobsbawm, *Industry and Empire*, p. 177.
13. Richardson, p. 16.
14. Lewis, p. 87.
15. Hobsbawm, *Industry and Empire*, p. 180.
16. Richardson, p. 130; Hart, p. 118.
17. Richardson, p. 152.
18. Branson and Heinemann, pp. 45–6.
19. Branson and Heinemann, p. 92.
20. Phelps Brown and Browne, p. 241.
21. Branson and Heinemann, p. 85.
22. Branson and Heinemann, p. 10.
23. Martin, p. 113.
24. L. Trotsky, *On the Trade Unions*, Merit Publishers, New York, 1969, p. 54.
25. Martin, p. 175.
26. Pollard, p. 340.
27. Pollard, p. 343.
28. Pollard, p. 331.

29. W. A. Robson in Robson (ed.), *Problems of Nationalised Industries*, Allen & Unwin, London, 1952, p. 286.
30. Roberts, p. 149.
31. Feinstein, p. 129.
32. Deane and Cole, p. 247.
33. Phelps Brown and Browne, p. 145.

Chapter 3

Most of the data we used in the chapter are explained in Appendices C–F in great detail. Facts on shares of world exports, costs and export prices are taken from the *National Institute Economic Review* (e.g. February 1971, Table 20).

References

1. C. Kaysen, quoted by Baran and Sweezy, *Monopoly Capital*, Penguin, Harmondsworth, 1968, which contains a good analysis of the modern corporation.
2. J. Revell's figures quoted in J. E. Meade, *Efficiency, Equality and the Ownership of Property*, Allen & Unwin, London, 1964.
3. K. Marx, *Capital*, Volume I, Chapter 22.
4. D. Morgan and A. D. Martin, 'Imports of manufactures into the U.K. and other industrial countries', *National Institute Economic Review*, May 1971.
5. M. Panic and A. H. Rajan, *Product Changes in Industrialised Countries' Trade*, N.E.D.O., London, 1971.
6. R. Gross and M. Keating, 'Analysis of Competition in Export and Domestic Markets', *O.E.C.D. Economic Outlook*, December 1970.
7. I. Kravis and R. Lipsey, *Price Competitiveness in World Trade*, National Bureau for Economic Research, New York, 1971.
8. N.E.D.O., *Imported Manufactures*, London, 1965.
9. Panic and Rajan, op. cit., Table 3.

Chapter 4

Our basic sources of information for individual countries were the annual reports by O.E.C.D. on member nations. In the list of detailed references below we refer to these reports by giving the country and the year the report was issued, e.g. 'O.E.C.D. Italy 1965' means that the quotation comes from O.E.C.D.'s Survey of the Italian Economy published in 1965. In addition for Germany we used the Annual Reports of the German Central Bank which are translated in English; and for the U.S. the Annual Reports by the Council of Economic Advisers (C.E.A.). O.E.C.D. also publishes a twice-yearly analysis of developments in member nations called *Economic Outlook* and the British National Institute of Economic and Social Research carries regular articles on the world economy in its quarterly review. Before listing the references we give a list of books which may be useful to people wanting to read more on the subject.

General References

(a) *Growth in the Capitalist Countries*

Denison, E. F., *Why Growth Rates Differ*, Brookings Institution, Washington, 1967.

Kuznets, S., *Postwar Economic Growth*, Harvard U.P., 1964.

Kuznets, S., *Modern Economic Growth*, Yale U.P., 1966.

Maddison, A., *Economic Growth in the West*, Allen & Unwin, London, 1964.

Maddison, A., *Economic Growth in Japan and the U.S.S.R.*, Allen & Unwin, London, 1969.

O.E.C.D., *Economic Growth 1960–70*, Paris, 1966.

O.E.C.D., *The Growth of Output 1960–80*, Paris, 1970.

Mandel, E., *Europe Versus America?*, New Left Books, London, 1970.

(b) *Distribution of Income*

Marchal, J. and Ducros, B. (eds.), *The Distribution of National Income*, Macmillan, London, 1968.

Economic Commission for Europe, *Incomes in Post-war Europe*, Geneva, 1967.

Loftus, P. J., 'Labour's Share in Manufacturing', Lloyds Bank Review, April, 1969.

(c) *Inflation*

Brown, A. J., *The Great Inflation*, Oxford U.P., 1955.

O.E.E.C., *The Problem of Rising Prices*, Paris, 1961.

O.E.C.D., *Inflation: The Present Problem*, Paris, 1970.

O.E.C.D., *Present Policies Against Inflation*, Paris, 1971.

(d) *Arms Expenditure*

Baran, P. A. and Sweezy, P. M., *Monopoly Capital*, Penguin, Harmondsworth, 1968.

Kidron, M., *Western Capitalism since the War*, Penguin, Harmondsworth, 1970.

Melman, S., *Pentagon Capitalism: the Political Economy of War*, McGraw-Hill, New York, 1970.

(e) *Planning*

Cohen, S. S., *Modern Capitalist Planning: The French Model*, London, Weidenfeld & Nicolson, 1969.

References

1. O.E.C.D., Netherlands, 1966.
2. O.E.C.D., Netherlands, 1970.
3. *The Times*, 20 July, 1971.
4. O.E.C.D., Italy, 1963.
5. O.E.C.D., Italy, 1964.
6. O.E.C.D., Italy, 1965.
7. O.E.C.D., *Economic Outlook*, July 1971.
8. O.E.C.D., France, 1969.
9. O.E.C.D., France, 1971.
10. Quoted by Patrick M. Boarman, *Germany's Economic Dilemma*, Yale U.P., 1964.
11. *Report* of the Deutsche Bundesbank for 1961, p. 18.
12. O.E.C.D., Germany, 1970.
13. O.E.C.D., Germany, 1971.
14. O.E.C.D., *Economic Outlook*, December 1970.
15. O.E.C.D., Germany, 1971.
16. Quoted by Boarman.
17. *The Times*, 16 May 1971.
18. O.E.C.D., Germany, 1971.
19. O.E.C.D., *Economic Outlook*, July, 1971.
20. *Report* of Council of Economic Advisers, 1970.
21. O.E.C.D., U.S., 1971.
22. R. Rowthorn, *International Big Business 1957–67*, Cambridge U.P., 1971, Table 22.
23. O.E.C.D., *Inflation: The Present Problem*, Paris, 1970, pp. 8, 9.
24. O.E.C.D., *Inflation: The Present Problem*, pp. 34–5.

25. O.E.C.D., *Inflation: The Present Problem*, p. 37.
26. O.E.C.D., *Inflation: The Present Problem*, p. 42.
27. *Report* of Council of Economic Advisers, 1969, Table 8.
28. *Report* of Council of Economic Advisers, 1969.

Chapter 5

Data on personal incomes and consumption are published annually in the *National Income Blue Book* (e.g. 1971, Tables 20–26) and quarterly in *Economic Trends* also published by the Central Statistical Office. Data on wages are published in the *Department of Employment Gazette* (e.g. August 1971, Tables 122–131) and additional information particularly on wage settlements is published in the regular reports of Incomes Data Services. Calculations of tax payments and benefits received by families in different income groups are published each February in *Economic Trends*. Data on self-employment incomes, dividend and interest payments and receipts are published in the *National Income Blue Book* (e.g. 1971, Tables 13, 20, 22, 25, 29, 44, 58). Data on share prices and interest rates are published in the *Annual Abstract of Statistics* (1970, Tables 364–366) and monthly in *Financial Statistics* again published by the C.S.O. In addition to these regular series the Department of Employment conducted three very detailed earnings surveys in September 1968 (published in the *New Earnings Survey*) and April 1970 and April 1971 (published in the *Department of Employment Gazette* November to February after survey). Finally, in *Inland Revenue Statistics* published annually there are data on personal incomes in various size groups which we used to calculate proportions of the incomes of the rich which come from various sources (Tables 59, 63).

References

1. H. A. Turner and F. Wilkinson, *New Society*, 25 February 1971.
2. Vincent Hanna, *Sunday Times*, 28 March 1971; National Board for Prices and Incomes, *General Problems of Low Pay*, Report No. 167, Cmnd 4648, 1971.
3. P. Townsend, *The Times*, 10 March 1971.
4. N.B.P.I., op. cit.
5. P. Townsend, *The Times*, 10 March 1971. M. Meacher, *The Times*, 29 December 1971.
6. K. Marx, *Capital*, Vol. I, Modern Lanuages Publishing House, Moscow, p. 644.

7. *Top Salaries in the Private Sector and Nationalised Industries*, National Board for Prices and Incomes, Report No. 107, Cmnd 3970, 1969.

Chapter 6

Data on fixed investment are published annually in the *National Income Blue Book* (e.g. 1971, Tables 51–70) and quarterly in *Economic Trends*. Data on financing and liquidity, based on the Department of Trade and Industry's analysis of company accounts, are published annually in *Business Monitor M3* and some additional information is available from *Financial Statistics*. Some data on bankruptcies are published by the D.T.I. in *Companies, General Annual Report*.

References

1. For example N. Dimsdale and A. Glyn, *Bulletin* of the Oxford University Institute of Economics and Statistics, August 1971.
2. E. Heath reported in *The Guardian*, 19 June 1971.
3. Reported in *The Times*, 1 July 1971.
4. *Sunday Times*, 3 February 1971.

Chapter 7

Data on prices, retail and wholesale, are published in the *Monthly Digest of Statistics;* and on unemployment and employment in the Department of Employment *Gazette*. We calculated the cost breakdown for the company sector from the 1968 input–output table (*National Income Blue Book* 1971, Table 19) with the help of some dubious assumptions. The Department of Trade and Industry's analysis of mergers is published quarterly in *Business Monitor M7;* for earlier years there are overall figures for acquisitions of subsidiaries as part of the analysis of company accounts and published in *Business Monitor M3* (*Economic Trends* April 1962 for the period up to 1960). There is a detailed analysis of mergers for the period 1958–68 published by the Monopolies Commission in 1970, called *A Survey of Mergers 1958–68*, which we used for most of the detailed information in the text. Data on flows of foreign investment into the U.K. and by the U.K., and on earnings on these investments, are published annually in the *Balance of Payments Pink Book* (e.g. 1971, Tables 21, 22, 26–9, 42, 48–51). In addition there are detailed recent surveys in *Business Monitor M4* and in the *Board of Trade Journal* (now *Trade and Industry*), 23 September 1970. We also drew quite extensively on data in:

Reddaway, W. B., *Effects of U.K. Direct Investment Overseas*, Interim and Final Reports, Cambridge U.P., 1967 and 1968.

Dunning, J. N., *Studies in International Investment*, Allen & Unwin, London, 1970.

Data on financial companies are published annually in the *National Income Blue Book* (e.g. Table 30) which also (1971, Table 22) gives data for life assurance and superannuation funds. A series for profits of different groups of financial companies is published monthly by the *Financial Times* and data for lending by different types of institutions are published in the *Annual Abstract of Statistics* (e.g. 1970, Tables 351–378) and also in *Financial Statistics*. Facts about expenditure on durables and mortgages by different income groups are in *Family Expenditure Survey 1970*.

References

1. *The Times*, 25 May 1971.
2. National Board for Prices and Incomes, Report No. 123, *Productivity Agreements*, Cmnd 4136, 1969, p. 29.
3. H. A. Clegg, *The System of Industrial Relations in Great Britain*, Blackwell, 1971, Oxford, p. 179.
4. T. Cliff, *The Employers' Offensive: Productivity Deals and How to Fight Them*, Pluto Press, London, 1970, p. 50.
5. *Incomes Data*, 109.
6. R. Caves, p. 321 in Caves (ed.), *Britain's Economic Prospects*, Allen & Unwin, London, 1968.
7. In a series of pamphlets, *The Structure of British Industry* (1970), *The Growth of Competition* (1970), and *The Control of Monopoly* (1971).
8. Reddaway Report, p. 359.
9. Dunning, p. 290.
10. J. Arnison, *The Million Pound Strike?*, Lawrence & Wishart, London, 1970.
11. See an interesting exchange on this subject between Robin Murray and Bill Warren in *New Left Review*, 67 and 68.

Chapter 8

Data on the effect of changes in company and personal taxation we took from post-budget issues of the Economist and from our own calculations in Appendix F. For public expenditure we used the White Paper (Cmnd 4518) *New Policies for Public Spending*. Facts about recent developments in the nationalized industries come from the financial press. Assessments of the impact for various industries of joining the Common Market come from *The Guardian*, 8 July 1971, *Investors Chronicle*, 21 May 1971, *Financial Times*, 21 July 1971, and in the case of the City from various articles in *The Pound into Europe*, The Banker, London, 1971. Data on the overseas earnings of the City are given in the *Balance of Payments Pink Book 1971*, Annex 5, and there is an exhaustive analysis of sterling's role in maintaining these earnings in B. J. Cohen, *Sterling's Role as an International Currency*, Macmillan, London, 1971. Unemployment data are given in the Department of Employment *Gazette*, which also provides information on overtime, short-time, vacancies, etc. There is a good deal of information on attempts to run an incomes policy in H. Clegg's book, *How to Run an Incomes Policy*, Heinemann, London, 1971, and in the chapter by David C. Smith in R. Caves (ed.), *Britain's Economic Prospects*, Allen & Unwin, London, 1968. On the Industrial Relations Act we drew on:

S. Chomet (ed.), *Industrial Relations Bill: A Basis for Agreement?*, Transcripta Books, London, 1971.

Confederation of British Industries (working party under L. F. Neal), *Guidance to Employers on Industrial Relations Bill*, London, 1971.

Joan Henderson, *The Industrial Relations Act at Work*, The Industrial Society, London, 1971.

Peter Paterson, *An Employer's Guide to the Industrial Relations Act*, Kogan Page Associates, London, 1971.

Trades Unions Congress, *Industrial Relations Bill: Report of the Special Trades Union Congress*, London, 1971.

References

1. M. Miller, *National Institute Economic Review*, August 1971, who gives an exhaustive analysis of alternative estimates.
2. S. Brittan, *Financial Times*, 1 July 1971.
3. The United Kingdom and the European Communities, Cmnd 4715.
4. Peter Oppenheimer in *The Pound into Europe*.

5. In *The Pound into Europe*.
6. *The Times*, 26 April 1971.
7. *National Institute Economic Review*, August 1971.
8. *The Times*, 11 June 1971.
9. *Guardian*, 7 July 1971.
10. *Guardian*, 7 July 1971.
11. Joan Henderson, op. cit., p. 21.
12. S. Chomet, op. cit.
13. Peter Paterson, op. cit.
14. *Guardian*, 19 March 1971.
15. *Workers' Press*, 15 March 1971.
16. *Guardian*, 21 March 1971.
17. *Guardian*, 21 March 1971.

Chapter 9

Most of the figures for wages, employment, hours and strikes in this chapter have been taken from the following sources:

Department of Employment, *British Labour Statistics: Historical Abstract*, 1886–1968, H.M.S.O., 1971.
Department of Employment, *Gazette* (monthly publication).
Incomes Data Services, *Incomes Data* (weekly publication).

On industrial relations questions we have made extensive use of:

H. A. Clegg, *The System of Industrial Relations in Great Britain*, Blackwell, Oxford, 1971.
Report of the Royal Commission on Trade Unions and Employers Organizations (the Donovan Report, published in 1968, Cmnd 3623).

Other sources are listed in the references. On trade union strategy much of the information comes from the annual reports of the T.U.C.

References

1. Clegg, p. 230.
2. Clegg, pp. 15–16.
3. H. A. Turner, G. Clack and G. Roberts, *Labour Relations in the Motor Industry*, Allen & Unwin, London, 1967, pp. 222–3.
4. A. Flanders, *Collective Bargaining: Prescription for Change*, Faber, London, 1967, p. 25.
5. *Incomes Data*, 12.

SOURCES AND REFERENCES

6. *Workers' Press*, 27 July 1971; *Guardian*, 14 May 1971; *The Times*, 11 May 1971.
7. *The Times*, 28 August 1971.
8. *Workers' Press*, 27 September 1971.
9. Clegg, pp. 312–14.
10. H. A. Turner, *The Trend of Strikes*, Leeds U.P., 1963, p. 18.
11. T. Lane and K. Roberts, *Strike at Pilkingtons*, Fontana, London, 1971.
12. *Financial Times*, 3 May 1971.
13. *Workers' Press*, 19 March 1971.
14. Quoted in T. Cliff, *The Employers' Offensive*, p. 167.
15. *Guardian*, 2 October 1971.
16. Report of Court of Inquiry on Electricity Supply Dispute, February 1971 (Wilberforce Report), p. 35.
17. *Financial Times*, 13 July 1971.
18. Report of T.U.C. Special Congress on the Industrial Relations Bill, 1971, pp. 3 and 77.
19. Cliff, p. 200.
20. *Financial Times*, 14 and 18 September 1971; *Guardian*, 28 September 1971.

Chapter 10

References

1. S. M. H. Armitage, *The Politics of Decontrol of Industry* (see list of books for chapter 2), p. 153.
2. T.U.C. *Annual Report*, 1968, p. 550.
3. L. Trotsky, *On the Trade Unions*, Merit Publishers, New York, 1969, p. 71.

List of Figures

Tables

More about Penguins and Pelicans

Penguinews, which appears every month, contains details of all the new books issued by Penguins as they are published. From time to time it is supplemented by *Penguins in Print*, which is a complete list of all available books published by Penguins. (There are well over three thousand of these.)

A specimen copy of *Penguinews* will be sent to you free on request, and you can become a subscriber for the price of the postage. For a year's issues (including the complete lists) please send 30p if you live in the United Kingdom, or 60p if you live elsewhere. Just write to Dept EP, Penguin Books Ltd, Harmondsworth, Middlesex, enclosing a cheque or postal order, and your name will be added to the mailing list.

Note: *Penguinews* and *Penguins in Print* are not available in the U.S.A. or Canada

Britain and the World Economy

J. M. Livingstone

In the world's market-place every country keeps a stall and every country goes shopping. The result – in currency, credit, and kind – is a network of transactions as intricate and alive as a printed circuit.

Britain and the World Economy is a short, readable survey of the part played by one country in this world network. Britain, partly by necessity, partly by choice, plays a variety of economic roles in the world and J. M. Livingstone emphasizes the country's growing dependence on events abroad in this examination of her contributions as an international banker operating the sterling system; as the leader of a still powerful Commonwealth; as a force in a revitalized Europe; as a world trader; and as a 'have' with responsibilities towards the 'have-nots'.

a Pelican Book